THE EARTH LIBERATION FRONT
1997-2002

THE EARTH LIBERATION FRONT
1997-2002

LESLIE JAMES PICKERING

arissa
media group

PORTLAND, OREGON

THE EARTH LIBERATION FRONT
1997-2002

Arissa Media Group
P.O. Box 6058
Portland, OR 97228
info@arissamediagroup.com
www.arissamediagroup.com

Printed and bound in the United States of America.

First Edition, 2003, Arissa Publications: New York.
Second Edition, 2007, Arissa Media Group: Portland.

Library of Congress Control Number: 2003112770
International Standard Book Number (ISBN): 0-9742884-0-3

Edited by Ariana Huemer.
Cover design by Matthew Haggett.

Printed on 100% recycled, acid-free paper.

Arissa Media Group, LLC was formed in 2003 to assist in building a revolutionary consciousness in the United States of America. For more information, bulk requests, catalogue listings, submission guidelines, or media inquiries, please contact Arissa Media Group, LLC, P.O. Box 6058, Portland, OR 97228. www.arissamediagroup.com

For

Bill Rodgers

A.K.A.

Avalon

CONTENTS

rage
against
state
oppression

On February 2, 2000, agents from the FBI, BATF and U.S. Forest Service raided the home, vehicle and former office of Earth Liberation Front (ELF) spokesperson Craig Rosebraugh. A virtual truckload of property was seized for the investigation into actions of economic sabotage against those who profit from the destruction of the earth and the exploitation of life. Rosebraugh has worked as a spokesperson for the ELF and ALF(Animal Liberation Front) for the last three years receiving anonymous communiques from the underground organizations and distributing them to media nationwide. At the time of the search Rosebraugh was issued another subpoena (his fifth in three years) to testify before a federal grand jury in Portland which convened to investigate multiple actions of both the ELF and ALF. In addition, Rosebraugh received notice February 18th that he is an official target of the grand jury and may be indicted on federal charges. He has been commanded to testify before the grand jury on February 29th in this unjust fishing expedition. Grand juries, first created and later outlawed in England, have been used historically as a harassment tactic in the U.S. to combat successful social movements. In the proceedings, witnesses called to testify do not have the usual constitutional rights to counsel or to remain silent during questioning. Witnesses who take the fifth amendment and refuse to answer questions have been subject to contempt charges and held for up to a year and a half in prison. In protest of this unjust government and system, Rosebraugh is refusing to cooperate or answer questions with the grand jury.
Express your outrage at the state while the grand jury proceedings begin.

February 29
11:00 am
@ the US Courthouse
SW Jefferson & 3rd

The ELF guidelines are as follows:

1) To cause as much economic damage as possible to a given entity that is profiting off the destruction of the natural environment and life for selfish greed and profit.

2) To educate the public on the atrocities committed against the environment and life.

3) To take all necessary precautions against harming life.

North American Earth Liberation Front Press Office
Mission Statement

The North American Earth Liberation Front Press Office (NAELFPO) is a legal, above ground news service dedicated to exposing the political and social motives behind the covert direct actions of the ELF. The NAELFPO receives anonymous communiqués from the ELF and distributes the message to the media and the public throughout North America. The NAELFPO provides a public face ideologically in support of the ELF and similar acts of economic sabotage against those who profit from the destruction of the natural environment. The NAELFPO is contacted by the media and public internationally to provide information on the political and social motives of the ELF actions, and the tactical necessity of covert direct action. Due to the work of the NAELFPO, individuals who are looking to learn more about these issues have a place to turn, and the public who may be ignorant to the actions and motives of the ELF are exposed to more frequent and in-depth coverage in the media.

teach-in on state repression & community solidarity

Where successful movements for social change exist so will repression against those movements from the system. Recent events in Portland prove that we are under attack by local, state and federal authorities who wish for us to remain passive and complacent as agencies and corporations profit off the destruction of our natural environment. Come learn about and discuss; forms of repression currently in practice in Portland such as the Grand Jury and intense harassment by Federal and State Agents, Government repression of past Social movements, and how we as a community can unite and fight this unjust system.

**tuesday, march 28th, 7-9 pm
p.s.u. smith memorial center
free. call 478-0902 for information**

are you down with the struggle?

INTRODUCTION

EARTH LIBERATION FRONT 1997-2002

In the summer of 1996 I joined a newly-founded organization in Portland, Oregon called Liberation Collective. The philosophical basis of the organization at that point was that all forms of institutional oppression are born of a single cause: the system. If it were not for the capitalism, racism, sexism, imperialism that the system perpetrates upon world and each one of us, then there would be no clear cuts, no vivisection, no Persian Gulf War, no Nike corporation. Our objective was "linking social justice movements to end all oppression," but our methods of achieving this righteous goal, however, were not so successful. For the most part we conducted attention-getting acts of civil disobedience and protests around vivisection and various other single issues and ran information tables that looked like a haphazard collage of every liberal handbill under the sun.

During approximately the same period, a group of unknown individuals was building another organization with a similar philosophy but very different methods. When The Earth Liberation Front (ELF) took its first action in the U.S., I remember the exuberance and the resurgence of hope that raced through me and many others in the movement. I had been very interested in the underground actions of the Animal Liberation Front (ALF) for a number of years, actively researched all the information I could find about the organization and even did significant fundraising for the ALF press office and support group. I imagined the potential of an organization using tactics similar to those of the ALF, but whose objectives went beyond the liberation of animals to the liberation of the entire Earth. Now, not only had this organization come into being but it also sent its first communiqué to our Liberation Collective.

Through the Liberation Collective, Craig Rosebraugh in particular handled the release of numerous ELF communiqués, from the first on November 29, 1997 until the official formation of the North American Earth Liberation Front Press Office (NAELFPO) in early 2000.

Internal conflict caused Rosebraugh, myself, and a handful of other members to leave the Liberation Collective early in 2000. Reflecting on our years with the collective, and now free to put our energy elsewhere, Rosebraugh and I concluded that the handling of ELF communiqués was extremely valuable work, and we thus founded the NAELFPO.

From the start, the NAELFPO was forced to deal with FBI raids and grand jury subpoenas, in addition to handling ELF communiqués. At first I put my energy as Press Officer into the production of ELF support literature

2

(such as much of what is reprinted here) and organizing against ELF-related grand juries. Rosebraugh continued handling ELF communiqués more directly and dealing with the local, national and international media as an official Spokesperson. Time passed and these roles broke down, as Rosebraugh grew increasingly frustrated with the media and I reluctantly stepped in front of the cameras. By the time of the second raid on the NAELFPO on April 5, 2001, we more equally shared the duties of Press Officer and Spokesperson.

On September 5, 2001, just days before the infamous 9/11 terrorist attacks, Rosebraugh and I jointly released a stepping down statement. While in reality our reasoning for stepping down was more akin to the politics of my final resignation statement (chapter 8) we decided to focus on relevant yet less pressing issues by releasing the following statement:

> ELF Press Officers Step Down
> Sept. 5, 2001
>
> Portland, OR - Both Craig Rosebraugh and Leslie James Pickering have stepped down from their duties as press officers for the North American Earth Liberation Front. Both have stated that if the Earth Liberation Front is to be a viable movement, public concentrations of support must not be centered on one or two people. The two have maintained that the ELF is one of the greatest demonstrations of the power the people can have if they so desire to take it. They sincerely wish to express their gratitude to all those who have expressed some form of support over the years and to the courageous individuals that have been involved in ELF actions.

After September 11, it became very clear that voices in opposition to the system were more needed than ever, due to massive nationalist and anti-terrorist propaganda. In addition, a House Subcommittee Hearing on Eco-terrorism-- to which Rosebraugh had been subpoenaed (chapter 6)-- was to be held on February 12th, 2002.

On February 2, 2002, I temporarily returned to my position as spokesperson for the NAELFPO, stating in part,

> Those who struggle for revolutionary change in North

America will not be intimidated by the system's alleged 'War on Terrorism,' its so-called Patriot Act or their 'House Subcommittee hearing on Eco-Terrorism'. If anything, these only exemplify the dire need for a revolutionary movement struggling on the side of the people here in North America. Direct action taken by the Earth Liberation Front, and similar underground organizations, is part of a larger struggle for revolutionary change. The system has long proven that it values profits and property over life, and this underground response is the voice and fist of the people rising in self-defense.

During this second bout as Spokesperson, I received increased criticism, as Rosebraugh was no longer working with me and I had decided to take a more honest and radical approach than I had done in the past. I no longer publicly proclaimed the ELF as a nonviolent organization, and I openly implemented the ELF as part of an urgently-needed revolutionary movement. A percentage of this criticism came from supporters of the ELF, who proclaimed that I was taking the attention away from environmentalist issues and taking too extreme of a stance. I knew my second term with the NAELFPO had run its course and released a substantial 'resignation statement' published in the June-July 2002 issue of the *Earth First! Journal* and elsewhere (chapter 8).

I have since been working with Arissa, an emerging effort to build a truly revolutionary movement in the US.

•

The communiqués (chapter 1) are the only words passed on to us from the guerrillas of the Earth Liberation Front. I take them as I would the wisdom of an elder or the brilliance of a child. Their knowledge, while not unquestionable, is invaluable. They display the sincerity, the desperation, the love and the anger of the revolutionaries, who armed themselves with not only the firebomb, but the pen as well.

The Frequently Asked Questions booklet (chapter 2) was published to give a deeper understanding of the ELF than would ever be allowed through the mainstream media. This also represented a bold, first step taken by the NAELFPO to attempt to define the "ideology" of the loose-knit underground cells as that of a revolutionary organization. While for editorial reasons it is the second chapter of this book, it may be important to note that it was published between the fourth and fifth issues of *Resistance*.

The three issues of *Resistance* that were published under the NAELFPO (chapters 3, 4 & 5) display the political line at their respective dates of publication. They also give information on various ELF-related legal events such as grand jury appearances. Not all articles and images from the original issues are reprinted in this book.

The 2/12/02 Subcommittee booklet (chapter 6) displays the unadulterated opinions of some of the people who are affected the most by the ELF through their presumably honest Congressional testimonies. Some are targets of the ELF who have suffered economically and psychologically from their actions. Some, as representatives of districts in which the ELF has struck, consider themselves victims. Others have taken it upon themselves to attempt to extinguish the flames of the ELF either as federal agents of repression or representatives of nonprofit organizations fronting for industry interests.

Craig Rosebraugh's statement gives a unique view into the making of a revolutionary in contemporary American society, and, in a more abstract way, a birthing of a homegrown guerrilla organization. The questions posed to him by the subcommittee show the intent and focus of the system and his responses to them display intelligence, honesty, strength and even humor.

The Guerrilla News Network interview (chapter 7) is literally one of thousands conducted during the times I was involved with the NAELFPO. But due to the timing of the interview and the integrity of the journalists, it gives a much deeper look into the political and personal issues involving the ELF and myself. In it I express personal opinions on revolution that I had previously held back due to pressure from the larger movement, which enjoyed the perception of the ELF as a nonviolent environmental organization.

In my resignation statement (chapter 8) I address the issues of nonviolence and single-issue politics directly, refusing to bow to what I continue to see as a disturbing and extremely self-defeatist trend in radical politics. Rather than continue in what I had grown to understand is a counterproductive direction, I resigned from my position as spokesperson for the NAELFPO and began searching for the next step towards liberation.

It is the case with this book that the whole is greater than the sum of its parts. Nearly all of the information herein has been previously printed but has grown difficult to obtain, as it was published with limited resources in relatively small quantities. This book is being published not only for posterity, but more to display an evolution in the ideology and tactics of the struggle that is not easily noticeable in studying any of the original publications on their own.

Whether under the cover of darkness, in the spotlight of the media or under pressures of the U.S. government, a lot has evolved over the last five years. A better understanding of this ideological and tactical evolution is of great value to us both now and as the struggle progresses into the future.

In particular, by studying the combined texts in this book, you will see an increasingly revolutionary assessment of the oppression from which we suffer and the liberation for which we strive. The struggle continues.

●

This book is not about where I feel the Earth Liberation Front succeeded and failed, or where I think the movement should go from here, although those are topics we should all be thinking about. This book has been reprinted because it is an important resource for understanding an important time and place in recent American history. These pages contain the texts of documents representing and influencing a movement that grew so significant as to be named the number-one domestic priority of the Federal Bureau of Investigation. This book is intended to give a brief glimpse into how things really were.

One of the first things I learned when I got involved in the struggle was how the movement deals with the media. I was to understand that how a movement is represented to the public helps determine how much support it gets, and proper handling of the media is expected to follow unwritten rules.

There was an ongoing debate within the movement over the theory that 'any media is good media.' The system would continue to pretend that life on Earth was in no danger unless we exposed the truth, and no matter how bad the media made us look, there would be at least one person out there somewhere who would see through the hype and get the message, which is one more person than we had before... or so the theory goes. Opposing viewpoints were that negative coverage taints the entire movement and radicals should either not bother with the mass media or go mainstream.

I'm sure it was assumed, because the North American Earth Liberation Front Press Office got so much bad press, that we followed the 'any media was good media' theory, but in reality I don't think we even had a stance on it. We were given a task and were just trying to do the best we could against the odds. When you're down with the struggle you do whatever you can, regardless of skill-level or odds.

We always assumed that the mass media was not on our side. It was expected that our most inarticulate statements would be the ones to show up in the news, so we tried our best to improve our articulation and to speak in sound bites. The idea was that if you only gave them short, concise statements, then that's all they would have to work with. Sometimes I would just ignore their questions and give a pre-rehearsed statement as if it were an answer. In our case this could work because when a million-dollar building burns to the ground they don't have a choice but to do a story on it, so they'd have to work with whatever we gave them. But there were numerous misquotes and completely fabricated statements (especially in the print media who rarely did more than jot down a few notes during interviews).

It's a rigged game. A two-minute debate edited and directed by your opponent. They layer your face with make-up and sit you under bright lights with cameras glaring from every angle. You try not to shake from nervousness and keep your focus, but you feel like you're going to pass out. They call you a violent terrorist, ask you incredibly leading questions, and then edit your responses out of their context and broadcast it to the nation. Even if they can't make you look stupid they are going to make you look crazy.

I can't complain though, because we were asking for it. Earth Liberation Front actions were sensational, so we never expected that the notoriously sensational US media wouldn't sensationalize their coverage. Our strategy evolved with the experience of being burned time and time again, and after a while I learned that we did hold a card or two in our hands.

Reporters are suckers for a big story, and the more radical we came off, the bigger the story. It was as if they didn't realize that part of our objective was to get attention and they were giving it to us, or maybe more that they didn't care because it sold so well.

We learned to play the rebel card. I tried to look cool, play cool, and I'd have them meet me in obscure little cafes or street corners instead of going their production studios. They would make a statement about terrorism and violence expecting me to argue against it, but instead I'd tell them about how they ain't seen nothing yet, and they'd be speechless, if only for a moment.

We never won. The major networks never ran a story about how the ELF is a modern day Robin Hood, and we never expected that they would. I don't think there was a single piece in the major media that didn't scream slanderous exaggerations of violence and terrorism, but at times you would swear there was a news editor out there trying to make us look cool, and more and more communiqués came, and the movement grew.

When the FBI first knocked on our door in 1997 I was nineteen. I was a high school dropout and a runaway looking for a revolution. The intensity of the government surveillance and harassment that followed helped shape the way we grew to see the world, and we'll never be the same.

Looking back over the documents published in this book is embarrassing. I never paid much attention in my public school English classes. I never had much of an interest in writing or public speaking until I went to work with the Press Office. My political analysis during those years was even more simplistic than it is today.

The first thing to cross my mind when re-reading this rhetoric is how inaccessible it is to outsiders. If you weren't throwing tear gas canisters back at riot police and sitting in old growth redwoods in the Pacific Northwest in the late 1990s the documents in this book just weren't written for you.

But it's real. These are the documents that came out during those first five hot years of the Earth Liberation Front. They are being republished because they are a resource necessary to understand a significant social justice struggle that is almost always misunderstood. We need to know our true past to find our true future.

1.

COMMUNIQUES

Beltane, 1997

Welcome to the struggle of all species to be free.

We are the burning rage of this dying planet. The war of greed ravages the Earth and species die out every day. ELF works to speed up the collapse of industry, to scare the rich, and to undermine the foundations of the state. We embrace social and deep-ecology as a practical resistance movement. We have to show the enemy that we are serious about defending what is sacred. Together we have teeth and claws to match our dreams. Our greatest weapons are imagination and the ability to strike when least expected.

Since 1992 a series of Earth-nights and Halloween smashes has mushroomed around the world. 1,000's of bulldozers, power lines, computer systems, buildings and valuable equipment have been composted. Many ELF actions have been censored to prevent our bravery from inciting others to take action.

We take inspiration from Luddites, Levellers, Diggers, the Autonome squatter movement, the ALF, the Zapatistas, and the little people – those mischievous elves of lore. Authorities can't see us because they don't believe in elves. We are practically invisible. We have no command structure, no spokespersons, no office, just small groups working separately seeking vulnerable targets and practicing our craft.

Many elves are moving to the Pacific Northwest and other sacred areas. Some elves will leave surprises as they go. Find your family! And let's dance as we make ruins of the corporate money system.

November 29, 1997

The Bureau of Land Management (BLM) claims they are removing non-native species from public lands (aren't white Europeans also non-native?) but then they turn around and subsidize the cattle industry and place thousands of non-native domestic cattle on these same lands...

...to help halt the BLM's illegal and immoral business of rounding up wild horses from public lands and funneling them into slaughter...

This hypocrisy and genocide against the horse nation will not go unchallenged! The practice of rounding up and auctioning wild horses must be stopped. The practice of grazing cattle on public lands must be stopped. The time to take action is now. From an investigation like the Associated Press', to writing the BLM, to an action like ours you can help stop the slaughter and save our Mother Earth...

June 21, 1998

This year for summer solstice the ALF and the ELF decided to honor the wildlife of the Pacific Northwest and the forests they call home by having a bonfire (or two) at the facilities which make it a daily routine to kill and destroy wildlife. The arrogant humans who make money by killing and destroying nature would have the public believe that beaver, deer and other wildlife are responsible for the decimation of our pubic lands – not clearcutting! That cougars just trying to survive their genocide – not human expansion and habitat decimation – are the problems! So one tax-payer-supported government facility researches more efficient and economical ways to destroy our wildlife while a second tax-payer-supported agency puts that research into practice. In addition a third tax-payer-funded organization – the State Department of Natural Resources – conducts insect control experiments and genetic research. This action was done in solidarity with Josh Ellerman and in recognition of his courage and commitment to the animals.

-The Real Wildlife Services

June 28, 1998

Minutes before midnight on June 28th, the building that houses the Mexican Consulate in Boston, MA, was targeted by the Earth Liberation Front. The unjust government in Mexico is complicit in murdering the indigenous population in Chiapas.

Red hand prints, symbolizing the blood on the hands of the Mexican government, were painted on the walls and spilled on the ground. 'VIVA EZLN' was spray-painted on the entrance.

Earth Liberation Front disappeared into the night but the blood on the hands of the Mexican government won't easily disappear.

TODOS SOMOS MARCOS

EARTH LIBERATION FRONT 1997-2002

REMEMBER GUADALUPE

July 3, 1998

Approximately 7 PM, in the evening of July 3 1998 the Animal Liberation Front and the Earth Liberation Front carried out a daylight raid on the United Vaccines experimental research fur farm in Middleton, Wisconsin, near Madison.

Two large holes were cut in the perimeter fence of the compound and one large section of fence was completely torn down. Inside were 3 sheds, one was empty, one containing cages mink and one containing animals resembling possibly the Black-footed ferret of a variety of pole-cat. Neat the sheds were two double rows of cages covered by liftable roof segments. All cages containing animals were opened, some requiring cage doors to be bent to allow for escape. All prisoners were seen climbing out of their cages. 310 animals liberated. Each cage in the fenced in area was numbered and each mink had small black tags on both ears. Light bulbs smashed out in all sheds and a weighing scale smashed.

"INDEPENDENCE DAY FOR FUR FARM PRISONERS" spray-painted on a storage barn. 3 windows smashed alarm to go off and force liberators to evacuate before causing more damage.

This facility also contained fenced in area with empty fox cages. On top of the research building were air ducts and ventilation. This room we suspect is where laboratory tests are conducted on the animals.

The experiments conducted at the United Vaccines laboratories and research farms are solely to decrease "profit-losses" incurred by premature deaths on fur farms. The cause of these deaths can be attributed to the widespread on the farms due to close confinement, malnourishment, poor sanitation and the psychological stress of captivity. The blatant disregard for the mink and fox nations' well-being is apparent in this industry, which cares only about fur quality and maximum "production" and death.

The Fur farming industry plays a crucial role in the devastation of delicate ecosystems. Fur farm waste run-offs contaminate local bodies of water, poisoning fish supplies and suffocating aquatic plants. Disruption of this balance adversely affects all plant and animal nations and their interdependent relationships with the ecosystem.

12

This action commemorates the worldwide struggle for independence from occupation and is dedicated to Josh Ellerman for his dedication to defend Mother Earth and her animal nations.

Returning the prisoners back home, the Fur War continues.

-ALF and ELF

October 19, 1998

On behalf of the lynx, five buildings and four ski lifts at Vail were reduced to ashes on the night of Sunday, October 18th. Vail, Inc. is already the largest ski operation in North American and now wants to expand even further. The 12 miles of roads and 885 acres of clearcuts will ruin the last, best lynx habitat in the state. Putting profits ahead of Colorado's wildlife will not be tolerated. This action is just a warning. We will be back if this greedy corporation continues to trespass into wild and unroaded areas. For your safety and convenience we strongly advise skiers to choose other destinations until Vail cancels its inexcusable plans for expansion.

-Earth Liberation Front (ELF)

October 26, 1998

As corporate destroyers burn in the west, wildlife nations will be liberated in the north...

...the farm held captive many different breeds of mink... many were seen leaving the compound and entering surrounding woods as the liberators left...

This action was done in defiance of recent government repression waged by the grand jury's indictment of two falsely accused activists from Washington state. The Earth Liberation Front will not be intimidated by this government's actions or fur farmers' recent threats of violence against liberators...

December 27, 1998

To celebrate the holidays we decided on a bonfire. Unfortunately for US

Forest Industries it was at their corporate headquarters office...

On the foggy night after Christmas when everyone was digesting their turkey and pie, Santa's ELFs dropped two five-gallon buckets of diesel/ unleaded mix and a five gallon jug with cigarette delays which proved to be more than enough to get this party started.

This was in retribution for all the wild forests and animals lost to feed the wallets of greedy fucks like Jerry Bramwell, USFI president... and it's a warning to all others responsible. We do not sleep and we will not quit.

December 25, 1999

Boise Cascade has been very naughty. After ravaging the forests of the Pacific Northwest, Boise Cascade now looks towards the virgin forests of Chile. Early Christmas morning elves left coal in Boise Cascade's stocking. Four buckets of diesel and gas with kitchen timer delay destroyed their regional headquarters in Monmouth, Oregon.

Let this be a lesson to all greedy multinational corporations who don't respect their ecosystems.

The elves are watching.

-Earth Liberation Front

December 31, 1999

The ELF takes credit for a strike on the offices of Catherine Ives, rm. 324 Agriculture Hall at Michigan State University on Dec. 31, 1999. The offices were doused with gasoline and set afire. This was done in response to the work being done to force developing nations in Asia, Latin America and Africa to switch from natural crop plants to genetically engineered sweet potatoes, corn, bananas and pineapples. Monsanto and USAID are major funders of the research and promotional work being done through Michigan State University.

According to local newspapers the fire cost some $400,000 in damage. Cremate Monsanto, Long live the ELF!

On to the next GE target!

COMMUNIQUES

January 23, 2000

Greetings from Bloomington, IN:

The Earth Liberation Front would like to take credit for a late night visit to the Sterling Woods development on the evening of January 23rd.

During our visit, we torched one house that was under construction. It was completely destroyed. The walls had caved in by the time the fire department had arrived. Damage has been assessed at $200,000. 'NO SPRAWL, ELF' was painted on the developers sign.

The house was targeted because the sprawling development it is located in is in the Lake Monroe Watershed. This is the drinking water supply for the town of Bloomington, IN, and the surrounding area. It is already being jeopardized by existing development and roads.

Once again the rich of the world are destroying what little we have left in terms of natural areas and collective holdings (the water). Hopefully they will get the message that we will not take it anymore.

February 9, 2000

In the early hours of February 9 the Earth Liberation Front paid a visit to Green Hall at the University of Minnesota in Saint Paul, MN. The target was trans-genic oat research crops. The research was being done by university professors David Sommers and Howard Rines.

All the oats found in the greenhouse were destroyed, messages were spray-painted and the locks were glued on the way out.

Oat research is simply on of the projects that the university is taking part in, in partnership with gross corporations that are adding to the destruction of life on Earth.

Let this action be a warning to the University of Minnesota and the entire biotech industry that if you continue to destroy biodiversity on Earth your profits will continue to fall.

The elves are watching. Stop genetic engineering or we will.

-For freedom and wilderness, the Earth Liberation Front

March 24, 2000

Over the weekend of March 24th, maintenance work was done to the vehicles belonging to CS McCrossan construction, and were being used for the construction of the highway 55 reroute in Minneapolis. 4 machines had wires and hoses cut, dirt and sand poured into gas tanks, oil tubes and exhaust pipes, engine parts smashed, removed and destroyed, which has happened several times before and gone unreported.

This site is only a quarter-mile from Coldwater Springs, a sacred site to the Dakota people, and the last source of fresh spring water in the twin cities. After cutting hundreds of old trees and decimating a once wild ares, the road now threatens to cut off Coldwater's underground source, which has already happened to other springs in the city because of road construction.

Also on 3 separate occasions, large amounts of rock and table salt was mixed into the sand piles being used for cement. The piles are now gone and it is assumed that they were used in the cement building the land tunnel. This is being told because salt will weaken the integrity of cement.

The road is not nearly done and neither are we.

-Earth Liberation Front

April 30, 2000

Greetings,

Early Sunday, April 30th, the Earth Liberation Front struck again in Bloomington, IN. We entered the site of a massive clearcut on the west side of town, and poured sand into the engines and cut hoses of 6 large Earth destroying machines. We then set afire to a trailer full of wood chips destined to become paper trash.

According to the local paper, the damages cause by our midnight soiree were in the vicinity of $500,000. Not bad for one night's work, though certainly no Vail. The reason that this site was targeted was the ongoing development of the wooded areas around Bloomington have turned what was once forested land into parking lots, luxury houses for rich scum and expanded roads. The government and developers are mad with greed and there will be no limit to what they destroy until we take away the profit from their schemes. The local paper was right when they wrote that we take direct action when we don't get what we want through the usual bureaucratic channels.

We dedicate this action to Craig Rosebraugh and other Earth warriors that are being persecuted for their beliefs.

For the wild and an end to sprawl!

    -ELF

June, 2000

The Earth Liberation Front would like to make public that we have place hundreds of spikes in trees in the timber sales that are about to be cut on Crooked Creek Road in Brown County and Buskirk Road in Monroe County. These spikes have been placed both high and low in the trees to prevent the cutting of the trees. The trees are now worthless to the mill and dangerous to be cut down.

We ask that this action be widely publicized in order to prevent injury to any timber workers who might be working in the area. It is not our intention to cause harm to anyone. We also hope that this action will discourage companies from buying timber sales in the State Forests. This is a warning to all those who want to turn the beings of the Earth into cash. We are committed to protecting every last square inch of our forests that remain. Too much has been lost, let the corporations beware, the ELF is everywhere.

July 20, 2000

On behalf of native forests everywhere, we attacked the US Forest Service's North Central Research Station Forest Biotechnology Laboratory in Rhinelander, Wisconsin last night. Over 500 research pine, and broadleaf trees and saplings were cut down, ring-barked and trampled. Additionally, ten Forest Service trucks were defaced and calling cards were left behind. Due to an overzealous security guard, we had to make an earlier than

17

anticipated exit.

In Rhinelander, the Forest Service is mapping the DNA of white pine and attempting to genetically engineer them to be resistant to pine rust. Why? To aid industry in creating disease-resistant trees suitable for tree farms that will increase their profits. Despite the obvious threat of genetic pollution by GE trees, these fools, aided by industry financing, prod ahead in the name of science.

Don't get us wrong – this action is against the Forest Service, not just one particular project or research program. What they do on a daily basis is sheer genocide: putting forth the notion that they are "managing" life, running an asinine timber program that destroys the last of the old-growth and mars everything else, cutting deep into roadless areas in Idaho, spraying biocides like Btk in forests in Eastern Oregon and Washington under the guise of "pest management," treating wildlife as some numbers on a graph. The list goes on.

On that note we strongly advise or allies to cease their quibbling with the Forest Service over details of their genocidal plans, i.e. roadless policy, promises of no logging on public land etc. The sooner we realize that the Forest Service, like industry, are capitalists driven by an insane desire to make money and control life, the better. Then we can start taking more appropriate action.

As for the feds – we know you are stepping up the pressure by harassing press officers and other absurdities. What you don't realize is that we are infiltrating your ranks and gathering our own information. We could be that temp worker typing away at your disgusting computer, we could even be your secretary or intern. We are everywhere and nowhere and we are watching.

For wilderness and an end to industrial society.

-ELF, Earth Liberation Front

September 9, 2000

Greetings,

Late Friday night the Earth Liberation front paid a visit to the GOP

18

headquarters in Bloomington, IN, leaving it in flames as we left.

The fire was set as a reminder to politicians such as John Hostettler that we are watching and we will not sit by as they push for plans like I-69. The construction would fill the coffers of multinational corporations at the expense of the environment and working people everywhere. I-69 is just one example of the willingness of the rich to bleed the Earth and the working class to fulfill their money lust.

We have no faith in the present system of electoral politics where every candidate, both Republican and Democrat, is funded with corporate blood money. Because there are no viable options on the ballet, we must find another means of voting. Our non-participation in, and active resistance against this system, controlled by the rich, is our means of voting.

We are everywhere and nowhere.

September 26, 2000

Greetings Allies,

Members of the Earth Liberation Front are glad to announce our late night visit to construction sites along Whisky Rd. in Coram, Long Island, on September 26th. During the festivities a bulldozer and a house under construction were spray-painted and damaged, and numerous survey stakes "disappeared." We will no-longer allow urban sprawl to destroy what little of the environment we have left on Long Island, especially so close to a nature reserve. Urban sprawl has lead to the virtual extinction of several animal species, such as the Blue Heron and the Box Turtle, from parts of the island.

So until next time???

    -The elves

October – November, 2000

To whom it may concern,

Around mid-October early-November, 2000, selected greens and fairways of Crown Isle started showing signs of damage to the grass plus other damage to the ball washers, etc. Members of the ELF (Earth Liberation Front) took these photos and are claiming responsibility for this action. This is in protest of Crown Isle's destruction of green space - a home for animals and a great trail system. This action was also intended for further protest by causing economic damage in hopes to delay Crown Isle's plans for expansion across Ryan Rd. in the form of more upper-class ugly housing and another nine hole golf course.

This development would surely mean the destruction of that existing woodland, an area used partly for cattle grazing. The present development has already upset the water ways around Mission Hill through absence of trees and the destruction of the soil; any more development would do further damage to this ecosystem. Building ugly over-priced development (much like the current Crown Isle) is not worth this cost.

October 18, 2000

Early on the morning of October 18, a small group of dedicated folks walked into the martin State Forest determined to do whatever it took to stop the cutting of the trees on our public lands. The two active cuts had already sliced and diced their way through a beautiful patch of Indiana forest, including some very large, old trees. As prevention was not possible revenge became necessary. The price of doing dirty business in the state forests just went up. But not without warning. In an effort to be fair and give our opposition time to reconsider their wicked deeds, several warning had been spray-painted earlier. They disregarded these well-intended cautions and proceeded with the cut. We were forced to retaliate. Three skidders and one loader were as thoroughly damaged as we could accomplish without endangering the surrounding forest. Hoses were cut, sand poured into engines and gas tanks, seats and belts were slashed and appropriate messages were spray-painted (Earth Raper, Go Cut in Hell, and We are Everywhere). Let all those who would profit from the destruction of our last wild places beware. We ARE everywhere, and we are watching.

This IS a timber war.

-ELF

November 11, 2000

In the early morning hours of November 11th, members of the Earth Liberation Front paid a visit to the construction sites off Whisky Rd. in Coram, Long Island. This has been the third hit on the construction site and the worst yet. Several houses were spray-painted extensively and had their windows shattered. We here elves are waging an unending war against urban sprawl and will fight to our last breath to protect our environment from greedy corporate interests.

-ELF

November 24, 2000

On November 24th, members of the Earth Liberation Front did a 4th action against the construction sites along Whisky Rd. in Coram, Long Island. During the action over 17 windows were smashed along with the spray-painting of various slogans. The ELF then proceeded to another site of urban sprawl in Miller place. They then created some havoc including the decommissioning of Earth raping equipment. On a property sale sign and post that was stuck through a bulldozer, our mark was left,'Earth Not For Sale – ELF.'

-Earth Liberation Front

November 27, 2000

Viva la revolution! The Bolder ELF burned down the Legen Ridge mansion on November 27th. We know that the corporate developers' No on Amendment 24 campaign is guilty of a $6 election buyout.

December 1, 2000
Greetings,

On December 1st, members of the Earth Liberation Front executed a massive strike on a large construction site building over 40 luxury houses in Middle Island, Long Island. During the action an immense number of windows, totaling over 200, were smashed, survey stakes were ripped out of our Earth, slogans were spray-painted profusely, and various other forms of ecotage were performed on the houses. The workers were kind enough to have lined up all their vehicles the day before to facilitate our monkeywrenching. An assortment of equipment from backhoes to bulldozers sustained crippling damage. The final number ranged to a little more than a dozen.

Urban sprawl not only destroys the forests and green spaces of our planet, but also leads directly to added runoff of pollutants into waterways, increased traffic that causes congestion and air pollution, and a less pleasing landscape. These luxury homes are being built precariously close to the 320 acre Cathedral Pines County Park. Long Island has the 2nd largest pine barren ecosystem in the world. Our greedy and corrupt politicians are more than willing to provide subsidies and allow construction in any area not under current protection by the Long Island Pine Barren Protection Plan.

Our forests also lay atop of our aquifer which provides a large expanse of drinking water that is actually contaminated by pollutants and runoff. We will not stand by idly while our Earth is butchered for the monetary gain and the luxury of the wealthy elite. As long as our planet continues to be raped, we will be out there

We are everywhere.

-Earth Liberation Front

December 7, 2000

At roughly 1:30 AM Friday, December 7th, members if the ALF and ELF descended upon McDonald's corporate offices in Haupauge (Long Island). Here we smashed over 10 windows and spray-painted anti-meat slogans against environmental destruction. We will not be stopped...

December 9, 2000

Greetings,

The Earth Liberation Front claims responsibility for the fires that ravages the Birchwood at Spring Lake housing development in Middle Island, Long Island. During the night of December 9th, members of the ELF crept into the construction site and placed incendiaries in four rows of condominiums. The structures were checked thoroughly for the presence of any occupants (human or animal) before being set. All of the incendiaries ignited successfully and the resulting fires gutted almost 16 nearly completed luxury homes, which were to be sold at several hundred thousand dollars each. Messages denouncing urban sprawl were scrawled on many of the remaining future dens of the wealthy elite. Survey stakes were also pulled up to prevent the planned expansion of the housing development along the boarder of a New York State Conservation Area.

The actions of those who orchestrated the construction are absolutely intolerable, so we are now declaring an unbounded war on urban sprawl. As the stakes of the struggle continue to expand, so will our methods and tactics. Window breaking and disabling vehicles can only do so much, and in a battle with our Earth in the balance we can not hold back or go soft on those pillaging the planet for profit. Hopefully the several million dollars in destruction will provide an unmistakable message to developers that their land rape will now be more costly than ever before.

-Earth Liberation Front

December 19, 2000

Greetings from the front, The Earth Liberation Front claims responsibility for the torching of a luxury home under construction in Miller Place, Long Island on December 19th. Anti-urban sprawl messages were spraypainted on the walls, then accelerants were poured over the house and lighted. Let there be no mistake that this was a non-violent action and the house was searched for any living thing before being set alight. This is the latest in a string of actions in the war against urban sprawl.

Urban sprawl not only destroys the forest and green spaces of our planet, but also leads directly to added runoff of pollutants into our waterways, increased traffic that causes congestion and air pollution, and a less pleasing landscape. Our earth is being murdered by greedy corporate and personal interests. The rape of Earth puts everyone's life at risk due to global warming, ozone depletion, toxic chemicals, etc. Unregulated population growth is also a direct product of urban sprawl. There are over 6 billion people on this planet of which almost a third are either starving or living in poverty. Building homes for the wealthy should not even be a priority.

Forests, farms, and wetlands are being replaced with a sea of houses, green chemical lawns, blacktop, and roadkill. Farmland is being bought out by land developers because of their inability to compete with cheap corporate, genetically-engineered, pesticide saturated food. The time has come to decide what is more important: The planet and the health of its population or the profits of those who destroy it.

The purpose of sloganeering is not self-righteous posturing as has been reported, but a direct warning to the Earth's oppressors. Apparently, Long Islands growing smog and cancerous water is not a good enough warning to those directly responsible for it. The site of this recent action was warned twice of impending actions with the monkeywrenching of several vehicles and spraypainted messages.

It's time for the people of Long Island to put their foot down and no longer passively tolerate our island's rape. It is time for Nassua and Suffolk County Police to realize we are but the symptoms of a corrupt society on the brink of ecological collapse. Law enforcement should be directing their time and resources towards the real terrorists. Those who commit murder and thest upon our populace daily. Big business is the enemy of the people, yet most people remain bllind due to the massive propaganda and the power they wield. Every major media outlet in Long Island is in their pockets. The time for action is upon us. We are watching.

-Earth Liberation Front

December 31, 2000

Greetings friends,

As an early New Year's gift to Long Island's environment destroyers, the Earth Liberation Front (E.L.F.) visited a construction site on December 29 and set fire to 4 unsold Luxury houses nearly completed at Island Estates in Mount Sinai, Long Island. Hopefully, this caused nearly $2 million in damage.

This hopefully provided a firm message that we will not tolerate the destruction of our Island. Recently, hundreds of houses have been built over much of Mount Sinai's picturesque landscape and developers now plan to build a further 189 luxury houses over the farms and forests adjacent to Island Estates.

This action was done in solidarity with Josh Harper, Craig Rosebraugh, Jeffrey "Free" Luers and Craig "Critter" Marshall, Andrew Stepanian, Jeremy Parkin, and the countless other known and unknown activists who suffer persecution, interrogation, police brutality, crappy jail conditions, yet stand strong.

Whether it's denying a prisoner vegetarian or vegan food, phone calls (which is a right), or even the terrorism of the Grand Jury, they stand strong. Oppression of our brothers and sisters will only make us uproot our tactics, by means, frequency, and cost. The more brutality you give our brothers and sisters, the more money we cause the oppressors. Our hearts go out to all of them.

Keep up the fight

/// Earth Liberation Front FAQ:///

Q: *Aren't there environmental groups to take care of these problems?*

A: Yes, but obviously they're not getting the job done; otherwise there wouldn't be houses for us to burn down! All successful movements in history have had a variety of methods, from education all the way to direct action.

Q: *Are you terrorists?*

A: No. We condemn all forms of terrorism. A common definition of terrorism is "to reduce to a state of fear or terror." We are costing them money. If change falls out of your pocket, you are not in a state of fear or terror. If you give money to the homeless, you are losing money, but you are not being terrorized. Even if your house is robbed, you are not being terrorized.

We are non-violent. Houses were checked for all forms of life and we even moved a propane tank out of the house all the way across the street just in case, in worst case scenario, the firefighters could get hurt. We show solidarity with our firefighters and we are sorry to wake you up in the middle of the night. Don't be mad at us; be mad at urban sprawl. We encourage all citizens to donate generous contributions this year to your local volunteer firefighters.

Q: *Don't companies have the right to property?*

A: We are just trying to cause the rich sprawl corporations enough money so they stop destroying the planet, and thus the health, well-being, and existence   of humankind. Corporations do not have rights. Humans do. Corporations lost their "right" to property the second the earth10 inhabitants lost their freedom to life and happiness. Cancer is not happiness. Dead animals are not life. Polluted air and mudslides affect people's lives. Property is theft.

Q: *Why don't you use legal methods?*

A: They don't work as well. Mahatma Gandhi disobeyed the law to free his people. Harriet Tubman used illegal methods to free slaves on the underground railroad. Nelson Mandela even used violent methods to end the Apartheid. John Brown killed slave owners and raided a federal arsenal to try to start a slave revolt.

How many successful movements in history can you think of off the top of your head that came about only by education? How do you "protest" against slavery? Holding signs and handing out flyers on southern plantations? Today, these "unlawful" people are all seen as martyrs, and someday we will too. Try to realize this NOW. Not all laws are just. Malcolm X says "By Any Means Necessary" in order to obtain freedom.

But, we do not hurt people, we never have in our long history, and we never will. We respect all life, even our worst enemies that give us cancerous drinking water. (If someone is going to shoot you in the back six times, do you nicely, kindly ask him to shoot you only three or four times? No, you freakin' turn around and punch them in the face, grab the gun from them, and shove it up their ass!)

The Earth isn't dying; it's being killed, and those who are killing it have names and addresses.

What are YOU doing for the earth tonight?

No Compromise in Defense of Our Earth! Stop Urban Sprawl Or We Will."

January 1, 2001

We torched Superior Lumber in Glendale, OR on January 1, 2001. Superior Lumber is a typical earth raper contributing to the ecoloaical destruction of the Northwest. What happened to them should shock no one.

This year, 2001, we hope to see an escalation in tactics against capitalism and industry. While Superior Lumber says, 'Make a few items, and do it better than anyone else,' we say, 'choose an earth raper, and destroy them".

-ELF, Earth Liberation Front"

January 23, 2001

Five windows were broken, and 18 vandalized, causing upwards of $800 in damages in the first wave of attacks against corporate sprawl in Louisville, Kentucky. the damage effected two nearly finished buildings including a PNC Bank. The once beautiful farmlands of Eastern Jefferson County, KY, are being destroyed by Earth rapers for corporate profit. This was the first, be it minor, direct action attempt to stop the sprawl. It will be a long fought battle and more actions are planned in the future.

-Louisville ELF

February 20, 2001

The Earth Liberation Front takes credit for torching the Delta & Pine Land Co. Research cotton gin in Visalia, California on February 20.

D&PL continues to pursue its "Terminator technology" despite global opposition to the genetic engineering of plants to produce sterile seeds. Engineering a suicide sequence into the plant world is the most dangerous new technology since nuclear power and needs to be stopped.

We chose this warehouse because it contained massive quantities of transgenic cotton seed in storage. But now, this seed will no longer exist to contaminate the environment, enrich a sick corporation, or contribute to its warped research programs.

After cutting through a padlock on a door to get into the warehouse, we placed 4 five-gallon buckets filled with half gasoline and half diesel in strategic locations. Windows were broken to provide the fire with oxygen and timers were set. Within just a few minutes the operation was complete.

We are the burning rage of a dying planet.

> -Earth Liberation Front (ELF) ...Terminate D&PL, cremate Monsanto, burn biotechnology...

March 2, 2001

Units 6 and 8 in the Judie Timber sale in the Hardesty Wilderness Area Umpqua National Forest) have been spiked. Also, all survey stakes have been pulled and destroyed on the road cutting into unit 8. We inserted 60-penny nails and 8 and 10 inch spikes both high and low in the trees to prevent cutting of this native forest.

The Salvage Rider sale threatens the Laying Creek watershed, which provides water to the nearby town of Cottage Grove. Scarred early in the century by fire, this vibrant forest provides habitat for rare plants, tree frogs, and elk (which we saw herds of during our excursion).

All responsibility for worker safety now lies with the owner of the sale, Seneca Jones Corporation and their accomplices, the Forest Service.

Cancel this sale immediately.

> -ELF, Earth Liberation Front

March 5, 2001

During the evening of March 5th, members of the Earth Liberation Front descended upon the Old Navy Outlet Center in downtown Huntington, Long Island, NY. We smashed over 8 10'x10' insulated plate glass windows and one neon sign. This action served as a protest to Old Navy's owners, the Fisher family's involvement in the clearcutting of old-growth forest in the Pacific Northwest. These actions will continue until the Fisher family pulls economic support from the lumber industry, regardless of whether with the Pacific Lumber Company or otherwise.

In the past week, Mother Nature has blessed the Northeast with snow, and we are reminded of our brothers and sisters in the Northwest, and their struggle to preserve what Mother Nature has blessed them with, the forests in the land that they call home. We will not sit idly by, and will do our best to amplify their voices, so that their message will get through to the Fisher family in the only language they know – economics.

Old Navy, Gap, Banana Republic care not for the species that call these forests home, care not for the animals that comprise their leather products, and care not for their garment workers underpaid, exploited and enslaved in overseas sweatshops. As more and more minds continue to be exposed to the true nature of their greed, fewer and fewer will sit idly by, and the cries of the Earth will not fall upon deaf ears. We will not stop.

> Love,
> The elves

April 2, 2001

Take actions against globalization now!!!

The Earth Liberation Front has very recently paid a visit to a Nike outlet in the town of Albertville, MN. This visit was in solidarity with all people of all nations to fight globalization, and to support the growing anti-global sentiment. This is also a call for direct action against globalization in solidarity with all of the anti-FTAA actions scheduled in Canada later this month.

After witnessing first hand the treacherous conditions that Nike workers experience daily in Sweatshops around the world, it was decided that no NGO organization could have the immediate impact necessary to end conditions that exist currently at any sweatshop.

Instead, direct action is a more efficient tactic to stop Nike in their footsteps. Unfortunately, due to weather conditions, the visit was short, and although the plan was to destroy the roof, only minor damages were sustained.

Although the roof of this Nike outlet did not go up in flames as planned, this action is still a message to Nike they cannot ignore. In fact, there are only two options for Nike at this point. Option 1. – You can shut down all of your sweatshops immediately, and immediately place all assets into the communities that you have stolen from. Along with this you must close down all Nike outlets, starting with the Albertville, MN, location (You are especially not welcome in this town!!!)… Or, Option 2. – People across the globe will individually attack Nike outlets, as well as retailers that sell

Nike (including college campus shops) until Nike closes down or adheres to demand #1.

It is important to point out to Nike that the violence they use against the poor, and especially those that do all the work for them will only be meet with violence towards what they hold dearest... their pocketbooks. All ELF actions are nonviolent towards humans and animals. But if a building exists which perpetrates, and sponsors violence towards people or animals (such as a Nike Outlet, or a Gap Outlet, etc.), then by God, it's got to be burned to the ground!!! The ELF wholeheartedly condones the use of violence towards inanimate objects to prevent oppression, violence, and most of all to protect freedom. Direct action is a wonderful tool to embrace on the road to liberation.

Sincerely,

Philip H. Knight, Chairman and CEO Nike inc.
One Bowerman Drive
Beaverton, OR 97003-6433
Fax: (503) 671-6300

April 15, 2001

The Earth Liberation Front claims responsibility for the fire that took place at Ross Island Sand and Gravel on Sunday, April 15th. For many years Ross Island Sand and Gravel has been guilty of stealing soil from the Earth, specifically the lagoon on Ross Island. Further, the recent acknowledgment of the drudging of toxic disposal cells has drawn our attention to the exploitation that Ross Island Sand and Gravel commits against our Earth. In their Easter basket we decided to leave four containers of gasoline and a time delayed fuse packed under two of their cement trucks.

If Ross Island Sand and Gravel mines the Columbia River Gorge, then the ELF will take necessary action. Let this be a warning to all the greedy corporations who exploit the Earth's natural resources, especially those who plan on doing it under the FTAA and the title of "free trade."

-the elves and the Easter bunny

May 21, 2001

COMMUNIQUES

Part 1

At 3:15am on Monday, May 21, the research of Toby Bradshaw was reduced to smoke and ashes. We attacked his office at the University of Washington while at the same time another group set fire to a related target in Clatskanie, Oregon, 150 miles away.

Bradshaw, the driving force in G.E. tree research, continues to unleash mutant genes into the environment that is certain to cause irreversible harm to forest ecosystems.

After breaking into Bradshaw's office at the Center for Urban Horticulture, we inspected the building for occupants and set up incendiary devices with a modest amount of accelerant. Although we placed these devices specifically to target his office, a large portion of the building was damaged. This extensive damage was due to a surprisingly slow and poorly coordinated response from the fire department, which was evident by their radio transmissions.

As long as universities continue to pursue this reckless "science," they run the risk of suffering severe losses. Our message remains clear: we are determined to stop genetic engineering.

From the torching of Catherine Ive's office at Michigan State University to the total incineration of GE seeds at the D & PL warehouse in Visalia, CA, the Earth Liberation Front is growing and spreading. As the culture of domination forces itself into our very genes, wild fires of outrage will continue to blaze.

-ELF

Part 2

Early Monday morning, May 21, we dealt a blow to one of the many institutions responsible for massive hybrid tree farming in the Northwest. Incendiary devices at Jefferson Poplar in Clatskanie, Oregon, burned an office and a fleet of 13 trucks. Unfortunately, due to a design flaw, one targeted structure was left standing. We torched Jefferson Poplar because hybrid poplars are an ecological nightmare threatening native biodiversity in the ecosystem. Our forests are being liquidated and replaced with monocultured tree farms so greedy, earth raping corporations can make

31

more money.

Pending legislation in Oregon and Washington further criminalizing direct action in defense of the wild will not stop us and only highlights the fragility of the ecocidal empire.

As we wrote in Clatskanie "You cannot control what is wild."

-ELF Earth Liberation Front

June 13, 2001

To whom it may concern,

During the early morning hours of June 13th members of the Animal and Earth Liberation Fronts attacked various Bank of New York branches and offices in efforts that massive economic damages will dissuade them from further management of American Depository Receipts belonging to Huntingdon Life Sciences. HLS is responsible for the deaths of over 500 animals daily and hundreds of thousands annually. These animals are murdered in crude attempts for pesticide and pharmaceutical corporations to pursue avenues to legalize their products. Monsanto and other earth destroyers use HLS' fraudulent practices to place potentially lethal and environmentally hazardous chemicals on the public market.

This is a message to the general public. HLS does not care about the health of people, does not care about the preservation of wild lands and life, and brutalizes, probes, tortures, and murders thousands of lonely, frightened and beautiful creatures.

The Earth will be Revered; We will deliver! These Animals Need Love; We will deliver! HLS must close; and We will deliver!

The following attacks were made on June 13th:

1. Bank of New York, Huntington, Long Island Branch - Had locks glued and the slogans "BNY Invests in Murder", "Investors in Murder", and "ALF" spray painted.

2. Bank of New York, Kings Park, Long Island Branch - Was spray painted with the slogans "Bank of NY Kills Puppies" and

"ALF".

3. Bank of New York, Commack, Long Island Branch - Exterior ATM machine damaged by glue and plastic strips in card slot and glue in keypad. On the building's side wall the slogans "Investors in Murder", and "Stop the Torture" were spray painted in bold letters.

4. Bank of New York, Babylon, Long Island Branch - Two exterior ATM machines were damaged by glue and plastic strips in card slot and glue in keypad. On the bank's main building various slogans were spray painted.

5. Bank of New York, Suffolk County Office Building, Farmingdale, Long Island - Over 25 windows were smashed out and the slogans "ALF" and "ELF" were spray painted behind as a warning that these actions were not random vandalism, they were planned and calculated.

Unless BNY stops trade in HLS' American Depository Receipts, they can look forward to many more nights of broken glass.

These actions were dedicated to the 130 thousand animals who will perish this year for HLS' greed, and dedicated to Jeffrey "Free" Luers, an outspoken forest preservation activist, and green anarchist who was just recently incarcerated.

Love, Life, Action

        -The Earth Liberation Front
        -The Animal Liberation Front

June 10, 2001

The University of Idaho Biotechnology building, currently under construction, was targeted in the early hours of the morning on June 10th by a cell of the Earth Liberation Front calling themselves the Night Action Kids. Survey stakes were removed and the exterior of the new building painted with such sentiments as 'NO GE!' and 'Go Organic'.

This is the second action against the Biotechnology building. The first of which individuals entered the building and caused an unknown amount of damage.

An anonymous ELF Night Action Kid compares research in Genetic Engineering and Biotechnology to the scientific studies which lead to the creation of the nuclear bomb. 'Biotechnological research may be intended for good ends by the scientist, as was nuclear research, but in our free enterprise police state society it will be used almost solely for greed and control. With Genetic Engineering we are creating another bomb.'

Monsanto and other large corporations are patenting seeds and forcing farmers to sign contracts that they will continue buying these GE, and many times pesticide resistant, seeds from the same corporation year after year, effectively taking control over our food sources. Genetically Engineered food on our grocery store shelves is not labeled as such, so the individual does not know what he or shi is eating. Genetically Engineered fish are escaping into the wild populations with the chance of killing off the entire species. Genetic testing for predisposition to certain diseases, such as cancer, may soon keep you and your children from getting insurance or a job.

GE corporations and their supporters have claimed that we [anti-GE activists] are using scare tactics to further our viewpoint. The fact is that Biotechnology and Genetic Engineering are scary prospects when placed in the hands of large corporations who care only about profits and not about the health and safety of the people, or the effects they are having on the environment. Through the University of Idaho Biotechnology Program we are teaching our children to work in a field which is developing faster than its effects, both physically and ethically, can be monitored and has the potential for causing catastrophic harm to all humans and the planet,' claims another Night Action Kid, who continues, 'Get Biotech out of Moscow! It is not wanted in our community.'

July 27, 2001

We are claiming responsibility for spiking 60-penny nails high and low into hundreds of trees in Units 5, 6, and 7 of the Upper Greenhorn Timber Sale in the Cowlitz Valley Ranger District in the Gifford Pinchot National Forest. This timber sale contains 99 acres of old growth and is home to at least 3 pairs of spotted owls, grizzly bear, lynx, wolf, goshawk, just to name a few of its many inhabitants. This is truly a beautiful area, unfortunately one of the last of its kind because of the system we all live under.

We want to be clear that all oppression is linked, just as we are all linked, and we believe in a diversity of tactics to stop earth rape and end all domination. Together we can destroy this patriarchal nightmare, which is currently in the form of techno-industrial global capitalism. We desire an existence in harmony with the wild based on equality, love, and respect. We stand in solidarity with all resistance to this system, especially those who are in prison, disappeared, raped, tortured....we are all survivors and will not stop!!!

The forest service was notified of this action BEFORE this year's logging season so we could take all precautions to assure worker safety. We must ask why they never made this public. We were trying to let them cancel this sale quietly. However, as bosses jeopardize worker's lives every day we realized we needed to make this public. Also, as repression against us increases, such as the recent laws in Oregon, we promise to be even stronger and encourage others to join us.

We are everywhere and nowhere. We are your parents and your children. We are alive!!!

Please do not label us...We are anonymous.

October 17, 2001
Corvallis, California

In opposition to the Bureau of Land Management's (BLM) continued war against the Earth - the Earth Liberation Front targeted the Wild Horse Holding Facility in Corvallis, California on October 17th, 2001. For years, the BLM has rounded up thousands of wild horses and burros to clear public land for grazing cattle. Many of these wild animals are sent to slaughter.

We cut through and removed four 60 foot sections of wooden fence to corrals holding more than 200 wild horses in order to free them from captivity.

After moving domestic horses to a safe distance we set four timed incendiary devices aimed at destroying two barns, two vehicles and one office building.

In the name of all that is wild we will continue to target industries and organizations that seek to profit by destroying the Earth.

-Earth Liberation Front

November 5, 2001

Hello;

This is a communique from a nameless Earth Liberation Front Cell. We claim no issue or area as our own, we just act. This is to announce we have spiked countless trees in the Otter Wing Timber Sale, located in the Nez Perce National Forest.

For too long, the forests of Central and North Idaho have been under assault from industrial forestry. The Boise, Payette, Clearwater, Idaho Panhandle, and Nez Perce are some of the National Forests in Idaho that have been scarred from excessive logging. The timber sale program - nothing but a financial drain as well as a ecological disaster - must end.

The Otter Wing Timber sale has destroyed a once pristine ecosystem on the South Fork of the Clearwater River. It is an area which hosted abundant wildlife, such as fish, birds, mammalian predators, ungulates and a beautiful mosaic of different forest vegetative patterns. Now most of that area has been logged-aside from the spiked units.

We are serious. This is our first act of sabotage in Idaho. We may feel compelled to act again. The forest service of Idaho should know that has long as they continue to destroy Idaho's last remaining wildlands, they risk action on behalf of the E.L.F.

January 26, 2002
St. Paul, MN

The construction site for the new Microbial and Plant Genomics Research Center at the University of Minnesota had incendiaries left in the main trailer and two pieces of heavy machinery, including a bulldozer. Heavy damage was caused to the machinery and trailer by the fire, which then spread to the adjacent Crop Research building.

The construction of this research building is being funded by biotech giant Cargill Corporation who develop, patent, and market genetically modified crops, making people dependent on GE foods. We are fed up with capitalists like Cargill and major universities like the U of M have who have long sought to develop and refine technologies which seek to exploit and control nature to the fullest extent under the guise of progress. Biotechnology is only one new expression of this drive.

For the end of capitalism and the mechanization of our lives,

-Earth Liberation Front

August 15, 2002

Hundreds of metallic and non-metallic spikes have been placed in units 28 and 29 of the Kirk Timber Sale in the Gifford Pinchot National Forest. The spikes were placed at all levels of the trees. Most trees have both metallic and non-metallic spikes.

The Douglas Fir, Hemlock, Cedar, and Yew trees are an average of 300 years old. The 16 acre grove is a refuge of Cascadian native forest and is adjacent to the Dark Divide Roadless area. It is home to Elk, Owl, and Bear among other wild beings. Logging this grove would require rebuilding a road and replacing a bridge over a major creek.

The Kirk Timber Sale is one of many sales currently proposed in the Gifford Pinchot National Forest. Industrial logging of public lands is primarily a public subsidy for timber companies. The US Forest Service timber sale program has never been economically viable and loses money yearly at the people's expense. The main beneficiaries are the owners and managers of a handful of timber companies.

This system does provide jobs for a few local residents, but fewer all the time because of unsustainable logging practices. That short term benefit is outweighed by the long term losses of topsoil, clean water, fisheries, and biodiversity which greatly reduce the chances that local people can make a sustainable living on the land. The timber sale program is the same as industrial resource extraction around the world in that its short term profits are enjoyed by only a few while the costs are felt by all. Acts of resistance like this spiking are part of a larger worldwide struggle to defend land and communities against clearcuts, war, and other acts of greed.

37

This action seeks to keep these old growth trees from ever being cut. It is not intended to put any timberworkers at risk. This message is being sent out before any trees are felled.

August 11, 2002

The Earth Liberation Front is claiming responsibility for the 8/11/02 arson attack on the United States Forest Service Northeast Research Station in Irvine, Pennsylvania.

The laboratory was set ablaze during the early morning hours, causing over $700,000 damage, and destroying part of 70 years worth of research. This lesson in "prescribed fire" was a natural, necessary response to the threats posed to life in the Allegheny Forest by proposed timber sales, oil drilling, and greed driven manipulation of Nature.

This facility was strategically targeted, and if rebuilt, will be targeted again for complete destruction. Furthermore, all other U.S. Forest Service administration and research facilities, as well as all DCNR buildings nationwide should now be considered likely targets.

These agencies continue to ignore and mislead the public, at the bidding of their corporate masters, leaving us with no alternative to underground direct action. Their blatant disregard for the sanctity of life and its perfect Natural balance, indifference to strong public opposition, and the irrevocable acts of extreme violence they perpetrate against the Earth daily are all inexcusable, and will not be tolerated. If they persist in their crimes against life, they will be met with maximum retaliation.

In pursuance of justice, freedom, and equal consideration for all innocent life across the board, segments of this global revolutionary movement are no longer limiting their revolutionary potential by adhering to a flawed, inconsistent "non-violent" ideology. While innocent life will never be harmed in any action we undertake, where it is necessary, we will no longer hesitate to pick up the gun to implement justice, and provide the needed protection for our planet that decades of legal battles, pleading, protest, and economic sabotage have failed so drastically to achieve.

The diverse efforts of this revolutionary force cannot be contained, and will only continue to intensify as we are brought face to face with the oppressor in inevitable, violent confrontation. We will stand up and fight

COMMUNIQUES

for our lives against this iniquitous civilization until its reign of TERROR
is forced to an end - by any means necessary.

In defense of all life - Pacific E.L.F

2.

ELF FAQS

EARTH LIBERATION FRONT 1997-2002

The ELF realizes the profit motive caused and reinforced by the capitalist society is destroying all life on this planet. The only way, at this point in time, to stop that continued destruction of life is to, by any means necessary, take the profit motive out of killing.

- North American Earth Liberation Front Press Office

What is the Earth Liberation Front (ELF)?

The Earth Liberation Front (ELF) is an international underground organization that uses direct action in the form of economic sabotage to stop the exploitation and destruction of the natural environment.

How and when did the group begin?

It has been speculated that the group was founded in the early 1990s as an offshoot of Earth First! in England. The ideology of the ELF spread to North America in the mid 1990s. In November 1997, the ELF officially claimed responsibility for the group's first action in North America. The claim of responsibility was sent to aboveground supporters, who released the information to the media. In the communiqué, the ELF claimed credit for releasing wild horses and burning down a Bureau of Land Management Horse Corral near Burns, Oregon on November 29, 1997. The communiqué appeared as follows:

> The Bureau of Land Management (BLM) claims they are removing non-native species from public lands (aren't white Europeans also non-native?) but then they turn around and subsidize the cattle industry and place thousands of non-native domestic cattle on these same lands...to help halt the BLM's illegal and immoral business of rounding up wild horses from public lands and funneling them to slaughter...
>
> This hypocrisy and genocide against the horse nation will not go unchallenged! The practice of rounding up and auctioning wild horses must be stopped. The practice of grazing cattle on public lands must be stopped. The time to take action is now. From an investigation like the Associated Press' to writing the BLM to an action like ours, you can

help stop the slaughter and save our Mother Earth...

This action caused an estimated $450,000 in damages to the facility and the release of 448 wild horses and 51 burros. Since November of 1997, there have been over two dozen major actions performed by the ELF in North America alone, resulting in nearly $40 million in damages.

Where is the ELF based geographically?

The ELF has no centralized location. Actions have been taken by the ELF all across the United States, in Canada, throughout Europe, and in South America. The number of locations targeted by the ELF continues to increase.

How is the organization structured?

The ELF is organized into autonomous cells that operate independently and anonymously from one another and the general public. The group does not contain a hierarchy or any sort of leadership. Instead the group operates under an ideology. If an individual believes in the ideology and follows a certain set of guidelines, she or he can perform actions and become a part of the ELF.

This cell structure has been extremely effective in ensuring the continuation of the organization with minimal arrests. Law enforcement, particularly in North America, is trained to recognize and deal with organizations that have a leader, a hierarchy and a central headquarters. The ELF does not contain any of these.

Due to the autonomous and underground aspects of the ELF cells, an infiltration into a cell by no way means the entire movement will be stopped. If one individual or even one entire cell is captured by authorities, other individuals and cells will be free to continue their work, as they operate independently and anonymously from one another. The cell structure is a type of guerilla tactic that has been successfully employed by various movements around the world for ages. It can be a successful tactic when used properly against a greater military power.

How many members are in the ELF?

It is next to impossible to estimate the number of ELF members internationally or even country by country. Since 1997, in the United States, the ELF actions have steadily increased and have appeared in a growing number of differing geographical areas. Therefore, it is safe to assume the group continues to grow in size.

More and more people around the world are realizing the horrifying state of the environment and the extreme, continuous exploitation of people and life in general caused by the greedy individual wanting more numbers to appear in the bank account. Simultaneously, people are becoming increasingly frustrated with the exhausted state-sanctioned, legal means of social change because on their own they do not work.

If people are serious about stopping the destruction and exploitation of all life on the planet then they must also be serious about recognizing the need for a real direct action campaign and their own personal involvement.

One ELF cell can consist of just a few people who have the ability to cause extreme amounts of economic damage with just one action. It doesn't take a trained expert to become involved in the ELF, just individuals who really care about life on the planet to the degree that they want to take actions to protect it. Environmental protection is a matter of self defense, and ELF actions are a natural response to the very real threats to life on Earth.

Is the ELF primarily an environmental organization?

The organization is an environmental group but also one that realizes the true cause of murder and destruction of life. Therefore, it is not enough to work solely on individual environmental issues; the capitalist state and its symbols of propaganda must also be targeted. It may be more realistic to refer to the organization as one that works to protect all life on the planet.

What is the ideology of the ELF?

The ideology is what lies at the heart of the ELF. As previously mentioned, the group does not have any sort of hierarchy or physical leadership but instead revolves around an ideology. This ideology is the key to the group's existence, purpose, and longevity. So what is it?

The ELF realizes that the destruction of life is not a mere random occurrence but a deliberate act of violence performed by those entities concerned with nothing more than pursuing extreme economic gain at any cost. With this realization in mind, the ELF maintains that it is only logical to work to remove the profit motive from killing the Earth and all life on it.

Anyone seeking to create actual positive social and political change must reflect on past attempts throughout history to learn what worked, what didn't, and what can be taken to aid in the current pursuit. A refusal to make this reflection is also a refusal to make an honest life commitment to the cause of justice and protection of life on this planet.

The ELF recognizes that the popular environmental movement has failed miserably in its attempts to bring about the protection needed to stop the killing of life on this planet. State-sanctioned means of social change rarely on their own have (or will have) any real effect in obtaining the desired results. This is due to the obvious fact that the legal means of protest in solving grievances do little more than reinforce the same system, which is a root of the problem.

The state system is not going to allow any real change within it unless the state structure (government), big business, and finally the mainstream consumer society feels that change is really necessary. Yet it is this same state structure, big business, and consumer society that is directly responsible for the destruction of life on the planet for the sake of profit. When these entities have repeatedly demonstrated their prioritizing of monetary gain ahead of life, it is absolute foolishness to continue to ask them nicely for reform or revolution. Matters must be taken into the hands of the people who need to more and more step outside of this societal law to enforce natural law.

One definition of natural law refers to our dependence on the substances in the natural environment which enable all life to exist, primarily clean air, clean water, and clean soil. Clean air is needed for life to breathe, clean water is needed for life to drink, and clean soil is needed to grow food for life to eat.

Particularly with the advent of the industrial revolution, the westernized way of life has been in complete violation of natural law. There is a major difference between taking actions for the immediate sustenance of you, your family and your close-knit community and actions taken to stockpile wealth and to demonstrate power and domination over, and often times at, the expense of others.

Yes, everyone should have access to basic necessities of living, a suitable shelter (not only for you but for the natural environment), access to healthy food (not only for you but for the natural environment consisting of organically and locally grown items using sustainable permaculture practices free of genetic engineering), access to proper healthcare, etc. But there is no excuse for, out of pure greed and selfishness, desiring more than you need to live a free and happy life. The majority of stockpiling, greed, and monetary wealth comes at the expense of others whether humans, non-human animals or the natural environment.

The ELF ideology considers the various social and political problems facing the world today to be mere symptoms caused by a larger overall problem. Thus, in a sense, to work individually on separate justice issues is to attempt to toss water out of a sinking ship with a teaspoon. (If you are serious about stopping the ship from sinking it would only be wise to find the hole and plug it!) The only way to stop the symptoms of the problem is to identify the main root cause and directly work to abolish it.

The ELF ideology maintains that it is the very social and political ideology in operation throughout the Westernized countries that is creating the various injustices on this planet and ultimately the destruction of life. That ideology is capitalism and the mindset that allows it to exist. Capitalism and (what we have referred to in the states for years) the American Dream have long symbolized a form of economic opportunity and freedom. The idea that no matter who you are, if you worked hard all your life, you too could have the perfect husband or wife, the 2.3 kids, new BMW, the beach house on Maui and penthouse in New York City and loads of cash to play with.

What wasn't and still isn't told to the millions seeking the American Dream is that dream comes at a price; it always has and always will. That price consists of everything from taking advantage of slave labor, to dumping toxic waste into our waterways, to murdering those who take a stand for justice, to destroying cultures, to destroying environments and exploiting and oppressing anyone or anything that poses to be a threat, nuisance, or a bump along the path to riches.

What also isn't revealed to the seekers of power and wealth is that those material possessions represented in the American Dream cannot buy happiness. The quest for monetary gain has left millions of people suffering from depression and other illnesses and has been responsible for countless suicides and murders and for the demise of the community and family structure, leading to (or at least being partially responsible for) such atrocities as the numerous school shootings.

True wealth and real happiness come from good health and a strong community. They come from knowing the history of your people and your place in the world, and from living a life of realism with a sense of what it means to be alive. Finally, they come from living a life that is not irreversibly harmful to other life forms or the natural environment.

The real symbolic statement of reference to the Westernized world (especially the U.S.) is apple pie, baseball, and screw anyone or anything you can to make a profit. Sound absurd? Ask the vast amounts of rainforests and old growth, natural areas who destroyed them. Ask the sun why its path to the Earth is far less obstructed due to the depletion of the ozone layer. Why did this depletion take place? Ask the citizens of Burbank, California how they enjoy the chromium in their drinking water. Why and how did it get there?

Ask the families of the murdered individuals why, when they took a stand against corporations like Shell and Chevron, they were killed. Ask the many Native American tribes who it was that murdered their families and virtually destroyed their cultures. Ask the relatives of black slaves why slavery was legal years ago.

Ask an Iraqi civilian why the U.S. government continues to bomb the country, killing innocent people. Ask the executives of the General Motors Corporation, Ford, and the others why the Gulf War was fought. Ask the executives of General Electric who it is that has profited massively from virtually every war that has been fought around the world. This is real violence. This is real injustice. This needs to be stopped by any means necessary.

The ELF realizes the profit motive, caused and reinforced by the capitalist society, is destroying all life on this planet. The only way, at this point in time, to stop that continued destruction of life is to by any means necessary take the profit motive out of killing.

Using real direct action in the form of economic sabotage, the ELF is targeting what the greedy entities care about: their pocketbooks. By inflicting as much economic damage as possible, the ELF can allow a given entity to decide it is in its best economic interests to stop destroying life for the sake of profit.

Capitalism as a target is not easily identifiable due to its being an ideology rather than a physical object. But forms and symbols of capitalism can be targeted successfully to greatly influence the impact the capitalist state has on life. These symbols and forms can take the shape of individuals, businesses, governmental and non-governmental organizations and items which aid in directly destroying life and/or the spread of the destructive propaganda of the American Dream. The list is endless but could include such symbols in the U.S. as Mt. Rushmore, the Statue of Liberty, Disney, Wall Street, etc.

Whatever the target may be, the ELF ideology promotes efficiency and effectiveness. It promotes the idea of choosing the most effective target possible and using strategies and tactics to cause the most amount of economic damage as possible. In addition, the idea of momentum is pushed to create an actual movement that continues to grow to successfully stop the destruction of life. More and more actions need to be taken by the ELF in order for this success to become a reality.

What are the various issues that the ELF has targeted?

The specific target areas of the ELF are constantly increasing and will continue to grow to include any threat to life on this planet caused by greedy quests for monetary gain. The ELF targets have included such issues as deforestation (for human development of roadways, for luxurious living and/or recreation areas, for profit by selling or using trees, etc.), urban sprawl, genetic engineering, natural habitat and ecosystem destruction, the use of slave labor by corporations and more.

What are some of the actions in North America performed by the ELF?

The most notorious action performed by the ELF in North America to date is the October 18, 1998 fires set at Vail Resorts, Inc. Vail, known as one of the premiere ski resorts in the world, had proposed an 885-acre expansion into one of the last remaining habitats for the Canadian lynx in the United States. Despite clear opposition from a vast majority of the local community and a ten-year legal battle by local environmentalists, Vail was still moving forward with the expansion plans. Members of the ELF felt it was time to increase the opposition. The action caused an estimated $12-$26 million in damages to Vail and brought the issue of expansion into wilderness once again into the international spotlight. The communiqué sent by the ELF taking credit for this action appeared as follows:

> On behalf of the lynx, five buildings and four ski lifts at Vail were reduced to ashes on the night of Sunday, October 18th. Vail, Inc. is already the largest ski operation in North America and now wants to expand even further. The 12 miles of roads and 885 acres of clearcuts will ruin the last, best lynx habitat in the state. Putting profits ahead of Colorado's wildlife will not be tolerated. This action is just a warning. We will be back if this greedy corporation continues to trespass into wild and unroaded areas. For your safety and convenience, we strongly advise skiers to choose other destinations until Vail cancels its inexcusable plans for expansion.
>
> - Earth Liberation Front

On December 27, 1998, the ELF burned down the corporate headquarters of U.S. Forest Industries in Medford, Oregon. This particular target served as the corporate headquarters for four mills: a White City veneer mill and a Grants Pass plywood mill in Oregon, a sawmill in Florida and a studmill in Colorado. The action caused an estimated $500,000-$800,000 in damages to U.S. Forest Industries. The communiqué sent by the ELF taking credit for this action stated:

> To celebrate the holidays we decided on a bonfire. Unfortunately for U.S. Forest Industries it was at their corporate headquarters office...

> On the foggy night after Christmas, when everyone was digesting their turkey and pie, Santa's ELFs dropped two five-gallon buckets of diesel/unleaded mix and a gallon jug with cigarette delays; which proved to be more than enough to get this party started.

> This was in retribution for all the wild forests and animals lost to feed the wallets of greedy fucks like Jerry Bramwell, U.S.F.I. president... and it is a warning to all others

responsible, we do not sleep and we won't quit.

Just under a year later, on December 25, 1999, the ELF targeted the Northwest regional headquarters of Boise Cascade in Monmouth, Oregon. A $1 million fire set by the ELF burned the 8,000-square-foot building to the ground. A few days after the fire the ELF sent the following communiqué:

> Boise Cascade has been very naughty. After ravaging the forests of the Pacific Northwest, Boise Cascade now looks towards the virgin forests of Chile. Early Christmas morning, elves left coal in Boise Cascade's stocking. Four buckets of diesel and gas with kitchen timer delay destroyed their regional headquarters in Monmouth, Oregon. Let this be a lesson to all greedy multinational corporations who don't respect their ecosystems. The elves are watching. - Earth Liberation Front

Boise Cascade had recently teamed up with Maderas Condor, a Chilean company, to continue expanding its practices of deforestation in the Puerto Montt area of Chile, one of the few remaining areas in the world which had remained free from massive cutting.

Just six days later, on New Years Eve, 1999, the ELF for the first time turned to the subject of genetic engineering. At Michigan State University, Catherine Ives worked as a researcher, according to her to help feed the starving people of the world through biotechnology. One of her programs funded in part by Monsanto and the U.S. Agency for International Development involved attempts to coerce farmers in less Westernized countries to give up sustainable agricultural practices for reliance on the biotech industry-- in particular Monsanto, who among numerous other creations brought the terminator seed to life. These seeds, which do not reproduce, require farmers to purchase new seeds annually from Monsanto.

The idea that there just is not enough food in the world to feed the current population is an absolute myth being used by the biotech industry as one of their reasons to continue into the area of gene manipulation. The public relations departments at Monsanto and in other firms within the biotech industry are being far from truthful in presenting this appearance of altruism as though they are helping people in (as they refer to them) the

50

"developing nations" to improve their lives.

It is nothing but another form of largely U.S.-based imperialism attempting to control and destroy non-Westernized cultures for the sake of monetary gain. Is it just a mere coincidence that Monsanto, the U.S. Agency for International Development and Catherine Ives, are not teaching and promoting organic permaculture in less-Westernized countries? And is it just another coincidence that instead they are manufacturing the desire for genetically-altered seeds, which Monsanto conveniently sells? In response to this program and Catherine Ives' work, the ELF set fire to her offices at Michigan State University causing an estimated $400,000-$900,000 in damages. Ives herself admitted the fire destroyed years of her work. A communiqué sent by the ELF stated:

> The E.L.F. takes credit for a strike on the offices of Catherine Ives, Rm. 324 Agricultural Hall at Michigan State University on Dec. 31, 1999. The offices were doused with gasoline and set afire. This was done in response to the work being done to force developing nations in Asia, Latin America and Africa to switch from natural crop plants to genetically altered sweet potatoes, corn, bananas, and pineapples. Monsanto and USAID are major funders of the research and promotional work being done through Michigan State University. According to local newspapers, the fire cost $400,000 in damage. Cremate Monsanto, Long live the E.L.F. On to the next G.E. target!

Just under a month later, on January 23, 2000, the ELF set fire to a new luxury home under construction in the Bloomington, Indiana area. This home, which was to be valued at between $750,000-$1.5 million upon completion, threatened the Lake Monroe watershed, which supplies clean, fresh drinking water to the Bloomington area. Damage from the fire was assessed at over $200,000 and it marked the first time the ELF had targeted what the group chose to call urban sprawl. The communiqué sent by the ELF claiming responsibility for this action stated:

Greetings from Bloomington, IN:

> The Earth Liberation Front would like to take credit for a late night visit to the Sterling Woods development on

the evening of January 23rd. During our visit, we torched one house that was under construction. It was completely destroyed. The walls had caved in by the time the fire department arrived. Damage has been assessed at $200,000. When finished the house was to be worth $700,000. 'No Sprawl, ELF' was painted on the developers sign. The house was targeted because the sprawling development it is located in is in the Lake Monroe Watershed. This is the drinking water supply for the town of Bloomington, IN and the surrounding area. It is already being jeopardized by existing development and roads. Once again the rich of the world are destroying what little we have left in terms of natural areas and collective holdings (the water). Hopefully they will get the message that we will not take it anymore.

In addition to the actions listed above, the ELF has taken responsibility for spiking trees in Eugene, Oregon and in Bloomington, IN. They have burned and caused severe economic damage to a series of homes on Long Island, New York and torched Superior Lumber Company in Glendale, Oregon. In addition, the ELF has continued on with its work against genetic engineering, targeting the Delta & Pine Land Company Research Cotton Gin in Visalia, California (a Monsanto subsidiary) and the University of Minnesota at St. Paul. More recently the ELF continued to broaden its targets with actions taken against a Nike Outlet store in Albertville, Minnesota, against an Old Navy Outlet Center on Long Island, and more. The ideology of the ELF reveals that any entity (whether it be an individual, corporation, governmental or non-governmental agency) that continues to destroy the natural environment for the sake of profit and greed may be considered the next target of the group.

How does one become a member of the ELF?

The ELF does not have any sort of physical membership list or meetings you can attend to become involved. Remember, the ELF revolves around not a physical base or classically-designed structure, but instead an ideology. If you believe in the ELF ideology and you follow a certain set of widely-published guidelines, you can conduct actions and become part of the ELF.

The ELF guidelines are as follows:

1) To cause as much economic damage as possible to a given entity that is profiting off the destruction of the natural environment and life for selfish greed and profit.
2) To educate the public on the atrocities committed against the environment and life.
3) To take all necessary precautions against harming life.

As you can see the guidelines are every similar to the goals of the ELF with one major exception. The third of three guidelines states that one must take all necessary precautions against harming life.

The ELF considers itself a nonviolent organization as no physical harm has come to a human as a result of the group's actions. This is by no means a sheer coincidence but in fact a commitment to the guidelines. Individuals interested in becoming active in the ELF need to follow the above guidelines and create their own close knit anonymous cell made up of trustworthy and sincere people. Remember the ELF and each cell within it is anonymous not only to one another but also to the general public. So there is not a realistic chance of becoming active in an already existing cell. Take initiative, form your own cell and do what needs to be done!

Are ELF actions successful?

Perhaps the most important and logical question which needs to be asked is, are the actions of the ELF successful? If the group does not stop a given entity fully with one action that does not mean the action was unsuccessful. The ELF actions have at least three major goals in mind:

1) To cause as much economic damage as possible to a given entity that is profiting off the destruction of the natural environment and life for selfish greed and profit,
2) To educate the public on the atrocities committed against the environment and life,
3) To make it known that any entity profiting off the destruction of life for profit may be considered the next target.

With these three goals in mind every action taken by the ELF has successfully met at least one or more of these goals.

Aren't the ELF targets covered by insurance?

A common argument against the actions of the ELF has been that each target has been covered by insurance so the given entity fails to suffer little if any economic loss. While it is largely true that most if not all of the ELF targets have been insured it is completely ludicrous to believe that insurance companies can suffer losses of hundreds of thousands to millions of dollars without greatly raising the rates of insurance. If the given entity or even industry was targeted repeatedly by the ELF, insurance companies would either cease to cover these entities or raise the cost too high for a profitable business.

The only problem with ELF actions at this point is there are not enough of them occurring.

Is the ELF a terrorist and violent organization?

Federal authorities and mainstream media particularly in the United States have done an outstanding job at feeding the public false rhetoric largely associated with the term "ecoterrorism." Any action taken by the ELF has been labeled as ecoterrorist by the press and law enforcement for a particular, very conscious purpose.

What would happen if a major ELF action were taken and instead of instantly labeling it as ecoterrorism, the press and authorities took an unbiased perspective and honestly revealed the entire story, including the motives for taking that action? Perhaps the public might be a little too eager to support the action and a lot less likely to quickly condemn the group.

What happens, though, in today's fast-paced, media-savvy society is that news and mainstream media are used to control the minds and actions of the mainstream public. Large news agencies and the federal government learned their lesson during the Vietnam War era, when pictures a little to true to reality were brought home into the living rooms of the public. As a response to the atrocities committed by the United States in Vietnam, the public within the States became angry and fought back. This was largely due to the fact they had more access to real information, less censored and controlled by societal forces.

A major difference could be seen in comparing the images shown to the public in the United States during the Vietnam War and those shown during the Gulf War in the early 1990s. The American public did not

54

see the murder of countless civilians, nor did they see the constant bombings of urban areas filled with civilians. Instead, what NBC, CBS, ABC, CNN and the others showed the public were heavily censored and filtered computerized images that appeared like a video game. This was an obvious attempt to build the patriotism level or at least maintain it within the States.

When a news event takes place it should be the responsibility of the news agency to provide a balanced, objective view of the events to the public, free from labels and other forms of mind coercion. If this did occur, the mind of the individual would be allowed to remain open to receive and process information, thus allowing the individual to come to his/her own conclusions. This is in direct contrast to the reality of today's news world where the public is made to feel like they are making free conscious decisions when in fact they are succumbing to mind control and preformed opinions created by the state and societal forces based around commerce.

By labeling an action or a news event, the media forces the public to adopt the media-created stigma, either positive or negative, in response to that label. Think of what goes through your mind when you hear the term "terrorist." Usually it relates somehow to racist beliefs and stereotypes about Arabs, about airline hijackings, violence, and about how terrorists need to be caught and/or killed to be kept away from society. So when the federal government and the mainstream press immediately label actions of the ELF as ecoterrorism, it could only create a negative stereotype in the minds of the public.

Unfortunately as the pressures of mind control through labeling increase, it becomes more difficult to allow the mind to remain open to independently process information and form less-biased opinions. This is precisely what the federal government and law enforcement want: to make sure that the mainstream public immediately equates the ELF with ecoterrorism.

Can you imagine just what might occur if the ELF were not labeled negatively? What if people were honestly told why the group exists and who its targets are? Obviously, more and more people would support and take part in ELF actions. The ELF is not an ecoterrorist organization or any sort of terrorist organization, but rather one that is working to protect all life on planet Earth.

It is amazingly hypocritical for mainstream media and the federal government to label the ELF as a terrorist group, yet at the same time ignore the U.S. government and U.S.-based corporations, which every day exploit, torture, and murder people around the world.

Why don't members of the ELF use more traditional tactics to achieve environmental protection?

The mainstream public has been fed an extreme amount of false and misleading propaganda in regards to "traditional tactics," those which are strictly legal and sanctioned by the state. In reality, a more honest definition of traditional tactics would include illegal direct action such as economic sabotage, due to its crucial role in numerous successful social and political movements throughout history.

The ELF does not engage in more traditional tactics simply because they have been proven not to work, especially on their own. The popular, modern mainstream environmental movement, which began arguably in the early 1960s, has failed in its attempts to bring about the needed protection to stop the destruction of life on this planet. This fact cannot be rightly disputed. The quality of our air, water, and soil continues to decrease as more and more life forms on the planet suffer and die as a result. How much longer are we supposed to wait to actually stop the destruction of life?

A belief in state-sanctioned legal means of social change is also a sign of faith in the legal system of that same state. The ELF clearly do not have any faith in the legal system of the state when it co comes to protecting life. The state has repeatedly shown itself to care far more for the protection of commerce and profits than that of its people and the natural environment. To place faith in that same state as though it will do what is in the best interests of justice and life is utter foolishness and a grave mistake. The state is a major portion of the problem. There is also a certain intelligence and logic to the idea that with one night's work, a few individuals can accomplish what years of legal battles and millions of dollars most likely did not.

Are ELF tactics, such as economic sabotage, new to social movements?

No, in fact very few (if any) major successful social movements globally have been able to progress using strictly state-sanctioned tactics. In Westernized societies, it is quite normal for schools to push the mythical propaganda that state-sanctioned means are the only way social change has ever been achieved.

One of the most famous examples usually cited by state-sanctioned, nonviolence absolutists is the Independence Movement in India while under British rule. Classically, people-- especially in privileged, Westernized societies-- have been taught that Gandhi's nonviolence tactics were the only methodology used to gain India's independence from Britain. Yet, in addition to the work of Gandhi, there was a strong militant faction of the Independence Movement that played just as important a role as the work of Gandhi himself.

The British government understood Gandhi's tactics and knew what broadly to expect from him. The more militant sector of the movement posed a far greater threat to the government simply due to the reality of the British not knowing what to expect or what might result if the road to India's independence was not traveled down. In fact, Gandhi himself was released from prison on at least one occasion only on the direct order from the British that he would try to calm the more militant sector of the movement. Both the nonviolence tactics employed by Gandhi and his followers and the threat of more severe tactics from the militant sector brought about India's eventual independence.

Most schooling systems also do not teach and educate students about the Luddites. Perhaps one of the earliest (if not the first) groups to target the Industrial Revolution and its effects was the Luddites. From 1811 to 1816, the Luddites caused extreme economic damage to the weaver industry in England. Angry at the threat to life and culture that the new machines of the industrialized revolution posed, the Luddites fought back using tactics very similar to those performed by the ELF today. Some factories were forced to shut down and others agreed to stop running the industrialized machines due to the Luddite activity and threat.

In the abolitionist movement in the United States, there are numerous accounts of slaves sabotaging the property of their "masters" and engaging in various tactics to disrupt the flow of commerce in the slave system. Slave revolts were fairly rare, but even one would create a chilling threat that actually forced some slave owners to give up the practice.

The suffragette movement, particularly in England, used sabotage in addition to other tactics to successfully gain rights for women. One example occurred in February 1913, when Emmeline Pankhurst, the founder of England's suffragette movement, bombed the villa of the Chancellor of the Exchequer David Lloyd George in Surrey. Pankhurst accepted responsibility for the event and described it as "guerrilla warfare."

In the United States, most everyone has heard of the Boston Tea Party which consisted of bands of men boarding English ships in Boston Harbor (among others) and dumping British tea into the water. Seldom is this referred to as economic sabotage, but that is indeed an accurate description of it.

In the protests in the U.S. against the Vietnam War, economic sabotage was once again used, in addition to other tactics, to place a great amount of pressure on the U.S. Government. In the end-- due in part to the protests but more to the reality that the U.S. lost the war-- the U.S. troops began withdrawing from Vietnam.

The above examples represent just a mere fraction of the historical instances in which economic sabotage has been effectively employed. The tactic has a rich and plentiful history in movements around the globe and makes sense from a purely logical standpoint. If an item or piece of property is threatening life for the sake of profit, shouldn't it be destroyed?

Why don't ELF members come forward and publicly take responsibility for their actions?

Frequently, when this question is asked there is usually some reference made to the ELF members showing cowardice by not publicly taking responsibility for actions. This is complete nonsense. The ELF is made up of brave, utterly courageous individuals who are risking their freedom to protect all life on Earth. ELF members make a conscientious decision to go underground and remain underground to create the highest level of effectiveness. The idea is not for the members to be rotting away in prisons but rather to be free each and every day to continue their heroic actions.

One school of thought under the broad scope of nonviolence theory states that an individual must allow an entity in opposition to see the evil in his or her own ways and voluntarily change. This, according to the theory, will create lasting change. This belief places an extraordinary amount of faith in the human conscience, which at this time has more than proven to be misguided. If an individual had a working conscience in the first place, would s/he actually engage in activities that threaten and destroy various forms of life on this planet? This is not a demonstration of a working conscience, and therefore all the attempts in the world to appeal to the oppressor's conscience will not work. There needs to be something more.

The ELF recognizes this flaw in conventional nonviolence theory and also realizes that remaining safely inside state-sanctioned societal law while attempting to create social and political change will never work. Laws are set up as a mere reflection of the morals and norms of the majority of mainstream society. Unfortunately, as a result of massive conditioning and the manufacture of desire, the mainstream public (especially in the United States) is living a life of extreme over-consumption, ruthlessly attacking what we all need to survive: clean air, clean water, and clean soil.

At this point in time there exists the immediate need for individuals to step outside of societal law and work to directly stop the destruction of life, by any means necessary. The ELF recognizes that the destruction of the planet is caused by the quest for profit, and therefore the only appropriate response at this stage is to completely remove the profit motive from killing life. When an unjust entity is severely attacked financially, it will see that it is in its best interests to stop the unjust acts. Due to the nature of the court systems, particularly in the U.S., there is little (if any) chance of a just trial. If an ELF member is caught and prosecuted s/he stands the chance of spending a ridiculous amount of time in prison because of newer and newer laws backed by big business and government to protect commerce.

The decision to not take public responsibility for each action is purely a strategic one. Why would anyone want to be caught and unjustly locked up, when s/he could instead be free to continue destroying that which is killing life? For the individual to come forward and take responsibility for an ELF action, this would require a sound faith in the legal structure. The ELF understands that this legal structure is part of the same system of government and now Westernized world domination that is causing the death of all life. It can never be trusted an ultimately needs to be abolished.

Do ELF actions alienate other groups and individuals within the environmental movement?

The members of the ELF have never stated that the tactics of their group will on their own achieve full change. Of course, there needs to be public education. The ELF considers itself one part of a global movement that uses a variety of tactics to stop the destruction of life. The ELF actions on their own do not alienate the environmental movement.

The problem arises when aboveground organizations, who claim to be for the same cause, come out publicly against the actions. Regardless of their motives, these groups have (whether they meant to or not) created a rift in the movement. A split in a social and political movement classically signifies a weak point that has historically been, and can continue to be, exploited by the authorities and entities who are interested in the movement's demise.

Grassroots and mainstream organizations who have come out publicly against the actions of the ELF do so either for economic reasons (to continue receiving donations from the public, members, or grants from charities or governmental or non-governmental organizations) and/or they have a firm belief and an exceptional amount of faith in the system of government in operation in their particular area. Either way, this attitude demonstrates a clear misunderstanding and/or a great reluctance to accept the seriousness of the threats to life on this planet and to make a firm commitment to work to actually stop that destruction of life. All of us must remember that the movement to protect all life must not be a means of monetary gain for individuals and organizations but rather one that produces concrete results.

In addition, rarely is the distinction made-- which is crucial for any movement seeking to actually produce change-- between actions that make an individual simply feel good and actions that are truly effective and challenge the oppressing party. Actions that make individuals feel better about themselves are most often safer and pose little actual threat to the entity that needs to be changed. Especially in the global movement to protect all life, this is in direct reference to the continued belief in and use of state-sanctioned tactics, which have not only been proven ineffective but may only aid in prolonging the real problem.

This movement to protect all life requires all of us to step out of our comfort zones and realize what actually needs to be done. The Westernized individual who may support more extreme forms of direct action abroad and outside of the Westernized countries, such as the armed self defense of the Zapatistas, while simultaneously denouncing direct action domestically to protect life, is practicing one of the sickest forms of hypocrisy, if not a form of racism and imperialism.

No one in his right mind can honestly state that the popular environmental movement using state-sanctioned tactics has been successful. It is very obvious something more is needed.

There is no tolerable excuse for an individual or organization that claims to be a part of the movement to protect all life on the planet to come out publicly against the actions of the ELF.

If the individual or particular organization disagrees with the tactics, it is just as easy to come out publicly when asked and respond with a statement such as, "Although neither I nor my organization take part in actions like those of the ELF, we can understand the motivations because the threat to life on this planet is very real and serious."

What this statement does is to, rather than publicly show a major rift in the movement, give at least the perception of a varied movement, strong and rich in diversity.

What if someone is injured by an ELF action? Has that ever happened?

The guidelines for the ELF specifically require members to take all necessary precautions to ensure no one is physically injured. In the history of the ELF internationally, no one has been injured from the group's actions and that is not a coincidence. Yes, the use of fire as a tool is dangerous. But when used properly, it can tremendously aid in the destruction of property associated with the killing of life.

If an action similar to one performed by the ELF occurred and resulted in an individual being harmed, this would not be considered an ELF action. It may have been done for social and political reasons and even may have had the same motives as the ELF, but since a life form was injured, it would not be considered an actual ELF action. Remember, the ELF exists to protect life on this planet. The choice to use economic sabotage is a very deliberate and purposeful strategy to target the real underlying threat to life: the quest for profit and power. The ELF does not engage in state-sanctioned tactics or those that physically harm people or life in general, due to the group's belief that economic sabotage is the best, most direct way to take the profit motive out of destroying the planet.

The real violence and danger come from businesses clear-cutting forests and destroying ecosystems; from pollutants carelessly pumped into our air by industrial and consumer society; from water being poisoned to the point of being undrinkable' from people eating commercially-grown, non-organic food; and many, many more. Very often, by labeling the ELF as 'violent,' mainstream society, government, and big business can attempt to forget about the real violence that occurs everyday: the violence against life.

Is the ELF concerned with the workers at a given business who may be forced into unemployment by an action?

The ELF supports the right for all individuals to have proper access to adequate nourishment, health care, shelter, and the basic necessities of life. There is, however, no excuse for individuals to be working at a job that directly threatens the ability for all life on the planet to exist. If an individual-- whether an executive, owner, or bottom-of-the-ladder employee-- is profiting off the destruction of the natural environment, aiding in the stockpiling of wealth into the hands of a few, the least he deserves is to lose his job. Individuals cannot blindly enter into any form of employment, regardless of the pay, without first considering who and/ or what that work is going to hurt. The victim / benefactor ratio must be greatly considered and occupations that pose a threat to life must be abolished.

What approach has law enforcement taken to stop the work of the ELF?

From 1997 through 2000, not a single person was arrested and charged with an ELF-related crime in North America. Then, on January 25, 2001, the first ELF-related arrest in North America came. Since that time, there have only been a few others. The ELF, by all accounts, has been extremely successful in evading law enforcement due in much part to its anonymous cell structure.

Law enforcement, from the federal down to the local level, has been extremely frustrated. Out of this frustration, aboveground individuals around the country have been harassed, subpoenaed to grand juries, had their homes and offices raided and property seized, and more.

The U.S. Department of Justice has particularly focused its interest since 1997 on the North American ELF Press Office, foolishly believing that the office might have some direct connection to ELF members. It doesn't. After years of surveillance, harassment, two major raids and property seizures, and numerous grand jury subpoenas, the U.S. Department of Justice continues to place pressure on the press office to shut down. They don't seem to be having much luck.

Another step that the protectors of the state and commerce have taken is to have the Federal Bureau of Investigations classify the ELF as a domestic terrorism group. In fact, the FBI has referred to the ELF as the leading domestic terrorism threat in the United States. This classification has allowed heightened surveillance and investigative techniques to be legally used against the ELF. In addition, this move by the FBI allowed the formal creation of "joint terrorism task forces" in most larger, urban areas throughout the U.S. One such example follows.

On November 25, 2000 the NAELFPO received notice the Portland City Council had approved a terrorism task force. This new force involves both the FBI and the Portland Police Bureau. The original ordinance passed by City Council has a particularly interesting mission statement. Mission statement #3 (of 4) states, "The mission of the PJTTF is to identify and target for prosecution those individuals or groups who are responsible for Right Wing and/or Left Wing movements, as well as acts of the anti-abortion movement and the Animal Liberation Front/Earth Liberation Front."

Public outcry in opposition to the above mission resulted in a rewording, but the idea remains the same. The state is beginning to recognize that the ELF poses a major threat to commerce so they are reacting accordingly.

In addition, certain U.S. states, including Oregon and Washington, are adopting "ecoterrorism" laws. These laws greatly increase the sentencing limits for crimes largely associated with the interference of commerce. With every step that the state takes to try to stop the unstoppable, loving work of the ELF, it once again proves its priorities are to protect commerce at any cost, regardless of the people and life in general.

The FBI's classification of the ELF as the most serious domestic terrorism threat in the U.S., as well as the increasing number of "ecoterrorism" laws being passed, is a definite sign that the authorities are considering the ELF a viable threat to the Westernized way of life and to the idea of profits and commerce at any price. It is a clear sign that the ELF is successfully threatening the nation state that is destroying life on this planet.

What is the future of the ELF?

The future of the ELF depends largely on the growing number of people globally concerned about the destruction of life. Once the ideology of the ELF is understood, anyone who is honestly concerned about the destruction of life should feel compelled to either support and/or become a member of the organization.

As the amount of exploitation and destruction of life continues to increase, so will the response from concerned global citizens. It is this individual involvement from people all over the world that justice and the protection of life relies upon.

Using real direct action in the form of economic sabotage, the ELF is targeting what the greedy entities care about: their pocketbooks. By inflicting as much economic damage as possible, the ELF can allow a given entity to decide if it is in its best economic interests to stop destroying life for the sake of profit.

– North American Earth Liberation Front Press Office

3.

RESISTANCE #3

Capitalism teaches us that heroic acts of sabotage against those profiting from the destruction of the natural environment are acts of terrorism. It teaches us that the systematic destruction of everything that keeps us alive-- air, water, and soil-- is progress.

The system murders and destroys the lives of those who dare to do what it's going to take in order to maintain life on this Earth. It lays down a path to follow to achieve positive social change that is a complete waste of energy by design, because positive social change is fundamentally in contrast to the capitalist ideology. And those who recognize this contradiction and forge new and effective ways of combating the deadly force of capitalism are vilified by the system.

The Earth Liberation Front (ELF) is an underground organization that commits acts of economic sabotage against those who profit from destroying the Earth, often in the form of break-ins, vandalism and arsons, while taking extreme precautions to make sure that no human or animal life is harmed in the process. They have claimed responsibility for over a dozen actions in North America over the last three years through anonymous communiqués sent to the targets, the media and to aboveground supporters who have passed the message on to the public nation-wide. The message is simple: The true "terrorism" comes from a system that makes commodities out of the Earth and those living on it, and it must be stopped by any means necessary.

Since 1997, the ELF has been responsible for well over $30 million in economic sabotage. Given the relatively low number of individuals estimated to be taking part in these actions, the ELF, and the use of covert tactics in general, have proven extremely effective. While thousands follow the system's path to achieve social change, an increasing number are realizing that it is simply not enough to reform the system and that a much more fundamental change is desperately needed if we wish to sustain life on this planet.

The government doesn't want the public to know the social and political motives behind these actions. It wishes to foster a common opinion that the ELF is a violent terrorist organization, hence the term "ecoterrorism" widely spread throughout the media. But the true violence and terrorism is coming from the hands of governments and corporations that value power and greed over the Earth and those who inhabit it.

This can be seen in the rapid deforestation and species extinction, genocide of indigenous peoples, the tampering with the genetic makeup of our food, the continued drive for technological advancement despite the obvious side effects of physical and psychological illness, those murdered overseas over economic disputes and those murdered at home by policing agencies and the death penalty.... The list goes on and on, and the damages massively outweigh any of the supposed "terrorism" against those perpetrating these injustices.

This issue is dedicated to the Earth Liberation Front. *Resistance* promises to speak the truth about the motives and actions of both the ELF and the system against which it struggles. In a cesspool of corporate-controlled media and government-spread misinformation, *Resistance* vows to tell it like it is.

Grand juries Target ELF Activity
Three years of Harassment with No Success
-Craig Rosebraugh

I was first subpoenaed to testify as a witness before a federal grand jury in Portland, Oregon in September 1997. At that time I had spoke out in support of two acts of eco-sabotage committed in Oregon by an underground organization known as the Animal Liberation Front (ALF). The organization I worked with at the time, Liberation Collective, had received two communications from the ALF claiming responsibility for these occurrences. After many visits by the FBI and the ATF, a subpoena was finally issued to me to give information to aid in the investigation of the crimes.

The subpoena commanded my appearance in federal court less than a week later. After realizing this I immediately called the Assistant U.S. Attorney in Portland and asked to have the date delayed so I could have time to obtain and consult an attorney. My request was granted and the proceedings were delayed for a month.

Early on an October morning, on my way to the U.S. Courthouse, I delivered a formal letter of objection to the U.S. Attorney's office on the grounds that I was being harassed. A protest against the grand jury was held outside the courthouse and attended by forty or so individuals angry at the secret government proceedings that were about to occur inside.

At 11:00 a.m. I went inside, confident that the grand jury, being members of my local community, would be able to see I had done nothing wrong and that the U.S. government was simply grasping at extremely small straws. U.S. Marshals immediately led me into a waiting room filled with FBI, ATF, and other government agents. Shortly thereafter, I was taken into another room and led up to the front, where I was told to sit. In front of me were the twenty-three members of the grand jury. To my left was the Assistant U.S. Attorney and to my right the court reporter and three forepersons of the grand jury.

As soon as I sat down the questioning began from the Assistant U.S. Attorney. By the time the third question was asked I began to take the Fifth Amendment, using my right to protection from self-incrimination but knowing full well that this could be challenged at any time.

(In grand jury proceedings, witnesses called to testify do not have the right to take the Fifth Amendment unchallenged. Those who do take the Fifth and refuse to answer the questions run the risk of imprisonment on contempt charges for up to eighteen months. Furthermore, in federal grand juries witnesses called to testify do not have the right to counsel inside the grand jury room.)

After an hour or so, questions began to come from the grand jurors themselves.

The first thing I noticed about the grand jury was that it was entirely white, hardly an accurate representation of the Portland area. (Compared to other cities Portland is an extremely white town but definitely not to the extent represented by that jury). Secondly, each individual seemed over the age of forty and many quite older than that. I had no knowledge of what was said about me prior to my appearance but it was clear by the tone of the grand jurors' questions that they considered me guilty of some sort of serious crime before I ever walked into that room.

To roughly seventy-five percent of the questions I took the Fifth Amendment and remained silent. The questions I did choose to answer related directly to the philosophy of the social movement and information about my organization, both of which were already public knowledge.

The grand jury seemed more interested in arguing with me over the ethics of a particular social movement than focusing on their task at hand--investigating the two crimes that had occurred. I was frequently cut off when trying to answer ideological questions and often snickered at when offering my viewpoint on a given issue. It became extremely frustrating, especially when I noticed two jurors dozing off in the back row. It was comforting to know that tax dollars were spent to have these individuals sleep during a court proceeding.

After an hour and a half of questioning, I was led outside the room and told to wait in the hall while the Assistant U.S. Attorney spoke with the grand jury to determine if there was any interest in asking more questions. I was soon taken back inside, where I sat through another fifteen minutes of questions, again exercising my Fifth Amendment right.

At this point I was told that I was finished for the day and reminded that I could be called back at any given time to face more questions. A U.S. Marshal then escorted me down the elevator and out of the building. I did not expect to be released that day or really for a length of time as I figured my Fifth Amendment protection would be challenged and I would be held in contempt. As I walked out the doors of the courthouse my mind was in a complete daze. The psychological stress that was invoked in that hostile atmosphere was simply unimaginable, especially from individuals who consider themselves to uphold the law.

Two months later, On December 12, I received two more subpoenas at my personal residence. One was for me to testify again, and the second was for the production of materials and/or objects belonging to Liberation Collective that relate in any way to the now-three incidents listed in the subpoena: (1) The November 29-30, 1997, trespass, burglary and fire at the U.S. Bureau of Land Management Wild Horse Corral in Harney County, Oregon; (2) The July 21, 1997, trespass, burglary and fire at the Cavel West, Inc. facility in Redmond, Deschutes County, Oregon; and (3) The May 30, 1997, trespass, burglary and "mink release" at the Arritola Mink Farm in Mt. Angel, Marion County, Oregon. These three incidents alone totaled over $1.5 million in damages.

Once again the date for my appearance was less than a week away so I called the Assistant U.S. Attorney and asked for a delay to obtain counsel. I was denied this delay without hesitation over the phone. After putting my request in writing, I faxed it to the U.S. Attorney's office asking once again for a delay. This too was denied.

On December 16, one day before I was commanded to testify, I put forth a motion to the court to disclose illegal electronic surveillance and to quash the subpoena. My interest in doing this was to attempt to learn whether or not illegal electronic surveillance had been used to gather information to obtain the subpoenas. Early the next morning, the court clerk called and told me a judge had denied my motion that very morning and that I was still commanded to appear.

The same day, another demonstration was held outside the U.S Courthouse in Portland. I had made up my mind that I would not even go into the courthouse due to the continued harassment I was feeling from the situation. At 11:00 a.m., an ATF agent came outside and asked me if I was planning on going up to testify. I said I was not. He went back in only to re-appear ten minutes later when he informed me that the Assistant U.S. Attorney had commanded me to testify. The ATF agent then asked me again if I was going to testify. I told him I was not. The agent went back in the courthouse and almost immediately came back out with a U.S. Marshal. Together they proceeded to arrest me, placing me in handcuffs claiming I was going to be held in contempt of court.

I was taken to the second floor and into a large room where the Assistant U.S. Attorney, U.S. Marshals, an ATF agent and a court reporter were all present. Soon a judge entered the room and, still in handcuffs, I was told to sit down at a table near the Assistant U.S. Attorney. The judge then asked why I was refusing to testify. I told him that I had three reasons that I felt were more than adequate for my refusal. The first was that I had only been given five days, two of which were on the weekend, to obtain and consult an attorney. Secondly, I had put forth a motion the day before asking for disclosure of illegal electronic surveillance and I felt that should be dealt with before proceeding. Finally, I had been in the hospital during the prior week and a half with paracarditis, and I was in no condition to sit through another grand jury inquisition.

Needless to say, the judge did not find any of these reasons valid enough to excuse me from testifying. He ordered the U.S. Marshals to take me down to the grand jury room where I would be forced to sit through more questioning. They led me into the room, sat me down, and took off my handcuffs. In front of me once again was the grand jury. This time, to my right was the Assistant U.S. Attorney and to my left were the court reporter and the three forepersons of the grand jury.

Immediately I noticed that the atmosphere seemed worse than the first time. Not only was I back in front of this group of people that had been led to dislike me, but the lighting was unbelievably oppressive. I was in what felt like a spotlight with the Assistant U.S. Attorney, while the grand jury sat in wrap-around audience-style seating with dim light. It was a spectator sport and unfortunately I was the unwilling subject at hand.

The questioning began once again form the Assistant U.S. Attorney. This time to just about all the questions I took the Fifth Amendment, as I felt I was going to be held anyway for contempt. An hour later the Assistant U.S. Attorney asked where the materials and objects were that were subpoenaed from Liberation Collective. I replied that the only items Liberation Collective had were copies of press releases that were already in possession of the court. The Assistant U.S. Attorney then told me that I had been commanded to bring all copies of any relevant materials. In addition, he said that if I was willing to go and get the copies and be back in a couple of hours, I would be free to leave.

At this point I did not know whether to believe him or not. I figured that there would be no harm in giving copies of documents to the U.S. Attorney's office that the Court already had. So I was released to go and get the press releases.

Upon retuning I was led back into the grand jury room where I sat through another fifteen minutes of questioning, and then sure enough, I was told I was done for the day. Both to the disbelief of myself and my support committee outside, I walked out the front doors of the courthouse after being handcuffed just hours earlier.

In January 1998, I received a fourth subpoena from an FBI agent. This time it commanded me to submit to fingerprinting by the FBI on or before February 28, 1998. I began working on a motion to quash this subpoena based on my belief that giving my fingerprints would be in violation of my Fifth Amendment protection against self-incrimination.

On January 26, I put forth this motion in Federal Court hoping to quash the given subpoena. I received word from the court the next day that once again my motion had been denied and I was still commanded to give my fingerprints or be subject to contempt charges.

At 9:00 a.m. on January 28, I was fingerprinted by agents of the FBI in the U.S. Marshal's office in the U.S. Courthouse. Many states already had my prints on file, and I figured if I were arrested for contempt the FBI would get a new full set anyway so I agreed to the fingerprinting. An hour later I walked out of the courthouse wondering just how long it would be before I was further harassed.

For the next couple of years the pressure from the grand jury slowed down a bit in Portland. While there were no subpoenas issued, the FBI and ATF occasionally showed up attempting to question me about the ongoing actions.

In other U.S. cities, especially in 1999, activists were not so fortunate. Strictly relating to Earth Liberation Front activity, a grand jury convened in Boulder, Colorado to investigate the October 1998 fire that caused some $26 million in damages to Vail Resorts, Inc. Local aboveground activists, largely from Ancient Forest Rescue, were severely targeted by the grand jury. When push came to shove, the U.S. Attorney's office in Colorado decided not to hold any activists in contempt of court for refusing to cooperate with this grand jury. That particular grand jury term was scheduled to expire in March of 2000.

On February 2, 2000, I was just getting out of bed when I heard loud knocking from my front door. Before I could get my clothes on a second knock came with a man's voice yelling, "FBI! Search Warrant! Open Up!"

As I began to head for the door, instantly it flew open and agents came pouring in, guns drawn, screaming at me and my roommates to gather in the kitchen. We were lucky the door was unlocked as the agents had a battering ram ready and waiting. They proceeded to search us explaining they had a search warrant for property relating in any way to several ELF and ALF actions.

The warrant stated that a wide variety of items were to be seized in the raid. It cited the following actions as those under investigation in the grand jury: (1) The December 31, 1999 fire at the Agriculture Hail of Michigan State University; (2) The December 25, 1999 fire at the Northwest headquarters of Boise Cascade in Monmouth, Oregon; (3) The December 27,1998 fire at U.S. Forest Industries in Medford, Oregon; (4) The October 18, 1998 fire at Vail Resorts, Inc. in Colorado; (5) The November 29, 1997 fire and horse release at the Bureau of Land Management Horse Corral in Burns, Oregon; (6) The July 21, 1997 fire at the Cavel West Horse Slaughterhouse in Redmond, Oregon; and (7) The May 30, 1997 release of some 12,000 mink from a fur farm in Mt. Angel, Oregon.

We were then told that we could either leave the house (and if we left we would not be permitted back in until the search was completed) or we must all sit on the couch in the living room-- coincidentally out of view from the rest of the house. So there I sat for six hours while a team of twelve or so federal robbers picked through every nook and cranny of my home.

During the search I was presented with another subpoena to testify before a new federal grand jury in Portland on February 29 at 11:00 a.m. A grand jury, which had convened in January 1999 in Portland, had taken over the investigation into ELF and ALF activity. That investigation had grown immensely.

About halfway through the search, more agents arrived and entered my home carrying briefcases. They stayed for roughly an hour or so and then left without any explanation to me. One agent also went outside and searched the interior of my vehicle during this process. To my knowledge nothing was found or taken from the vehicle. After six hours, the agents began bringing full, closed, moving boxes out into the living room. I was then presented with an inventory list, which I was not allowed to compare to the actual physical property. The items listed included three computers, videos, magazines, books, address books, media directories, mailing lists, photographs, receipts, and much more. The boxes were then taken and loaded into a government vehicle and finally the agents left.

Two rooms in particular were purposefully trashed by the agents during the raid. One was the basement, which contained a great number of files, computer equipment, and more. The other was my bedroom, which also contained a home office. The bedroom afterwards looked like a classic burglary scene from a movie in which the entire area was trashed. It appeared as though agents made a special attempt in the bedroom to make it known they were there. Left on top of the pile among other items were a torn painting made by my partner, Elaine Close, and a crumpled funeral announcement regarding my recently-deceased grandfather.

On February 15, FBI agent Daniel Feucht re-appeared at my door with a letter from the U.S. Department of Justice stating that I was considered a target of the grand jury. This meant that the grand jury not only wanted me as a witness but also sought to file federal charges against me.

The federal charges, which are being looked into by the grand jury and the U.S. Attorney's office, include 18 U.S.C. Section 844 (I), Use of fire or explosive to damage property used in interstate commerce; 18 U.S.C. Section (f) (1) Use of fire or explosive to destroy United States property; 18 U.S.C. Section 1951, Interference with commerce by threats of violence (Hobbs Act); 18 U.S.C. Section 43, Animal Enterprise Terrorism; 18 U.S.C. Section 371, Conspiracy to commit (such) offense; and 18 U.S.C. Section 2, Aiding and abetting.

Before leaving Feucht told me that he didn't like being referred to as "Agent Bastard," a remark obviously intended to inform me that the federal government was still reading my e-mail.

On February 29, a protest was held outside the U.S. Courthouse in Portland, attended by some 150 people. Leslie Pickering, one of the individuals working with the North American ELF Press Office, was arrested at this action for allegedly blocking traffic as he crossed the street an hour earlier. Support protests were also held that day in front of the U.S. Embassy in England and in front of federal buildings in ten other cities, including Minneapolis, Eugene and Bloomington.

With my attorney I entered the U.S. Courthouse in Portland and made my way up to the grand jury room. As I entered, the familiar oppressive atmosphere hit me. Instantly, the questioning began from Assistant U.S. Attorney Stephen Peifer. The questions covered a broad range of subjects and actions (see questions below). To all of the questions, excluding my name, I took the Fifth Amendment and remained silent.

After about an hour I was told to go out and wait with my attorney and that Peifer wanted to speak with my attorney before I left. When Peifer came out, he handed my attorney an order compelling testimony applying towards me. This order related directly to information surrounding the fire at Boise Cascade and would apply toward my future appearances before the grand jury. At that time, Peifer also notified my attorney that I was going to be commanded back to the grand jury in a month or so.

In late March I received word that I had been commanded back to the grand jury on April 26. Once again, the organizing began for another national

74

day of action against state repression. A call was put out internationally for actions on or around April 26 targeting U.S. federal buildings and embassies. The response was even greater this time, and not only from supporters.

I received a call on April 20 from a reporter on the East Coast asking if I had a response to the press release issued by members of Congress the day before. I replied I had no knowledge of such a release. The reporter then faxed me a copy of the release issued by Representative George Radanovich, a Republican from California. Its headline read, "Federal Buildings Threatened by Environmental Extremist; Western Caucus Chairman Writes Reno Seeking Protection." It continued:

> Rep. George Radanovich (R-California) joined Congressman Don Young (R-Alaska) and others in sending a letter to Attorney General Janet Reno seeking additional protection for federal buildings following an e-mail received from the North American Earth Liberation Front. The e-mail called on "militant demonstrations targeting U.S Federal buildings and embassies" on Wednesday, April 26th and was dated April 1, 2000.
>
> "We are requesting the Attorney General Janet Reno institute a criminal Investigation of those responsible for sending out this e-mail threat and we ask her to respond to us by 4 PM EST today with her intentions," said Radanovich, who serves as chairman of the 56 member Western Caucus.
>
> "As we remember the 5th anniversary of the Oklahoma City bombing today, it is important that we take every threat seriously. The Clinton-Gore administration has aligned themselves with the organized national environmental extremists in the past; however, I hope they do the right thing and investigate this e-mail before somebody gets hurt," he concluded.
>
> The Congressman seeks to have the Justice Department use the Racketeer Influenced and Corrupt Organization (RICO) prohibitions against interstate criminal organizations. Copies of this e-mail sent by Craig Rosebraugh from the North American Earth Liberation Front are available upon

request.

The e-mail Radanovich was referring to was a tame, usual organizing notice that appeared as follows:

> April 1, 2000
>
> I received notice two days ago that I have been commanded to appear before the grand jury in Portland once again on April 26th. They have already granted me immunity and are commanding my testimony regarding the burning of the Northwest headquarters of Boise Cascade in Monmouth, OR, which happened on December 25, 1999.
>
> As soon as I take the Fifth Amendment or refuse to answer any questions I will be immediately subject to a contempt hearing.
>
> We are organizing a national day of action against state repression on April 26. All individuals and groups concerned about government harassment and/or who support the Earth Liberation Front are asked to hold militant demonstrations targeting US Federal buildings, embassies, etc.
>
> If you are interested in setting up a demonstration please contact us in Portland to coordinate actions. Literature on grand juries, the ELF, and government harassment is available upon request.
>
> Craig Rosebraugh
> North American Earth Liberation Front Press Office

The letter from members of Congress to Janet Reno was a bit much, I would have to say.

A few days before the 26th of April, my attorney put forth a motion in court to have my subpoena dropped due to a procedural error on the side of Peifer. On February 29, Peifer already had the order compelling testimony completed before I ever testified. Usual procedure is that one waits to see what actions or inactions a witness takes before such an order would be completed.

However, Peifer was effectively able to argue that based on my prior dealings with him and the grand jury he had reasonable suspicion to believe that I would be taking the Fifth Amendment on the 29th of February. Therefore, a judge declared that Peifer was not out of line by having the order completed ahead of time. Thus, I was still commanded to appear on April 26 and would be under the order compelling testimony for Boise Cascade.

When April 26 rolled around, support protests were held in Portland, Sacramento, Los Angeles, Washington D.C., Denver, Minneapolis, London and other cities. The Portland protest attracted another 100 or so participants. As I entered the grand jury room yet again, I knew I had a very slim chance of leaving a free person that day.

With my attorney's assistance, I worked through question after question one at a time for two hours. After each question was asked I went outside and discussed the matter with my attorney. To questions outside the scope of the order compelling testimony I took the Fifth Amendment again. To other questions within the realm of the order I replied that I could not recall the answers. With all of the stress from the grand jury harassment and pressure from federal authorities, I simply had and continue to have a major memory problem. Of course what this meant is that legally I could not be held in contempt of court for not answering the questions. The answers I gave, though frustrating to Assistant U.S. Attorney Peifer, were the answers I had to the questions presented. (See questions below.)

After two hours of repetitive questioning, Peifer told me he needed to talk to my attorney and that I would be called back. He told my attorney that I would be called back in a month or so for further questioning. At that point, I walked out of the U.S. Courthouse and back into the world. This was another day of success in two areas: First, I did not cooperate once again with the grand jury and second, I remained out of prison.

So the U.S. Attorney's office and the grand jury commanded me to return to the grand jury on May 24. Only this time a second individual had been subpoenaed for the same time on the same day in Portland. I was uncertain as to how this would work but figured one individual would just be made to wait outside while the other was in the room of much hell.

Josh Harper, a Northwest activist who had been working with Ocean

Defense International in the Olympic Peninsula trying to stop the Makah whale hunt, received a subpoena also for May 24. He was actually in a boat on the water when coast guard cutters surrounded his vessel. Agents then boarded his boat and issued him the subpoena. This was Harper's first subpoena to a grand jury.

Prior to the 24th, more organizing was done to try and place some pressure on the grand jury system. When the day rolled around support protests were once again held in Portland, Los Angeles, Bloomington, Minneapolis, and San Diego.

I received notice late in the afternoon on May 23 that my subpoena had been called off. The reason given was that apparently the grand jury did not have time to deal with both Harper and myself on the same day at the same time. Peifer told my attorney that I would be called back to the grand jury some time either in June or July. Harper was still commanded to appear the next day.

The next morning, some 100 people gathered once again in front of the U.S. Courthouse at 8:00 a.m. to protest the ongoing harassment of the grand jury system. At 9:00 a.m., there was no sign from Harper so I read a statement from him to the crowd detailing his reasons for resisting the grand jury:

WHY I AM RESISTING THE GRAND JURY

My name is Josh Harper. I am a green anarchist currently residing in Seattle, WA. I was recently attempting to interfere in the killing of whales off of the Olympic Peninsula when the vessel I was aboard was surrounded by the coast guard. I was boarded and issued a subpoena commanding me to appear May 24th in Portland, OR. I have decided to defy this subpoena and wish to explain my decision to fellow activists.

First and foremost, this world is dying. All that is beautiful about the world is being destroyed and paved over. The animals are being either killed or turned into machines for human consumption. Our society, which was for thousands of years mostly peaceful and egalitarian, is now filled with neurosis, discontent, and alienation. But there is more out there! All of our rage, all of our anger at this system can be focused into positive action. This grand jury wants to stop that positive action. Although the ALF and ELF are only small parts of a larger effort for autonomy, freedom, and a progression to an intact Earth, they are important because they show us that we can fight back, and WE CAN WIN! I wilt not betray them by speaking with their enemies.

Secondly, as an anarchist I would never willingly cooperate with the grand jury system. The very idea that this government presumes they can command me to do anything shows how very little they know me. My life is my own, my thoughts are my own, and what I decide to do will not be dictated to me by judges, attorneys, and their lackeys with guns. If they want me, let them come and get me. They can drag me to the grand jury room, but they can never make me speak.

I send Craig Rosebraugh all of my respect. He has faced down this grand jury, and even though he has chosen a different tactic than me, I understand his motivations. The media he is gaining is invaluable; he is awakening even more people to the path of resistance. To the ALF and ELF - I do not know you, but I send you my endless admiration. Keep fighting. You are my sisters and brothers; perhaps someday you can remove the masks so that we may celebrate victory together. Until then, let us all remain in utter defiance of those who would try to stop us.

Harper, in his admirable complete resistance to the grand jury, decided not to show up at all. He has not been heard from since. Later in the day on the 24th, I received a call from my attorney, who said that Peifer had called, demanding the original of Harper's statement. I told him I did not have the original.

As of this writing (June 9, 2000), I have not heard anything new from the U.S. Attorney's office. This grand jury term is set to expire in late June and a new one will convene most likely in July. The possibility of endless harassment from the grand jury is great, considering the seven-year statute of limitations on arson.

The beauty in all of this misery is the plain, simple fact that in all of the U.S. ELF actions (as far as we at the press office know), not one individual has been caught. Although the grand jury harassment is annoying, it is pleasing to realize that I have been heavily targeted because the U.S. Attorney's office has no real suspects. Long Live the ELF. Down with Grand Juries.

Questions Asked of Craig Rosebraugh at the February 29, 2000 and the April 26, 2000 Grand Juries

February 29, 2000:

1) Regarding the development in the Bloomington, IN area, who committed the crime (of burning down a new house)?
2) Did you have any prior knowledge of the crime before it was committed?
3) A communiqué from the ELF claims that on October 23, 1999, six pieces of logging equipment were damaged in the Bloomington area. Did you receive prior notice of this crime? Who committed this crime?
4) Re: fire at MSU, December 31, 1999. Did anyone communicate with you about this incident before? Who communicated with you over e-mail about this? Do you have any knowledge about who did it?
5) Who is Sandy Banks? Re: Nturebatslast@yahoo.com. Who is this? Is this a false name used by someone you know?
6) Re: National Review magazine article on MSU fire. What is your philosophy on arson? Did you have a grand jury appearance in 1997? Here? Do you recall this?
7) You once supported nonviolence, have you had a change in philosophy?
8) Re: Boise Cascade fire, December 25, 1999. Are you familiar with this? Did you receive a communiqué about this? What was the source of that communiqué? Who did it? Did you know about it before it happened?
9) Why do you have no association now with Liberation Collective?
10) Re: U.S. Forest Industries fire. Did you issue a news advisory? What was the source of the communiqué? Who did it?
11) Do you know Darren Thurston? Is he an ELF member? Is he out

of Canada? Did he send you an e-mail asking you to conduct a press release?

12) Re: Vail fire. What was the source of the communiqué? Who did it? Did anyone tell you before hand? Did you have any prior knowledge?

13) Re: November 29, 1999 Bureau of land Management incident: Did you issue a news advisory? What was the source of the communiqué? Do you have any knowledge of the individuals involved? Did you have any prior knowledge?

14) Re: July 21, 1997, Cavel West fire. What was the source of the communiqué? Did you have any prior knowledge of the incident? Did anyone tell you about the incident?

15) Re: Arritola mink release. What was the source of the communiqué? Did you have any prior knowledge of the incident? Did anyone tell you about this incident?

16) Re: February 9, 2000 University of Minnesota. On the Animal Liberation Frontline Information Service, why was there not an association with your name regarding this incident? What was the source of the communiqué? Did you have any prior knowledge of this incident? Who did it?

17) Re: Schumacher Fur vandalism in Portland last week. Do you know anyone involved? Did you have any prior knowledge of this incident?

18) Do you ever verify information you receive from the ELF/ALF?

19) Re: letter received from someone in Monmouth, OR. Who is Lucas Szabo (sp?)? Did you respond to his letter? Did you encourage his activity in animal liberation? Do you know him?

20) Re: aerial photographs of mink farms on the Oregon coast. Why were you in possession of these? Why were they taken?

21) Re: e-mail stating that you wanted to close the Oregon Regional Primate Research Center at any cost. What are your intentions?

22) Re: aerial photographs of the Oregon Regional Primate Research Center. What is the purpose of having these? Where did you get these?

23) Re: vendor lists from the Oregon Regional Primate Research Center. What was the source of these? Why were you in possession of these?

24) Re: videos of raids of laboratories. Why were you in possession of these?

25) Re: e-mail from Josh Harper. Did he talk about a rabbit farm raid in Philomath, OR? Did he give specific information to you before

the raid? Didn't you give information seeking housing for rabbits on your website? Did Josh Harper live in the same house as you?

26) Do you know David Barbarash? Why did he e-mail you asking for photographs of ELF/ALF?

27) Re: e-mail stating that you want to disrupt the Americans for Medical Progress. Do you want to disrupt this organization? What is your intention?

28) Re: private computer e-mail list. Are you a member? Don't individuals have to be nominated by at least two people to be on the list? Do you know Alison Smith? Did you send an e-mail nominating Alison Smith to the list?

29) What is your affiliation with People for the Ethical Treatment of Animals (PETA)? Doesn't PETA post bail for those committing violent acts? Did you get an offer for full-time employment for PETA?

30) Do you know Katie Fedor? Did she e-mail you asking for your assistance in sending a press release in Illinois?

31) Was the fire in Redmond at the same time they were slaughtering those wild horses there?

32) Has anyone ever been harmed or killed in these incidents?

33) Are there ever mice in building that burn down? Does this concern you?

*additional comments from the grand jury included, "Yeah, he's got no vocabulary!" and "I bet those shoes are leather!"

April 26, 2000:

State your name.

1) Are you aware of the order compelling testimony regarding the Boise Cascade fire? Do you recall appearing in front of Judge King? Are you aware the order is in full force?

2) Did you receive any written notice claiming responsibility for the Boise Cascade Fire?

3) Did you use the Animal Liberation Frontline Information Service website to promote the Boise Cascade fire?

4) Why is your name on the internet posting retrieved from the Frontline Information website?

5) How did you receive the communiqué?

6) Did you have any part in composing the press release?
7) Why did you send out the press release? Why was it newsworthy? Why was it important?
8) Was it your purpose by putting forth the press release to further the goals of the ELF in burning down the Boise Cascade office in Monmouth, OR?
9) Do you consider the Boise Cascade fire to be economic sabotage? What does economic sabotage mean to you in relation to Boise Cascade?
10) (The assistant attorney reads the ELF communiqué for the Boise Cascade fire.) Do you recall this communiqué?
11) When you received the communiqué did you consider it economic sabotage?
12) Did anyone assist you in writing the press release? If so, who?
13) In 1999 were you aware of anybody who resided in Monmouth. OR?
14) Were you still with Liberation Collective in December of 1999?
15) Did you communicate with Lucas Szabo (sp?)?
16) Was a search warrant executed on your home on February 2, 2000?
17) Did you receive or have any knowledge of the fire at Boise Cascade prior to it occurring?
18) Where did you send the press releases?
19) Do you support the burning of Boise Cascade?
20) Does your memory lapse concern you? Have you seen a doctor about your memory? How do you function on a day-to-day basis with such a memory problem?

ELF Supporter Arrested by Squad of Riot Police while Peacefully Demonstrating against the Grand Jury

When authorities are unable to capture underground guerrillas, they turn to repressing their public supporters. Those who work to ideologically support covert acts of sabotage have been finding their Constitutional rights cut short and have found themselves facing government harassment and false arrests.

On February 29th, 2000 after a demonstration against the grand jury convened in Portland, Oregon investigating several actions claimed by the ELF and the Animal Liberation Front (ALF), Leslie James Pickering was detained by an "Arrest Squad" consisting of twelve riot police in formation. Leslie was dragged away, held for over two hours and charged with "disorderly conduct," a misdemeanor that holds a potential six-month jail sentence.

Officer Mack, who authored the report on the incident, stated that at several specific times throughout the demonstration Leslie allegedly disrupted the flow of traffic, both pedestrian and automotive. According to Officer Mack's report, "Pickering's action's showed a total disregard for other citizens. He was blocking the sidewalk.... and then entering the roadway.... causing traffic to stop."

While Leslie supports and at times engages in that type of action, during this particular demonstration his conduct was anything but "disorderly." The incidents described, which occurred nearly an hour earlier, are referring to exact moments when Leslie put his foot of the curb to take a photograph or cross the street while no traffic was present.

When referring to why the arrest didn't take place until the end of the demonstration, Officer Mack's report states, "Pickering was not arrested initially as this action would only serve to incite the crowd which is probably what he wanted."

The Portland police force knows that Leslie is an organizer of the resistance against this grand jury and recognize him as a force for change both locally and nationally. Leslie's arrest on February 29 was an attempt to stifle the resistance against the grand jury and to once again harass those who struggle on the side of the natural environment.

The arrest was also part of a coordinated effort to distract attention from the unexpected release of grand jury witness Craig Rosebraugh's from the proceedings. As Rosebraugh began to be lead out of the building, an agent of the FBI radioed down to officers outside that Rosebraugh was coming out. At that exact moment a suspicious man standing near Leslie was paged and left the demonstration as the riot police marched forward in formation and proceeded to surround Leslie and make the arrest. Few noticed moments later when Rosebraugh emerged from the building a free man, as the crowd had either scattered or was distracted by such a blatant form of political repression.

As this issue goes to print, Leslie faces a jury trial on charges relating to this incident. If authorities have it their way, everyone who struggles on the side of the natural environment will be subdued as agencies and corporations continue to profit from decimating the Earth.

4.

RESISTANCE #4

The ways in which we go about pursuing social change are unnatural. They have been developed to nullify the just desires we all have for autonomy, while placing no real threat to the structure that creates our vast universe of oppression. Our revolutionary spirits have been co-opted by fundamentally flawed methodologies, which prove unsuccessful time and time again.

When faced with oppression, is it a natural reaction to write a petition, mail a letter to your representative, lobby Congress or file a lawsuit? Is it a natural reaction to organize a protest, partake in a sit-in, lock your neck to a piece of equipment or go limp while the cops beat you and drag you off to jail to be fingerprinted? When faced with the current magnitude of oppression, is it logical to even consider single-issue reform as having any vague resemblance to a solution?

Preconceived concepts of what is and what is not proper action to take in pursuit of social change have mutated to a level of going unquestioned. These ideas have entire movements hypnotized; they have misdirected many individuals away from legitimate struggle. These avenues have been paved by the same governmental structures that cause the oppression they pretend to be solutions for. Activism detours potential revolutionaries while reinforcing the misconception that capitalist society can be reformed. It keeps us juggling the symptoms of an illness that goes untouched, all the while smiling like clowns.

It is important to ask ourselves if the methodologies we subscribe to have any chance of success. Have they been formed through a natural, logical and strategically-utilitarian process, or have they simply been handed down to us by those who have found them self gratifying in the past? Is it possible that our strategies have been designed and promoted by those in power in order to keep us chasing our own tails?

The argument that the movements led by Gandhi, Martin Luther King and others made gains through their practices of nonviolence is an uneducated misconception. These people and their philosophies were simply parts of larger movements, which utilized a wide variety of tactics. If we wish to gain even the limited success that these movements gained, we need to embrace an equally wide variety of tactics. If we wish to truly succeed, we need to learn from their mistakes.

Along these lines of thought, I have decided to make some significant changes to this publication. No longer will *RESISTANCE* report on the same tired voluntary arrests, which rely on a fundamental faith in the system and which simply aren't an effective means of achieving true revolutionary change. From now on *RESISTANCE* will report only on legitimate struggle-- struggle that has proven effective against those who work daily to destroy life.

On Wednesday, July 26, Terry Turchie, Deputy Assistant Director of the FBI Counter-terrorism Division, appeared before the U.S. House Government Reform Subcommittee to discuss domestic terrorism and national security. Turchie testified:

> The threat of special interest terrorism... most notably emanating from animal rights and environmental extremists... is emerging as a significant threat in a growing number of communities throughout the United States. During the past several years, special interest extremism... as characterized by the Animal Liberation Front and the Earth Liberation Front... has emerged as a serious terrorist threat.

The Federal Bureau of investigations can easily be viewed as the defense system of the machine that these organizations struggle to destroy. For the FBI to state that these groups pose a "significant threat" is to confirm the effectiveness of their actions. Threat to what? There has been no threat to any natural form of life posed by either of these organizations; in fact, they both struggle to "liberate" life. The threat they pose is to 'national security' and to the continuance of our genocidal and suicidal societal practices. They are a threat to those who kill and destroy everything that lies between them and profit. They are a threat to the power they hold over our lives and all life on Earth. This "threat" sounds an awful lot like a blessing to me.

Since 1997, the Earth Liberation Front has claimed responsibility for over 19 direct actions of economic sabotage, causing well over $34,131,000 in damages. These actions are being taken against those who profit from the destruction of the natural environment. No harm has ever been brought to any form of natural life, nor have any individuals been apprehended for any of the actions claimed by the Earth Liberation Front.

The Earth Liberation Front does not commit merely symbolic acts to simply gain attention to any particular issues. It is not concerned merely with logging, genetic engineering or even the environment for that matter; its purpose is to liberate the Earth.

The Earth, and therefore all of us born of it, is under attack. We are under attack by a system which values profit over life, which has and will kill anything to satisfy its never ending greed. We have seen a recent history rich in the destruction of peoples, cultures and environments. We have seen the results of millions of years of evolution destroyed in a relative blink of an eye. We watch as our governments justify murdering millions of people for oil while calling the Earth Liberation Front special-interest terrorists.

How can protecting the livability of our environment be called a special interest? How can self defense be called terrorism?

The only problems I can find with actions like these are that they aren't happening frequently enough and at severe enough levels. That the press offices aren't so flooded with communiqués and media calls that all forms of electrical communication are shut down. That entire industries aren't being driven to extinction due to profit losses caused by covert, direct-action campaigns. That areas of North America aren't completely protected from capitalist exploitation by clandestine guerrilla organizations. That the oppressive system itself isn't brought to its knees by the people taking direct action and fighting back. Though I can see all of this potentially becoming reality in the near future. What other choice do we have?

●

Grand Jury
Josh Harper Arrested by Feds; Faces Criminal Contempt Charges

Josh Harper was arrested in Seattle on September 27, 2000 for his refusal to cooperate and testify before a federal grand jury in Portland investigating the actions of the Earth Liberation Front (ELF) and Animal Liberation Front (ALF). Immediately after speaking to high school students about animal liberation and resisting grand juries, Harper was surrounded by federal agents and taken into custody. He was held at the SEATAC Federal Detention Center until Friday, September 29, 2000, when he was released on bail. Upon his release, Harper was commanded to appear in Portland on October 27, 2000, to face criminal contempt charges. He then released the following statement:

Dear Supporters,

As many of you may have heard, I was arrested on a warrant on September 27 by agents from the FBI, U.S. Marshall's office, and local police. The warrant stemmed from my refusal to appear before a grand jury convened in Portland investigating the actions of the Animal and Earth Liberation Fronts.

I was taken to a federal detention center and was expecting to be transported to Portland to await trial. Then, last Friday, a small miracle happened. The prosecutor in Portland and the one in Washington both tried to block me from getting bail. Federal agents were flown in to convince the magistrate not to release me, but due to overwhelming support from the animal, environmental, and anarchist communities I was released on bail! The courtroom was overflowing with supporters, and they managed to raise more than the amount needed for my bail in less than 20 minutes! I am overwhelmed by the generosity of everyone who helped me and cannot begin to express my gratitude.

Now that I am on the outside again I am preparing to fight the charge of criminal contempt. It is not likely that I will win, however, and chances are fair that I will be spending at least a year in federal prison, possibly more.

We must first put this in perspective. The crime I am accused of basically amounts to missing a court date. So why such a serious penalty? I say it is because they are afraid. All across the world people are rising up. Small cells of committed activists are fighting for human freedom, ecological sanity, animal liberation, and autonomy. Large protests are finally going past the tired, ineffective marches and sign holdings that kept the government safe from us all these years, and now are actually becoming a threat again! People are ignoring electoral politics and are taking action themselves. We are sick of the lie that tells us 4 minutes of action every four years will change the world. We are sick of watching as the last of the wild dies, as the animal nations are massacred, and as our communities become devoid of real life, happiness, freedom and personality. We don't want to live in a world owned by Starbucks, we don't want to work our existence away making profit for the rich bastards we all despise, and we don't want to be beaten down and arrested for finally speaking up! As we rise, they must try to knock us down. The grand jury system is being used all over this country to keep the power in the hands of the elite few.

We cannot let this happen without resistance! On Friday, the 27th of October, I am to appear in Portland at 9 a.m. before a judge. Let us show him that I am not alone. Come to the courthouse (1000 SW 3rd Ave, Portland, OR 97204) at 8 a.m. to show your support... And of course, the best thing you can do to support me is to keep the resistance growing.

On October 27, over 100 people showed up outside the U.S. Courthouse in Portland to give support to Harper and to resist the grand jury and government repression. At his arraignment date, Harper successfully asked for a postponement so he could obtain an attorney. The Court then rescheduled his arraignment for November 17, 2000.

The following statement was then allegedly released by Josh Harper, which provoked legal repercussions against his First Amendment right to free speech:

Hello again,

I am writing this update about my case to inform everyone of new developments and to thank all of those people who have helped me thus far. This is a very trying time for me, but it is made easier when I think that I am not alone. People from all over the world have written and sent donations. The Animal Liberation Front has shown support for me as well by breaking windows at a McDonalds and a Neiman Marcus in Long Island and Beverly Hills. All of this activity is inspiring, but sadly it doesn't change the facts of this case.

I am being charged with criminal contempt, a federal

felony, for failure to appear before a grand jury. Criminal contempt carries no maximum sentence, so any amount of jail time is possible if I am convicted. This case is a first in our movement and will set a precedent that could be very harmful.

The government is essentially saying, "Snitch on your friends or go to jail."

Failure to cooperate with a grand jury is going to start costing people years of their lives. That is why we must fight this charge to the best of our ability.

I have finally found counsel in this case, but I still need funds to pay for their assistance. We are working on making some support fund merchandise, but we need help setting up benefits elsewhere. Please contact us below if you can do anything-- a vegan bake sale, a show, anything at all. We also need to fight back on another front, and the ALF has certainly taken the lead. The prosecution in this case planned to have this grand jury be an end to underground direct action movement by knocking out the aboveground support structure.

Craig Rosebraugh was targeted and had his home raided because he speaks so eloquently on behalf of those with compassion and respect for the Earth. I have been targeted because of my video productions and speaking tours, as well as my association with militant aboveground action groups. The government fears that people like Craig and I are increasing the level of direct action in this country simply by telling people that it occurs. I don't know how true that is, but I do know that is difficult to argue with the success of direct action.

In one night an Earth raper can be forever put out of business. With a few hundred dollars in equipment, animals can be freed from a lifetime of slavery at the hands of a vivisector. With long term planning and security, a new movement could emerge to cast off the oppressive state and its industrial masters. If this charge of criminal contempt puts me away for the next few years, I at least hope that the grand jury doesn't reach its goal of crushing direct action.

I see so many people fighting for a day when the Earth is wild again and we live peacefully with each other and the animal nations. Right now it seems like such a far away dream, and I am at times frustrated when I think how impossible it all seems. But then I am given hope when I remember our radical history, and all the wonderful things we have already accomplished. It remains to be seen whether or not we will be willing to do what is necessary to bring about the changes that are so desperately needed on this planet, but I see a spark of hope in every broken window, every torched police car and every mink running free as their hearts desire. I cheer every time I hear that our movement has created a safe space for wimmin, fed the hungry, or cast off one more boss. Let us increase the momentum.

Thanks for your support,

Josh

The arraignment was then postponed again on November 17 due to Harper's then attorney not being licensed in Oregon. The court at this time placed another release order on Harper, which prevents him from ideologically voicing support for the ELF and/or the ALF. Assistant U.S. Attorney Stephen Piefer pleaded with a federal judge to place these extra restrictions on Harper after submitting into evidence a copy of the above email allegedly sent by Harper discussing his support of illegal direct action. If Harper violates this order he would be subject to arrest and held until his trial.

On December 1, Harper was officially charged with criminal contempt. His attorney acting on his behalf entered a Not Guilty plea and the case was set for trial on January 3, 2001.

Criminal contempt differs from civil contempt in the sense that in it has the possibility of a jury trial, and the sentence has no legal upper limit. Upon conviction, a judge may sentence an individual up to six months in prison without a jury trial. If the prosecution or judge sees fit to try for a longer sentence, a jury must legally be used. Most often, civil contempt

94

is considered before criminal contempt is used. Civil contempt does not involve a trial and commonly has an upper sentencing limit of eighteen months or the remaining length of the grand jury.

Let Harper's plight and the growing government repression be a motivating CALL TO ACTION. Harper was arrested for not cooperating with a government witch hunt attempting to stop the courageous efforts of the ELF and the ALF. Now is the time for more direct action than ever before. It is up to all of us to show this murderous government that it is impossible to stop the ideology of the ELF and the ALF: the idea that there is more to life than killing anything and everything for profit.

•

Bloomington Raid
By Marie Mason and Frank Ambrose

On July 19, 2000 at 6:30 a.m., five Indiana Conservation Officers (COs) and one FBI agent knocked on our door and announced they had a warrant to search our apartment and car. They came in and showed us the warrant and proceeded to search through every inch of our apartment looking for implements of tree spiking. The warrant authorized them to take any nails, nail heads, hammers, metal cutting tools, boots, computers, and any communication linking Frank Ambrose to the ELF.

During the raid, the majority of the items the State seized were not listed on the warrant. The vast majority of the material taken was organizational literature and address books belonging to Marie. They also took some spray paint, a crow bar from our car, Marie's family photo albums, a couple of household hammers, tin snips and a Leatherman multi-tool. They left Frank's boots on the floor without even looking at them, though they photographed the soles of all the shoes in the closet. When they were confronted about taking items that were not on the warrant, they claimed that they could do it, and there was nothing we could do to stop it.

It was clear which police agency was there and why. The COs largely stood around and watched us to make sure we didn't flush the foot-long tree spikes they were looking for down the toilet, while the FBI agent, Rob Woesner, did the bulk of the work looking through our file cabinets and car. Whenever the COs had a question about an item, they went to him for advice. He almost always advised them to take the items. It was clear the FBI is targeting us because of our political beliefs and our involvement in the takeover of a State Forest office in protest of the logging they were planning, and the COs were there just because the crime being investigated was a state-level crime and therefore their jurisdiction under the law.

Towards the end of the raid, the COs separated us and tried to get both of us to talk. They told Frank that he should cooperate with the State so that the Feds would not get involved. They said that the Feds were much worse and would not give him any deals. Meanwhile, they argued with Marie to have her try to convince Frank to turn himself in and throw his life at the mercy of the law and courts. We merely reminded them that we did not want to talk and that if they had evidence to lock us up, they would have just done that along with raiding our place.

The police promised us that they would be back later in the day with an arrest warrant for Frank (he was the one actually named on the warrant). They never showed. They also promised that they would talk to "everyone" (actually only a few individuals were harassed) in the environmental community and that someone would "rat" on him eventually. They have since visited several community members and tried to get them to say that he has been involved in illegal activities. They also have more concretely shown that they are not just interested in framing Frank, but also in framing Marie. They approached Heartwood, a local forest protection group where Marie had recently been employed. When their director, Alison Cochran, was asked questions about Marie, she cooperated and in the end agreed to give the FBI Marie's old computer. There was no warrant for this computer.

The raid and subsequent round of visits came in the wake of a series of Earth Liberation Front actions that have occurred in the Bloomington area this past year. Before the raid, there had been numerous Earth-destroying machines destroyed, a partially-built mansion burned to the ground, a wood chip truck burned, and trees spiked in two state forests. After the raid, the ELF took responsibility for attempting arson at the county's Republican headquarters and for destroying more forest-destroying machines in the Martin State Forest.

●

Beyond the ELF:
Creating a new direct action movement against capitalism and industrialization
By Craig Rosebraugh

While the Earth Liberation Front has shown to have quite an impact in the United States since 1997, its targets have arguably been limited in nature. As the ELF Is at least in theory an organization focused on environmental issues, its actions have stayed largely within that social movement. To their credit, the ELF has demonstrated a knowledge and understanding of a larger problem in society: the drive for profit and capital. Using economic sabotage the group has inflicted well over $34 million in damages since 1997 in the United States on entities profiting off the destruction of the environment.

But is this enough? The ELF is definitely on the right track as far as tactics of economic sabotage are concerned. Yet there is a clear difference, strategically speaking, between burning a building completely to the ground and causing minor damage through various forms of vandalism. Granted, I am under the assumption that the basic motives for all of these actions would be the same and therefore would applaud the brave and heroic individuals for working to save the environment and smash corporate greed.

The main difference in my mind, though, lies in not only the monetary amount of damage done to the given target, but also in the target itself. The idea should be that if an individual desires to engage in economic sabotage she/he should pick the best target possible at any given time. Then the best lactic should be chosen at each given time to ensure the most damage will be done. So how is this done? How are the best targets selected?

In my mind the best targets are those that will have the most effect in stopping the exploitation, destruction, and deaths of the natural environment and all life coexisting on the planet. One must make every effort to look beyond individual social issues, be they human, animal, and/ or environmental, to the higher cause of these problems. The desire, or manufactured desire, of the need for profit, material items, and ownership is at the heart of arguably many of these social issues.

Yet, instead of concentrating on fighting this desire most activists, largely of the leftist persuasion, appear content with continuing the exhausted state sanctioned legal means of protest, which have little effect. Underground organizations such as the ELF and the Animal Liberation Front have at least demonstrated a greater understanding of the role desire plays in the environmental and animal liberation movements. They have taken concrete steps to fight this desire within their own movements. Yet the real desire, the desire taught to us along with the American dream, apple pie and baseball, is most often overlooked or clearly unseen.

There needs to be a direct focus on fighting the desire created by industrialization and the westernized way of life. It needs to be a direct action focus using not state sanctioned forms of protest but underground guerrilla tactics in the form of economic sabotage and beyond.

So how do we go about combating this desire? How do we go about choosing targets that will have the most impact? The idea in the United States is to look at just what makes the country what it is. What symbols, what propaganda, what physical objects are involved in creating the atmosphere of desire? What makes the United States economically operate? Who and what are the information sources in the U.S. that push and create the propaganda? Are there targets that could be selected that involve and affect many corporations? Are there symbolic targets that if destroyed would place a major blow to the false reality?

Think big. Think Wall Street, the stock market, the Statue of Liberty, the U.S. Capitol, Mt. Rushmore, Disneyland, media conglomerates, military installations, governmental agencies (CIA, FBI, BATF, USFS, etc.), large multinational corporations, automobile manufacturers, etc. Realize the difference between pulling up an acre of G.E. crops and destroying Monsanto. The difference between sabotaging logging equipment and destroying MAXXAM/Pacific Lumber. The difference between spray-paint and fire.

When the ELF torched Vail Resorts, Inc. in 1998, the organization was on the right path toward targeting desire. Vail is known worldwide as the ritzy, only-for-the-rich, ski resort. A perfect symbol of desire. If you begin with nothing, work hard all your life, you too can become wealthy, powerful and can visit the planet's premiere facilities, including Vail. Those who can't are supposed to desire it.

The idea for a movement against capitalism and industrialization directly is nothing new. The Luddites (1811 – 1813) in England used direct action with some success to combat the beginnings of the Industrial Revolution. Before the revolution hit, many people for centuries had worked out of their cottages and small shops in villages on machines that could be run by one person. Suddenly, an industrial society appeared with new, complex machinery commonly housed in multiple-story buildings. This new way of working threatened and eventually killed the means by which livelihood had been achieved for years. The Luddites fought back using similar economic sabotage tactics seen today. Damages estimated at over $1 million were inflicted on business owners during this two-year time period. Some manufacturers agreed to actually stop using the new complex machines due to the Luddite threat of action.

The tactics of the Weather Underground in the U.S. in the late 60s to early 1970s also appeared to be focused against the ideology existing in the United States. While their operations appeared somewhat reactionary and their group politics arguably questionable, they did succeed in demonstrating that symbolic and real targets like those mentioned above are not impossible to hit. Here is a summary of the Weather Underground bombings from 1970-1972:

- Haymarket Police Statue, Chicago, October 1969 and October 1970
- Chicago Police Cars following the murder of Fred Hampton and Mark Clark, December 1969
- New York City Police Headquarters, June 1970
- Marin County Courthouse, following the murder of Jonathan Jackson, William Christmas and James McClain, August 1970
- Long Island City Courthouse, in Queens, in solidarity with prison revolts taking place in New York City, October 1970
- Department of Corrections in San Francisco and Office of California Prisons in Sacramento, for the murder of George Jackson in San Quentin, August 1971
- Department of Corrections in Albany, NY, for the murder and assault against the prisoners of Attica, September 1971
- 103rd Precinct of the New York City police, for the murder of 10-year-old Clifford Clover, May 1973
- Harvard War research Center for International Affairs, October 1970
- U.S. Capitol, after the invasion of Laos, March 1971
- MIT Research Center, William Bundy's office, October 1971
- The Pentagon, after the bombing of Hanoi and mining of the

harbors of North Vietnam, May 1972
- Draft and recruiting centers
- ROTC buildings
- ITT Latin America Headquarters, following the fascist revolution in Chile, September 1973
- National Guard Headquarters, Washington, D.C., after the murders at Jackson State and Kent State, May 1970
- Presidio Army Base and MP Station, San Francisco, July 26, 1970
- -Federal Offices of HEW (Health, Education, and Welfare), San Francisco, March 1974
- Liberation of Timothy Leary from California Men's Colony, San Luis Obispo, September 1970

The above actions are presented here to demonstrate the possibilities of direct action against the idea of desire. The Luddites and the Weather Underground are just two examples of earlier organizations targeting capitalism and industrialization through direct action.

The thought behind all of this is not to get discouraged but rather encouraged to get active and stay active in a way that will produce results. If the goal is to end environmental destruction and the suffering and murder of life on this planet, then a clear look must be taken at the real enemy. Whether the group is the Earth Liberation Front or some new organization, the importance lies in rethinking targets and choosing those that will produce the greatest success and damage. In either case the actions must not only become more strategic and of an intensified scale but they must also occur with a much greater frequency.

5.

RESISTANCE #5

When there is no legitimate argument for your actions it is often your best move to change the subject, to create a false debate in order to divert attention from the real issue at hand. In the case of the Earth Liberation Front (ELF) and of the direct action movement in general, a false debate over "violence" and "terrorism" is being employed by authorities and embraced by corporate mainstream media. In efforts to divert attention from the real issues being raised and to prevent public support of effective direct action, a propaganda campaign known as 'ecoterrorism' has been launched.

This false debate over 'ecoterrorism' is designed to steer attention away from the fact that we are systematically destroying the very elements we rely on for survival. A healthy, diverse, global ecosystem, billions of years in the making, has been almost completely devastated in just a few thousand years of anthropocentrism. In order to create rural, urban and suburban environments for humans, designed around the theory that money will bring happiness, our natural habitats (which support a countless number of species) are being "developed" faster than we can imagine. Our air, water and food are being poisoned directly and indirectly by industry and by the constant push for short-term profits through technological progress. If something drastic isn't done to change the way we live, we will have destroyed all opportunities for life to exist, including our own.

It's no coincidence that as we destroy the Earth, we suffer both physically and mentally. While Western medicine has succeeded at increasing the length of our lives, it cannot possibly keep up with the cancer, disease, illness and general unhealthiness caused by industrial/technological society that plagues us. Depression, hopelessness, social anxiety and alienation are natural reactions to a system designed around capitalist greed rather than the best interests of the people.

It's truly a question of quantity or quality. We can continue living as we do now, surrounded by our material possessions and alienated from our natural habitats and billions of others until we inevitably drive ourselves to extinction. Or, we can fight to our last breaths against the anti-Earth, anti-human agenda of capitalism. The system is guilty of nearly every misery we suffer as Individuals, as communities and as a planet. But instead of attempting to change this situation, we choose to ignore it and raise our debates over the "violence" involved in sabotaging a piece of property.

When a piece of property exists to bring profits by exploiting communities and destroying natural elements necessary for survival, it is in everyone's best interests to see that this situation no longer exists. One realistic way that the Earth Liberation Front has achieved this is by burning that piece of property to the ground.

Those who tell us that the change needed to bring about social and ecological justice can be achieved solely through legal, state-sanctioned means of protest have naively, if not purposefully, underestimated the magnitude of the problems we face. If you have bought into the propaganda telling us that destroying a piece of private property is wrong-- regardless of the oppression and injustice that that property perpetuates-- then you have essentially subscribed to the belief that property is more valuable than life. We must come to the obvious realization that the system exists for one purpose only: to exploit and exhaust every resource and opportunity possible, as rapidly as possible. It exists not to make the world a better place, not to provide resources and opportunities, but to steal them from us and from future generations.

Another obvious realization we must make is that the popular environmental movement has not and will not succeed along its current path. The vast majority of efforts made in the name of environmentalism are done so through state-sanctioned means of social change. But when the system itself is precisely what is enabling and promoting oppression, how is it logical to expect that same system to provide avenues towards liberation?

More and more of our natural habitats are destroyed each day, strictly for the economic interests of greedy corporations. The air that we need to breath, the water that we need to drink and the food that we need to eat become more and more poisoned each day as industry plows onward. Just take a sip of tap water; just get on the freeway at 5 PM. Observe as cancer rates skyrocket, our national parks are sold off by the board foot, and as the more 'environmentally-friendly' technologies are repressed until the last drop of oil is sucked from the Earth.

We cannot afford to continue along this path towards annihilation; it's suicide. What is more important to you: your money, your house, your car, your career, or your life and those of your children and grandchildren? If someone had his hands around your throat, strangling you, would you gather petition signatures to politely ask him to stop? Would you go limp as a symbolic gesture of your non-cooperation? Hopefully, you would defend yourself by any means necessary. The Earth Liberation Front realizes that the current environmental situation is just as desperate and takes direct action to defend all life on Earth.

The ELF is not a group of violent terrorists, as those who are responsible for the destruction of the Earth tell us. They are intelligent and courageous individuals who are taking necessary action in self-defense. They realize that the Earth is being destroyed because entities are making large profits off of its destruction. The ELF therefore engages in acts of economic sabotage in order to take the profit motive out of killing the Earth and its inhabitants.

The Federal Bureau of Investigation (FBI) considers the Earth Liberation Front "the number one domestic terrorist threat," precisely because the ELF is a threat. It is a threat to those who profit from the destruction of the natural environment. It is a threat to 'American Dream,' where property is more valuable than life. It is a threat to the system because its members realize that what is needed is revolution, not reform.

It's simple really. The Earth Liberation Front stands for the protection of our natural habitats and the preservation of the elements of the natural environment that we all need to survive: fresh air, clean water and healthy food. The system, on the other hand, stands for the destruction of these elements and the total annihilation of the natural environment for short-term monetary gains.

Down with the system! Long Live the Earth Liberation Front!

•

Feds Raid NAELFPO Again
Hundreds of Items Seized

On April 5, 2001, at approximately 6:00 a.m., agents from the FBI, BATF, and Oregon State Police conducted a six-hour raid simultaneously on the North American ELF Press Office (NAELPO), on two vehicles driven or owned by ELF spokespersons, and on a vegan baking company also owned by one of the spokespersons. Warrants issued by authorities called for the search of the residence of and vehicles Craig Rosebraugh, Leslie James Pickering and Elaine Close, as well as the NAELFPO and the building housing Rosebraugh's business, the Calendula Baking Company. The warrants also called for the seizure of any property relating in any way to the particular arson under investigation. The list of possible property items to be seized on the warrant was so extensive it covered just about everything you would find in an office or vehicle.

The particular arson under investigation occurred at the Joe Romania Chevrolet dealership in Eugene, Oregon on March 30, 2001. The following is the anonymous communiqué received by the NAELFPO claiming responsibility, by unidentified individuals, for the $1 million arson at Joe Romania Chevrolet in Eugene, Oregon, which destroyed over 3 dozen new SUVs:

> Claim for Romania Arson
>
> 1 million dollars worth of luxury SUVs were torched at Romania Chevrolet. Sucking the land dry, gas-guzzling SUVs are at the forefront of this vile imperialistic culture's caravan towards self-destruction. We can no longer allow the rich to parade around in their armored existence, leaving a wasteland behind in their tire tracks. The time is right to fight back.
>
> Romania Chevrolet is the same location that was targeted last June, for which two Earth warriors, Free and Critter, are being persecuted. The techno-industrial state thinks it can stop the growing resistance by jailing some of us, but they cannot jail the spirit of those who know another world is possible. The fire that burns within Free and Critter burns within all of us and cannot be extinguished by locking them up.
>
> In this continuous assault on both the planet and ourselves, SUVs destroy the Earth while the prison system tries to destroy those who see beyond this empty life. We must strike out against what destroys us before we are all either choking on smog or held captive by the state. Take the power into your own hands. It's your life.

At approximately 6:00 a.m. on April 5, a Portland police officer pulled over Rosebraugh in his vehicle. The officer claimed the stop was due to a broken tail light. After 30 minutes FBI agents approached the car and delivered copies of the search warrants to Rosebraugh. Simultaneously, agents began the raid on the personal residence in North Portland where both Pickering and Close were present. After Rosebraugh and his vehicle were searched, Rosebraugh was taken to the Calendula Baking Company where the FBI proceeded to break through a window to gain access. A four-hour search and seizure was conducted simultaneous with the six-hour search at the residence.

Agents seized hundreds of items of property, including computer equipment, phone books, videos, literature, and other items. Many Items stolen by the authorities-- such as keyboards, monitors, and printers-- had no relation whatsoever to evidence. Yet they were taken anyway as an attempt to stop the legal work of the NAELFPO.

April 5 was also the day on which Frank Ambrose was to have his pretrial in Bloomington, Indiana. Ambrose, the first person in North America to be arrested charged with an ELF-related crime, was facing accusations of tree spiking in the Bloomington area in 2000. The NAELFPO had previously called for a national day of action against state repression in support of Ambrose on April 5th.

In Portland, the NAELFPO had planned a press conference to discuss the case against Ambrose and the real motives behind the ELF. Both Rosebraugh and Pickering were scheduled to attend and speak at the conference. The FBI purposely chose this day to ensure that the press conference would not go on as planned. Rosebraugh was detained from 6:00 a.m. to 11:00 a.m., just enough time to miss the scheduled press conference. Pickering, however, was able to break away from his home to attend the conference where he immediately alerted the press about the raid.

The authorities' plans for yet another quiet, uneventful raid backfired, as media outlets raced to the home and caught the search and the authorities on tape. Throughout the day, televised live via satellite, news briefings took place as news helicopters flew above. At the end of the raid, authorities attempted to sneak out the back door into an alley to load the stolen items away from the watchful eye of the media. This plan failed as news cameras quickly made their way around to the back of the house and caught the loading of property stolen by the feds into their government-issued vehicles.

Authorities have claimed that the raid was an attempt to find information associated with those involved in the Romania arson and other ELF actions. Yet this is the second raid on the NAELFPO in just over a year. In February 2000, agents from the FBI, BATF, and U.S. Forest Service searched the home of Rosebraugh and Close, stealing hundreds of items of property. No arrests were made from information obtained in the 2000 raid, and there were no arrests made from the 2001 raid either. This is because the NAELFPO has no information that will aid the investigations into the ELF actions and other, politically-motivated direct actions. The authorities realize this and used the Romania fire an excuse to attempt to shut down the operations of the NAELFPO. Why else would they have stolen property such as keyboards and monitors?

Rosebraugh was also issued yet another subpoena—his 7th since 1997-- commanding him to appear before a federal grand jury convened in Eugene, OR to investigate the Romania arson. In response to Rosebraugh's request for a postponement, the U.S. Attorney told Rosebraugh (over the phone and in a confirmation letter to his attorney) that he could disregard the subpoena and that they would contact him through his attorney if they needed him in the future. And so, the harassment continues.

As the pressure from the authorities increases, the NAELFPO becomes further determined to bring news of the ELF and its ideology to the world.

●

Portland Grand Jury Harassment Ends for Now
By Josh Harper

Right now I am sitting in my second story apartment looking out the window. I live in a residential area like most others in big cities across the U.S. Where there once was an area vital to wildlife, now there is just a sea of cement. Sidewalks have replaced soil and gutters have replaced streams. The world I live in is certainly not what I would consider ideal, and yet right now I feel lucky to be looking through glass instead of looking through bars.

Earlier this year, I was arrested by FBI agents and Federal Marshals for resisting a grand jury investigating the ALF and ELF. Friends of mine put up the collateral and cash for my $10,000 bail, and I began the process of fighting the felony charge against me. It was a difficult time. The FBI had made it clear that although I was not a suspect in the seven direct actions they wanted to question me about, they did suspect me in other actions and were considering pressing additional charges. Luckily several anarchists, environmentalists, and animal liberationists were supportive of me, and my family and friends were willing to do whatever it took to keep me on the outside.

My lawyer and I discussed all of our possible defenses and whether or not to take a plea bargain, but I made it clear that answering questions about other people, or my private life was out of the question. After several court dates I was informed that the grand jury was going to convene again, and that the prosecutor was more interested in getting me into the grand jury room than sending me to jail. I was told that I could either walk into the grand jury room with a deal that would get my charges dropped, or I could be dragged in and still face a felony.

After discussing the situation with other activists I decided that refusing to show up again would only be a symbolic gesture, and would accomplish very little. The government knew where I was, and in the end, I would be taken before the grand jury. My lawyer and I began work on finding ways that I could still refrain from answering questions and hopefully stay out of jail as well. Thanks to his work, I am free today.

I signed an agreement basically stating that I would walk into the grand jury room and honestly answer questions. If the prosecutor was unable to prove perjury, then my charges would be dropped. On the day of the grand jury my lawyer prepared several excellent arguments to protect me from having to answer questions concerning other people. It worked. To all other questions I answered truthfully- "I don't recall," "Not to the best of my knowledge," and so forth. Stephen Piefer, the prosecutor, didn't look very happy when I walked out of the room without handcuffs.

So luckily my ordeal is over, almost entirely due to an incredible job done by Stu Sugarman, my attorney. We need to turn our attention to the new grand juries in Eugene and to protecting those brave warriors under fire from Santa Cruz to Long Island. The support I received was tremendous. If this energy can continue and accelerate, perhaps we have some chance

108

of ending this war on wilderness and freedom.

The following are the questions I was asked by the grand jury and the federal prosecutor, minus those questions involving individuals' names. All those named to me by the grand jury will be contacted privately. I also may have missed a few questions due to time constraints - I was writing them down as they were asked. Some of these were translated from my rough short hand, so the exact wording may not be the same. Still, this is a pretty accurate assessment of the proceedings. I was asked my whereabouts during each incident, and have not included those questions below for space reasons.

Aritola Mink Raid, Mount Angel, Oregon:

1. Were you aware that this crime occurred?
2. Did you know in advance that there was going to be an action at the Aritola mink farm?
3. Were you ever present on the farm?
4. Did you participate in any crime on the farm?
5. Did you write the communiqué?
6. Do you know who did write the communiqué?
7. Do you consider this a case of direct action?
8. Did you participate in the media release of the communiqué?
9. Did you solicit video footage of this action?
10. Did you receive video footage of this action?
11. Did you receive any written notes or still pictures?
12. Did you communicate with anyone regarding this action via e-mail?
13. Did you send an e-mail to anyone describing the interior layout of the farm?
14. Is there anything that you would like to tell us about this action, or any testimony you would like to clarify? (This question was asked again, after discussing each subsequent action.)

Cavel West arson:

1. Were you aware that this crime occurred?
2. Were you aware that it was going to happen before it occurred?

3. Did you ever discuss the identity of those involved with any person?
4. Did you have any prior information about Cavel West?
5. What do the initials EZLN stand for?
6. 6 Do you know which members of the Equine and Zebra Liberation Network or ALF were responsible for this action?
7. Did you write the communiqué for this action?
8. Do you know who did write the communiqué for the action?
9. Did you solicit video footage for this action?
10. Would you regard this as an instance of direct action?
11. Did you receive any written notes about this action?
12. Did you receive any audiotapes, or still photos of this action?

BLM Horse Corral arson and wild horse release:

1. How did you become aware that this crime occurred?
2. Did you participate in this crime?
3. Do you know who did this crime?
4. What details do you have about how this crime occurred?
5. Did you write the communiqué?
6. Do you know who did?
7. Would you consider this a direct action?
8. Did you nave advance knowledge of this action?
9. Have you ever been to the Burns horse corral?
10. Were you aware of its existence prior to the arson?
11. Did you solicit or receive any videotape?
12. Did you communicate with anyone about this action via e-mail?

U.S. Forest Industries arson:

1. How did you become aware of this crime?
2. What is the identity of those who were involved?
3. Had you had any discussion of this crime prior to jt happening?
4. Did anyone tell you they wanted to burn a place in Medford in advance?
5. Do you consider this to be direct action?
6. Were you a smoker at the time of this fire?
7. Did you ever receive a written account of this fire?
8. Did you receive notes from anyone about this crime?

9. Did you solicit any videotape of this crime?

Childers Meat arson, Eugene, OR:

1. Were you aware of the existence of Childers meat before the arson?
2. Have you ever been to Childers meats?
3. Do you know what sort of business happens at Childers meats?
4. Did you receive any tapes or written account of this action?
5. Did you hear anyone say they wanted to bum down Childers meats?
6. Do you consider this a direct action?

Boise Cascade arson, Monmouth OR:

1. Did you have any prior knowledge of the Boise Cascade office?
2. Did you take part in writing the communiqué?
3. Who did write the communiqué?
4. Did you solicit video of this action?

Superior Lumber, Glendale, OR:

1. Have you ever been to Glendale, Oregon?
2. Did you write the communiqué for this action?
3. Do you know who did write it?

Grand Jury Questions - What follows are most of the questions asked by the actual jurors. I have omitted those that were repetitious or involved people's names. I also have omitted the lectures and statements of any jurors and the prosecutor. (By the way, the prosecutor earlier in the day had yelled, "Stop playing games with me Mr. Harper! If you want to keep saying, 'I don't recall' I will just leave the room and try and get any sentence I can on the criminal contempt charge." I thought it was pretty funny.)

1. Are you a member of the ALF or ELF?
2. Can you please define direct action?
3. (Sarcastically) Do you possibly recall if you were you present at the WTO demonstrations?

4. Are you a member of a group called PAP?

That is pretty much it. It was over pretty quick. My lawyer, Stu Sugarman, really shut them down. Earlier in the day, he had upheld my right successfully against having to answer any questions regarding anyone else's identity. When I walked out of the grand jury room, the prosecutor looked pretty defeated.

When I saw the support demo outside I yelled, "WE WON!" I think in this case we did. The government spent a lot of time and money on this grand jury, and as far as I know, they have nothing to show for it. I think we have more reason than ever to be confident as a movement that their harassment is just a random attempt to find a weak link in the chain. They have no idea who is committing these actions; that much is for sure.

Josh

•

The Case of Frank Ambrose
By the Bloomington Defense Committee

Who is Frank Ambrose?

Frank Ambrose is a community activist from Bloomington, IN. He is involved with several mainstream and some radical groups such as Earth First!, Industrial Workers of the World, Speak Out for Animals, and the American Lands Alliance. He is employed by the latter forest protection organization, and has been become one of the foremost forest activists in the Midwest. Outside his employment, he has shown consistent support for people's struggles to rid themselves of those who wish to exploit them and the environment they depend upon. This commitment has made him a prime target in the government's attempts to harass the activist community into silence.

He was arrested on January 25, 2001 and is being charged with tree spiking in relation to an incident in a local State Forest that was claimed by the Earth Liberation Front (ELF). Tree spiking is a Class 'D' felony that carries a sentence of up to 3 years in prison and up to a $10,000 fine. This is the first arrest in the U.S. in relation to an ELF action. The ELF

112

has caused over $37 million in damages to businesses profiting from the destruction of the environment.

The harassment of Frank and his family began last February when FBI and ATF agents began visiting him and his friends to attempt to question them about a recent ELF action that had occurred in Bloomington. It continued in July when the FBI and State Conservation Officers raided Frank and Marie Mason's (his wife) house looking for implements of tree spiking. What they came away with was loads of organizational literature, address books, family photo albums and a few miscellaneous household items like spray paint and a pocketknife. The authorities told them at this time that they would find someone who would 'rat' on Frank and come back with an arrest warrant.

Now, 6 months later, the FBI and State Conservation Officers are attempting to frame Frank for the tree-spiking incident. They cite circumstantial evidence as the reason for their accusation. They are making Frank and others who take confrontational, but legal, approaches to stop the madness defend themselves in courts for their views. Frank has done nothing more than be vocal and be willing to put his body on the line to stop the logging program. (He was a part of a take over of a State Forest office during a timber bid.)

It is believed that the authorities are entering into the legal arena with a 'low-pitch' to make it more likely to get a conviction. With a conviction, they would have a name to place with the elusive Earth Liberation Front, and then they might move to add federal anti-terrorism charges or try to pin the other ELF actions in the Bloomington area upon him. It is very important that we fight this battle in every way possible.

Frank needs to have a good criminal defense to beat these charges. The activist community needs to stand united and show the authorities that we will not be scared into silence. We need to increase the number of effective campaigns that have made the moneyed interests take notice in the first place. This is a great chance to stand up and show those who view life as a commodity to exploit that we are not going away no matter what they do to us we are in this battle to win.

The Role of the FBI

The FBI's primary and founding purpose is to disrupt and destroy activist movements, having been formed to destroy the Industrial Workers of the World in the early part of last century. They continued to infiltrate and break apart many different social movements that have threatened the established power structure through a program called COINTELPRO (counter intelligence program). These movements and groups include the American Indian Movement, Black Panthers, Puerto Rican independence movement, and Earth First! They usually use the pretext of some crime that has been committed that has a political nature to it to begin to investigate social movements. Many times there is no crime, or the FBI committed the crime themselves to gain public support for their investigation.

In every movement they have 'investigated,' they have gone to all lengths to silence the activists involved. Many Blank Panthers and AIM members were jailed on manufactured evidence or even executed, and Earth First!ers have been bombed and framed by FBI infiltrators. Fred Hampton is a Black Panther who was assassinated by the FBI, the MOVE organization was bombed and burned by the government, and Leonard Peltier sits in jail today based on FBI lies. These incidents are well documented in other sources, such as *War at Home* by Brian Glick.

Frank's arrest is just a part of the FBI's modern day witch-hunt to destroy the growing movement against globalization and earth's destruction. They see the movement that has been growing exponentially since the WTO meeting disruptions in Seattle as a significant threat to the existing power structure. This arrest is larger than just a disruption of the Bloomington community, the FBI is also working with other law enforcement agencies across the country to use trumped up charges and threats of significant jail time against activists to make people afraid to join the movement. They want the movement to stop. The FBI is acting as the armed mercenary of the corporate world order, protecting their 'right' to destroy all that is living. It is up to everyone out there to resist their efforts and push forward.

•

Someone Remind me again please...
What are we fighting for?
Is it our job, our organization, our personal conscience, or the actual protection of the natural environment?

Since the official beginning of the Earth Liberation Front (ELF) in North America in 1997, there have naturally been critics of the group and its tactics who have spoken out publicly against the organization. I say "naturally," simply as a realization that the mainstream public, especially in Westernized societies, is not going to understand the necessity of property destruction or illegal activities, as they have been taught not to. In addition, the mainstream public will rarely, if ever, consider these tactics as legitimate because they threaten to the systems loved so dearly by these populations. These "systems" to which I am referring revolve around consumerism, over-consumption, and the sickening belief that profits come before life. Any threat to those practices and values is considered nothing more than terrorism by those benefiting from the system. So, in a sense, the mainstream population's objections to the beliefs, strategies, and tactics of the ELF are to be expected.

What is more surprising and perhaps nauseating is the unsound criticism of the ELF that has surfaced publicly from mainstream organizations that claim to be a part of what they refer to as "the environmental movement." Attached to this article are just a few examples of that to which I am referring. From the time I began acting as an ELF spokesperson in 1997, I have watched, listened to and/or read as so-called representatives of this environmental movement have spoken quite negatively of the ELF's tactics and beliefs.

"They [the ELF] are discrediting the movement" and "They [the ELF] are just making the legitimate work in the environmental movement that much harder" are two quotations I have heard repeatedly over the last few years. And all the while I was maintaining the public posture that the work of the ELF is not only beneficial but goes hand in hand with the important work that many aboveground, legal groups conduct.

No one can rightly argue that criticism is not healthy. I strongly believe that no matter what you are doing, you must constantly evaluate and re-evaluate your actions and work to ensure what you are doing is the most effective at any given time. Obviously, there are serious matters and questions involved when the ideology of the ELF is discussed. Those matters and questions need to be seriously considered and answered to ensure a proper focus is maintained. But there is a major difference between healthy criticism and that which comes from entities that have invested interests in discrediting the work of groups like the ELF.

The popular environmental movement, which arguably began in the early 1960s, has failed miserably in its attempts to stop the destruction of the natural environment and life on this planet. This is an undeniable fact. Our air, water, and soil qualities around the planet continue to decrease as more and more life forms are suffering as a result. The few futile attempts at legislative measures over the years have not only been discouraging and (arguably) a waste of time and resources, but more importantly they have perhaps been catastrophic in their continuance and reinforcement of the same system that is destroying life.

This has been the reality of what mainstream individuals and groups refer to as "the environmental movement." It is this very movement that has failed. In fact, it is not a movement in the sense of progressing for the greater good of life and natural law. Rather, the "movement," so to speak, has not moved anywhere except to allow the destruction of the natural environment and life to continue and grow. To be a movement, a body must move; it must progress forward to stop that profit-driven force that is annihilating the planet.

The ELF has a broad major goal: to stop the destruction and murder of life on the planet. The group recognizes that lives are being taken primarily due to the belief throughout most Westernized societies that profits must be had at any cost. It is the very profit motive that is driving individuals to act in conflict with natural law. The ELF then, as a matter of sound strategy, seeks to directly remove the profit motive from the destruction of life. The group engages in economic sabotage to directly inflict economic suffering on those who value profits more than life. If there is an actual environmental movement, it definitely consists of organizations like that of the ELF who seek not to further their own economic interests in the name of environmentalism, but to actually protect life.

Grassroots and mainstream organizations who have come out publicly against the actions of the ELF do so either for economic reasons (ie, they rely on donations from the public, members, or grants from charities or governmental or non-governmental organizations) and/or they have a firm belief faith in their government. Either way, this attitude demonstrates a clear misunderstanding and/or a great reluctance to accept the seriousness of the threats to life on this planet, and it demonstrates a reluctance to firmly commit to stop that destruction of life. All of us must remember that the movement to protect all life must not be a means of monetary gain but rather one that produces concrete results.

In addition, rarely is the distinction made that is crucial to actually produce change: the distinction between actions that make an individual simply feel good and actions that are truly effective and challenge oppression. Actions that make individuals feel better about themselves are usually safer and pose little actual threat to the entity that needs to be changed. Especially in the global movement to protect all life, this is in direct reference to the continued belief in state-sanctioned tactics that have not only been proven ineffective but may only aid in prolonging the real problem.

This movement to protect all life requires all of us to step out of our comfort zones and realize what actually needs to be done. The Westernized individual who supports extreme direct action outside of the Westernized countries (such as the armed self defense of the Zapatistas) while simultaneously denouncing direct action domestically to protect life is practicing one of the sickest forms of hypocrisy, if not a form of racism and imperialism.

No one in his right mind can honestly state that the popular environmental movement using state-sanctioned tactics has been successful. It is obvious something more is needed. There is no excuse for anyone claiming to be a part of the movement to protect all life to come out publicly against the actions of the ELF. If someone—whether an individual or an organization- - disagrees with ELF tactics, it is just as easy to state that although he does not participate in actions like those of the ELF, he can understand their motivations because the threat to life on this planet is very real and serious. Such a statement would avoid publicly showing a major rift in the movement and would give at least the perception of a varied movement, strong and rich in diversity.

The global movement to protect the natural environment and life must be considered as a matter of self-defense. When the quality of our air, water, and soil becomes increasingly poor, sickening and killing life, the only natural, realistic and strategically-sound option is self-defense. Those who are in an actual situation requiring immediate self-defense do not have the luxury or the privilege of deciding to wait until the proper laws are passed. They do not have the luxury or privilege of sticking only to those tactics that are considered appropriate by the State and mainstream society.

Only when the threat becomes real enough do individuals begin to actually see it as a matter of self defense, a matter of doing what is necessary to stop the ongoing murder and destruction. How much longer are we supposed to wait? How many more lives must be taken before the privileged begin to at least embrace those tactics which are aimed at the real problems in society? How much longer before it is too late?

If we are serious about stopping and the destruction of life, we must recognize the crucial value of targeting the profit motive directly. This is not going to occur at this point in time by lobbying or attempting legislation. This is not going to occur by lying nicely in the street, passively allowing the thugs of the state to beat and jail you into submission. This is going to occur by participating in and supporting public education and direct action in the form of economic sabotage. Property destruction is not violence. Property-- especially that which is used to aid in the destruction of life—is violence. Refusing to destroy what is threatening and destroying all life is sheer suicide at best, if not another form of hypocrisy.

●

The Only Thing Worth Fearing is the Outcome of Another Generation Living Out the 'American Dream'

The State's threats are microscopic in comparison

Clearly one of the primary tactics used by federal agencies against effective social movements is "divide and conquer." Most activists should be familiar with the FBI's "Cointelpro" activities against the Black Panther Party, the American Indian Movement, and others in the 1960-70s, where many efforts were made to create and widen divisions within effective movements.

This can also be seen in the fabricated notion of "left wing" liberalism and "right wing" conservatism. This has effectively split those who are opposed to the system in half and poised them against each other, diverting their attention from the system itself. It is not whether you are "left" or "right;" it is how far you are form the center. Clearly, organizations like the Earth Liberation Front embrace ideologies where liberation and conservation work hand in hand.

One very common "divide and conquer" tactic is the installation of fear and paranoia. The paranoia that individuals and organizations have in associating with other, possibly more-radical individuals and organizations only helps to create and widen divisions within a movement. And it seems that many avoid association with others who may be under more pressure by federal authorities simply because they fear similar pressure, not necessarily because of ideological differences. Unless you have a particular personal reason to avoid federal attention (in which case you should avoid association with aboveground activism all together) you are simply playing into the state's fear tactics designed to eliminate effective movements.

The more fearless an individual or organization is, the more of a threat they are to the system which oppresses them. This is true for individuals facing charges as well. Often lawyers will attempt to convince their clients that associating with politics will only hurt their case, but generally lawyers have an inherent faith in the system, and their priorities stem from that faith. Lawyers generally have no interest in challenging the system on any level. Their interests are in making their clients believe that they have done the job well, better than the clients themselves would have been able to do. Lawyers are generally afraid to bring politics into the court because they fear bias against the client's politics will equal bias against the client.

Of course this is legitimate to an extent, but bias is inescapable, and when someone finds himself indicted for a serious crime, bias is already strongly working against him. Many people figure that if someone is being charged with a major crime, he must be guilty of something in order to be in that situation. Politics can help to explain just why the individual was falsely indicted.

It is even more ridiculous for fear to interject on the activities of activists who are not facing charges. Activists should not be afraid to publicly support illegal activity, to go to public discussions on illegal activity, to possess literature supporting illegal activity, to associate with those known to publicly support illegal activity or even to attend protests. Fear should not deter activists from supporting direct action; it should only make them more determined to do those very things. We should be free to ideologically support anything we wish, to associate with anyone we wish and to openly practice those freedoms. And if we are not, then isn't it our duty to actively change that situation?

This paranoia works most effectively to isolate the most lively, passionate and radical aspects of a movement, and therefore strip it of its life and its power. In order for a political or social cause to be considered a "movement" it must be "on the move." Without radical aspect pushing a cause forward that cause isn't going anywhere, and is therefore not part of a movement at all.

In brief, don't be afraid to be a revolutionary; state repression is inevitable, but rather than fear it, we should accept it and move forward, preparing for this reality.

6.

U.S. HOUSE SUBCOMMITTEE HEARING ON ECOTERRORISM

There is no distinctly American criminal class except Congress.

~ Mark Twain

SUBCOMMITTEE HEARING ON ECOTERRORISM

Craig Rosebraugh served as a spokesperson for the North American Earth Liberation Front Press Office (NAELFPO) between the spring of 2000 and September of 2001. Prior to his official role in the NAELFPO, Rosebraugh served as an unofficial spokesperson for the underground Earth Liberation Front (ELF), beginning on November 29th, 1997 when the organization released its first communiqué claiming responsibility for an arson at the Bureau of Land Management in Burns, Oregon. Throughout this period (11/29/97 - 9/5/01), Rosebraugh relayed anonymous communiqués from the ELF to the public and worked to encourage ideological support for clandestine direct action, helping the movement gain international attention.

Since 1997, the ELF has been engaging in large-scale acts of economic sabotage in North America, totaling over $40 million in damages to those who profit from the destruction and exploitation of the Earth and its peoples. The ELF realizes that the Earth is being destroyed and the people are being oppressed because industries have been built around the commodification of life and will stop at nothing to further their economic agenda. Therefore, the ELF chooses economic sabotage as a primary tactic to effectively eliminate the profit motive driving the destruction and exploitation of life on Earth.

More importantly, the ELF is part of a larger revolutionary movement that is struggling for fundamental change in the way we live on Earth. The system represents and perpetrates a value structure that places profits and property above the people and the natural environment that sustains us. The ELF is essentially a clandestine task force fighting back against the massive oppression resulting from this warped set of values. It is for this reason that the system perceives the ELF and similar organizations as a threat.

Because of his outspoken support for the Earth Liberation Front, Rosebraugh has been victim of harassment by government agencies such as the Federal Bureau of Investigation (FBI); the Bureau of Alcohol Tobacco and Firearms (ATF); the Justice Department and several other federal, state and local authorities, as well as pro-industry organizations. Prior to being subpoenaed to the testify in Congress before the Subcommittee on Forests and Forest Health, Rosebraugh was subjected to seven federal grand jury subpoenas regarding illegal activities of the ELF as well as two FBI/ATF raids.

The February 12th, 2002 hearing of the Subcommittee on Forests and Forest Health was the first Congressional hearing to specifically focus on the growing movement of economic sabotage taken in defense of the Earth and its peoples. The Subcommittee Hearing on Ecoterrorism consisted of testimonies from different groups of individuals, members of Congress arguing for further legislation against "ecoterrorism," individuals representing corporations targeted by the ELF, pro-industry representatives arguing for increased government action against "ecoterrorism," law enforcement agencies arguing for more funding with which to combat "ecoterrorism," and Craig Rosebraugh. Rosebraugh was the only individual in the hearing who even vaguely had an interest in preserving "forests and forest health" and was also the only one there under force of subpoena.

The hearing was hosted by the Chairperson of the House Resources Subcommittee on Forests and Forest Health, Rep. Scott McInnis (R-CO 3rd). McInnis, a former police officer, represents the system and its twisted values. McInnis, the members of Congress and everyone else voluntarily participating at the subcommittee hearing for that matter, have built careers on shoving the American Dream down the throats of not only everyone in the U.S., but everyone on Earth. The Subcommittee on Ecoterrorism is an attempt by the system to prevent the liberation of the Earth and its peoples from its greedy stranglehold.

In condemnation of the hearing, Rosebraugh refused to cooperate with the Subcommittee's efforts to vilify and incarcerate this movement for liberation. When he first received a letter asking for his voluntary participation in the hearing, he replied in refusal. At the hearing itself he evoked his Fifth Amendment right to remain silent for every question asked of him, with the exception of two: one asking his citizenship and the other asking whether he submitted a written testimony.

It is important for everyone involved in the struggle for liberation to know what we're up against. To effectively fight the system, we need to know what these motherfuckers with their boots on our throats are thinking and what they're going to do next. Everyone voluntarily participating in the Subcommittee hearings is a pig, with a clear, vested interest in continuing the capitalist annihilation of life on Earth. By analyzing the testimonies given at the Subcommittee hearings and researching the true intentions and motivations behind the participants, we get a glimpse of the struggle to come.

Before his release from the Subcommittee Hearings on Ecoterrorism, Rosebraugh was informed that he would be receiving further questions to which he would be required to reply in written format. Later, the Subcommittee announced its intentions to charge Rosebraugh with Contempt of Congress.

As it stands today-- March 23rd, 2002-- Rosebraugh has received and replied to the additional written questions and has yet to hear the Subcommittee's response.

Long Live the Earth Liberation Front! Long Live Liberation! Long Live Revolution! Down With this System that is Strangling the Earth and its Peoples!

Leslie James Pickering
Spokesperson,
North American Earth Liberation Front Press Office

•

Craig Rosebraugh
Former Spokesperson for the Earth Liberation Front Press Office
Written Testimony Submitted on February 7, 2002 to the U.S. House Subcommittee on Forests and Forest Health for the February 12, 2002, Hearing on "Ecoterrorism."

> *When a long train of abuses and usurpations, pursuing invariably the same object, evinces a design to reduce [the people] under absolute despotism, it is their right, it is their duty, to throw off such government, and to provide new guards for their future security. The oppressed should rebel, and they will continue to rebel and raise disturbance until their civil rights are fully restored to them and all partial distinctions, exclusions and incapacitations are removed.*

- Thomas Jefferson, 1776

On April 15, 1972, I came into this world as a child of two wonderful parents living in Portland, Oregon. Growing up in the Pacific Northwestern region of the United States, I had the privilege of easy access to the natural world. Much of my childhood was spent in the fields and forested areas behind our home, playing and experiencing life in my time of innocence. I had no knowledge of societal problems, especially those pertaining to the natural environment.

Throughout my childhood and adolescent years, the education I received from my parents, schools, popular media and culture instilled in me a pride for my country, for my government, and everything the United States represented. I was taught about the great American history, our Constitution, Bill of Rights, and our legacy of being at the forefront of democracy and freedom. I considered myself to be just an average boy taking an active part in the popular American pastimes of competitive sports, consumer culture, and existing within a classic representation of the standard, middle-class suburban lifestyle.

Upon graduating from high school, I became exposed to new forms of education and ideas. Resulting from my exposure to people from differing socio-economic backgrounds and beginning college, I found my horizons beginning to widen. For the first time in my life, I was presented with the notion of political and social conflict coupled with the various issues contained within both categories. It was alarming yet, at the same time, invigorating as I began to feel passion burn within me.

George Bush, Sr. had just thrust the United States into what became known as the Gulf War. Now, as I was raised with a certain absolutist support of my country and government, my first inclination was to wave the stars and stripes and support unconditionally this noble pursuit of "promoting democracy and freedom" in the "less fortunate" and "uncivilized" lands. Yet, as I began to look further into the matter, I found myself asking questions such as, *Why are we there? Why are we killing civilians? What is the true motive behind the conflict?* After extensive research, I came to the logical and truthful conclusion that natural resources and regional power were the primary motives.

As news from independent sources slowly filtered out, I became increasingly horrified at the slaughter of Iraqi civilians by the U.S. military. With "NO WAR FOR OIL" as my personal guiding statement, I joined the local anti-war protests and movement existing in Portland, Oregon. Little did I realize that this first political activity would lead me to a life of devotion to true justice and real freedom.

While my anti-war involvement progressed, I also began to understand the disastrous relationship our modern society has with the many animal nations. Out of an interest inspired by both independent reading and early college courses, I became involved with a local animal advocacy organization. At first, I attended meetings to hear the numerous arguments for the rights of animals and further my own education. The more I learned, the more compelled I felt to involve myself fully in working for animal protection. My activities went from merely attending meetings, rallies, and protests to organizing them. Of all the issues I had learned about during the six years I spent with that organization, I focused the majority of my time, research, and interest on fighting against the use of animals in biomedical and scientific experimentation.

While a great percentage of the public in the United States had been convinced that animal research progressed and continues to improve human health, I soon realized that this myth was not only untruthful and single sided, but the work of a slick public relations campaign by the pharmaceutical industry in coordination with federal agencies such as the National Institutes of Health. I also learned that just like the factory farm industry, the use of animals for human entertainment and for the fashion industry, animal experimentation was motivated first and foremost by profits. Furthermore, I learned how the government of the United States not only economically supports these various institutions of exploitation and slaughter, but how it continues to perpetuate and politically support the dangerous lie that animal research saves human lives. My support for various governmental policies was slowly fading.

And then memories of innocence were torn away. In the early 1990s, I learned that the lush natural acreage I used to play in as a child had been sold to a development firm. It intended to bulldoze the entire area and create a virtual community of homes for the upper middle class to wealthy. Within two years, the land as I knew it was no more. The visual reminder I used to appreciate, the one that would take me back to the years when the fields and trees were my playground, was stolen by a development corporation who saw more value in the land as luxurious houses than for its natural beauty and life.

I remember asking myself what would happen to the various wildlife who made the area their home for so many years? Where would the deer, coyotes, skunks, wild cats, mice, raccoons, opossums, and others go? It was obvious that the developers had not even considered these questions. Rather, it appeared, the main pursuit of the corporation was working towards building incredibly large homes as close as possible to one another for maximum financial gain.

As the 1990s progressed, I became increasingly aware of the relationship between social and political problems in the United States. No single issue was truly independent but rather was affected by many others. In my work with the local animal advocacy organization, I realized that exploitation and destruction at the hands of human domination over animals also involved much more. Economics, politics, sociology, psychology, anthropology, science, religion, and other disciplines all played a significant role in understanding this unhealthy and unbalanced relationship between humans and other animals.

But, by far the most important realization I made was that the problems facing animals, the problems facing the natural environment, and those affecting humans all came from a primary source. Understanding this crucial connection, I co-founded a non-profit organization in 1996 dedicated to educating the public on this fundamental realization.

During the mid-1990s, through continued formal and informal education, I also began to understand that the history I had learned growing up was only one story of many. I gained insight into the fact that everything I had learned about the origins of the United States of America had been purely from the viewpoint of the colonists and European settlers. Thus, the history I was taught was from the perspective of the privileged white man, which not only told a mere fraction of the story, but also provided an extreme amount of misinformation as well.

I was never taught that the origins of this country were based upon murder, exploitation, and ultimate genocide. My teachers neglected to mention the fact that the white European settlers nearly annihilated the various indigenous peoples who had existed on this land for ages. Instead, I was taught about Thanksgiving and Columbus Day. I bought into this version of American history so much that I vividly recall my excitement over creating a paper model of one of Columbus' ships years ago.
No one ever seemed to provide the insight to me that the settlers, immediately upon their arrival, enslaved the natives and forced them to work and assist the European powers in their quest for gold and spices. Likewise, I failed to ever have access to a true African-American history

that began when blacks were captured and shipped as property to this land to work as slaves for white men.

While I was taught about the so-called "Great American Revolution," it was never mentioned that this war for independence against the European powers only served and benefited the privileged white male. Of course, all white men were privileged to some degree; however, many were enslaved initially just like the natives and blacks. Women, natives, blacks, and, to a limited degree, poor whites were considered property, bought, sold, and owned by the affluent white hierarchy.

In school, my teachers did explain to me the importance of the U.S. Constitution and the Bill of Rights and how our forefathers drew up these documents to serve the people. This, I learned, was the foundation of our supposed great democracy. Yet, in reality, these items were created by the white power structure and only served to benefit the privileged members of white society. Women, blacks, natives, and poor white men still were not enfranchised, nor did they have any accessibility to self-determination and freedom.

Land ownership—a notion completely foreign and absurd to most of the indigenous—became a deciding factor of power and privilege for white men. Those without land lacked the opportunity for the vote, for ultimate power and respect. As more and more settlers pushed westward through the country, the government committed endless treaty breaches and violations, stealing land that whites had allotted to the indigenous.

Perhaps one of the most disturbing facts was that these original agreements made between various indigenous nations and the United States government were supposed to have international standing. Each of the indigenous populations was recognized at the time each document was signed as being a sovereign nation, and yet, the U.S. government still exerted its power and domination to steal land for eventual development and drainage of resources. This genocide against the varied Native American nations by the United States continues today with innocent people such as Leonard Peltier being imprisoned for years simply due to the government's perception of him as a political threat. Free Leonard Peltier!

On July 4 annually, U.S. citizens celebrate the founding of our country, most either blatantly forgetting or ignorant of the true issues surrounding that date. The fact that the United States as a nation systematically committed mass genocide against the indigenous of these lands, to catastrophic extremities, is certainly no cause for celebration. Rather, it should be a time for mourning, for remembrance, and, most of all for education of our children so we are not doomed to repeat the mistakes of the past.

The plight of blacks and women throughout U.S. history, although perhaps not as overtly catastrophic, still constituted outright mass murder, enslavement, exploitation, and objectification. Early on, white European settlers found that natives were much more difficult to enslave and manage due to their ability to maintain at least partial elements of their cultures. When blacks began to first arrive on slave ships, chained in the darkness below the decks, white settlers theorized they would make better slaves because they would be further removed from their cultures. Thus, the enslavement of blacks began in this land and would, in its overt form, last for a couple hundred years. During this time and well beyond, blacks were considered property to be bought, sold, traded, used, and disposed of at will.

Even after the Abolitionist movement, which began in the 1820s, blacks continued to be considered second-rate citizens, restricted from voting and experiencing the free life which whites were accustomed. When the modern U.S. civil rights movement began in the 1940s, it took some twenty years of constant hardship and struggle to achieve some reform in the fascist policies of the United States. Even though blacks "won" the right to vote and exist in desegregated zones, there still was an absence of overall freedom, never any actual resemblance of equality.

Today, the saga continues. While African Americans have made incredible progress in obtaining certain rights and privileges, there continues to be a more hidden, underlying discrimination that is every bit as potent. A clear example can be seen by taking an honest look at the prison industrial complex and understanding who continues to be enslaved in mass to make that industry financially viable. Free Mumia Abu Jamal! Free the Move 9! Free all the political prisoners in the United States!

A similar and equally unfortunate history has haunted and continues to haunt women in U.S. society. Also once considered property, women were not even able to vote in this country until the 1920s. Even after, they continued to be faced with a patriarchal society consisting of white

130

men in power. While women have made many wonderful advances for themselves, they still exist today in the United States under that same sexist and patriarchal society. A quick glance at the profiles of the federal government as well as top CEOs from U.S. corporations fully illustrates this reality.

When I co-founded the non-profit organization in Portland, Oregon in 1996, I was becoming more aware that the similarities in the human, environmental, and animal advocacy movements stemmed from this rich U.S. history-- not of glory, freedom and democracy-- but of oppression in its sickest forms. I began to also realize that just as the U.S. white male power structure put itself on a pedestal above everyone else, it also maintained that attitude toward the natural environment and the various animal nations existing within it. As a society, we have continuously acted towards these natural life forms as though we owned them, therefore giving us the right to do whatever we wanted and could do to them.

Particularly with the advent of the Industrial Revolution in the United States, the destruction of the natural world took a sharp turn for the worse. The attitude, more so than ever, turned to one of profits at any cost and a major shift from sustainable living to stockpiling for economic benefit. This focus on stockpiling and industrial productivity caused hardship on communities, forcing local crafters and laborers to be driven out of business by overly competitive industries.

Additionally, with this new focus on sacrificing sustainable living for financial gain, natural resources were in greater demand than ever. Semi-automatic to automatic machinery, production lines, the automobile, the roadway system, suburbs, and the breakup of small, fairly self-sufficient communities all came about, at least in part, due to the Industrial Revolution. This unhealthy and deadly transgression, of course, was supported and promoted by the U.S. government, always eager to see growth in the domestic economy.

All of this set the stage for the threatening shortage of natural resources and the massive environmental pollution and destruction present today in the United States. In cities such as Los Angeles, Detroit and Houston, the air and soil pollution levels are so extreme that people have suffered and continue to face deadly health problems. Waterways throughout the country, including the Columbia Slough in my backyard, are so polluted from industries it is recommended that humans don't even expose themselves to the moisture let alone drink unfiltered, un-bottled water.

The necessary and crucial forests of the Pacific Northwestern region of the country have been systematically destroyed by corporations such as Boise Cascade, Willamette Industries and others within the timber industry whose sole motive is profits regardless of the expense to the health of an ecosystem. In Northern California, the sacred old growths-- dreamlike in appearance, taking your breath away at first glance-- have been continuously threatened and cut by greedy corporations such as Pacific Lumber/Maxxam. The same has occurred and still is a reality in states including Washington, Oregon, Idaho, and Colorado.

The first National Forests were established in the United States more than a century ago. One hundred fifty-five of them exist today, spread across 191 million acres. Over the years, the forest products industry has decimated publicly-owned National Forests in this country, leaving a horrendous trail of clearcuts and logging roads. Commercial logging has been responsible for annihilating nearly all of the nation's old growth forests, draining nutrients from the soil, washing topsoil into streams, destroying wildlife habitat, and creating an increase in the incidence and severity of forest fires. Only an estimated 4 percent of old growth forests in the United States remain.

The National Forests in the United States contain far more than just trees. In fact, more than 3,000 species of fish and wildlife, in addition to 10,000 plant species, have their habitat within the National Forests. This includes at least 230 endangered plant and animal species. All of these life forms co-exist symbiotically to naturally create the rich and healthy ecosystems needed for life to exist on this planet.

The benefits of a healthy forest cannot be overrated. Healthy forests purify drinking water, provide fresh clean air to breathe, stabilize hillsides, and prevent floods. Hillsides clearcut or destroyed by logging roads lose their ability to absorb heavy rainfall. If no trees exist to soak up moisture with roots to hold the soil, water flows freely down slopes, creating muddy streams, polluting drinking water, strengthening floods, and causing dangerous mudslides. Instead of valuing trees and forests for being necessary providers of life, the U.S. Forest Service and commercial logging interests have decimated these precious ecosystems.

The timber corporations argue that today in the United States more forests

132

exist than perhaps at any time in the last century or more. It doesn't take a forestry specialist to realize that monoculture tree farms—in which one species of tree, often times non-native to the area, is grown en masse in a small area for maximum production—do not equate to a healthy forest. Healthy forests are made up of diverse ecosystems consisting of many native plant and animal species. These healthy ecosystems are what grants humans and all other life forms on the planet with the ability to live. Without clean air, clean water, and healthy soil, life on this planet will cease to exist. There is an overwhelming battery of evidence that conclusively shows that we are already well on our path toward massive planetary destruction.

The popular environmental movement in the United States, which arguably began in the 1960s, has failed to produce the necessary protection needed to ensure that life on this planet will continue to survive. This is largely due to the fact that the movement has primarily consisted of tactics sanctioned by the very power structure that is benefiting economically from the destruction of the natural world. While a few minor successes in this country should be noted, the overwhelming constant trend has been the increasingly speedy liquidation of natural resources and annihilation of the environment.

The state-sanctioned tactics, that is, those approved by the U.S. government and the status quo and predominantly legal in nature, rarely, if ever, actually challenge or positively change the very entities that are responsible for oppression, exploitation, and, in this case, environmental destruction. Throughout the history of the United States, a striking amount of evidence indicates that it wasn't until efforts strayed beyond the state sanctioned that social change ever progressed.

In the abolitionist movement, the Underground Railroad, public educational campaigns, in addition to slave revolts, forced the federal government to act. With the Suffragettes in the United States, individuals such as Alice Paul acting with various forms of civil disobedience added to the more mainstream efforts to successfully demand the vote for women. Any labor historian will assert that in addition to the organizing of the workplace, strikes, riots and protests dramatically assisted in producing more tolerable work standards. The progress of the civil rights movement was primarily founded upon the massive illegal civil disobedience campaigns against segregation and disenfranchisement.

Likewise, the true pressure from the Vietnam anti-war movement in this country only came after illegal activities such as civil disobedience and beyond were implemented. Perhaps the most obvious, yet often overlooked, historical example of this notion supporting the importance of illegal activity as a tool for positive, lasting change, came just prior to our war for independence. Our educational systems in the United States glorify the Boston Tea Party while simultaneously failing to recognize and admit that the dumping of tea was perhaps one of the most famous early examples of politically-motivated property destruction.

In the mid-1990s, individuals angry and disillusioned with the failing efforts to protect the natural environment through state-sanctioned means began taking illegal action. At first, nonviolent civil disobedience was implemented, followed by sporadic cases of nonviolent property destruction. In November 1997, an anonymous communiqué was issued by a group called the Earth Liberation Front claiming responsibility for their first-ever action in North America.

Immediately, the label of "ecoterrorism" appeared in news stories describing the actions of the Earth Liberation Front. Where exactly this label originated is open to debate, but all indications point to the federal government of the United States in coordination with industry and sympathetic mass media. Whatever the truth may be regarding the source of this term, one thing is for certain: The decision to attach this label to illegal actions taken for environmental protection was very conscious and deliberate.

Why? The need for the U.S. federal government to control and mold public opinion through the power of propaganda to ensure an absence of threat is crucial. If information about illegal actions taken to protect the natural environment was presented openly to the public without biased interpretation, the opportunity would exist for citizens to make up their own minds about the legitimacy of the tactic, target, and movement.

By attaching a label such as "terrorism" to the activities of groups such as the Earth Liberation Front, the public is left with little choice but to give into their preconceived notions negatively associated with that term. For many in this country, including myself, information about terrorism came from schools and popular culture. Most often times, the definition of terrorism was overtly racist associated frequently in movies and on television shows with Arabs and the others our government told us were threatening. Terrorism usually is connected with violence, with politically-motivated physical harm to humans.

Yet, in the history of the Earth Liberation Front, both in North America and abroad in Europe, no one has ever been injured by the group's many actions. This is not a mere coincidence, but rather a deliberate decision that illustrates the true motivation behind the covert organization. Simply put and most fundamentally, the goal of the Earth Liberation Front is to save life. The group takes actions directly against the property of those who are engaged in massive planetary destruction in order for all of us to survive. This noble pursuit does not constitute terrorism, but rather seeks to abolish it.

A major hypocrisy exists when the U.S. government labels an organization such as the Earth Liberation Front a terrorist group while simultaneously failing to acknowledge its own terrorist history. In fact, the U.S. government by far has been the most extreme terrorist organization in planetary history. Some, but nowhere near all, of the examples of domestic terrorism were discussed earlier in this writing. Yet, further proof can be found by taking a glimpse at the foreign policy record of the United States even as recently as from the 1950s. In Guatemala (1953-1990s), the CIA organized a coup that overthrew the democratically-elected government led by Jacobo Arbenz. This began some 40 years of death squads, torture, disappearances, mass executions, totaling well over 100,000 victims. The U.S. government apparently didn't want Guatemala's social democracy spreading to other countries in Latin America.

In the Middle East (1956-1958) the United States twice tried to overthrow the Syrian government. Additionally, the U.S. government landed 14,000 troops to purportedly keep the peace in Lebanon and to stop any opposition to the U.S. supported Lebanese government. The U.S. government also conspired to overthrow or assassinate Nasser of Egypt. During the same time in Indonesia (1957-1958), the CIA tried to manipulate elections and plotted the assassination of Sukarno, then the Indonesian leader. The CIA also assisted in waging a full-scale war against the government of Indonesia. All of this action was taken because Sukarno refused to take a hard-line stand against communism.

From 1953 to 1964, the U.S. government targeted Cheddi Jagan, then the leader of British Guiana, out of a fear he might have built a successful example of an alternative model to the capitalist society.

The U.S. government, aided by Britain, organized general strikes and spread misinformation, finally forcing Jagan out of power in 1964. In Cambodia (1955-1973), Prince Sihanouk was severely targeted by the U.S. government. This targeting included assassination attempts and the unpublicized carpet bombings of 1969 to 1970. The U.S. government finally succeeded in overthrowing Sihanouk in a 1970 coup.

The examples continue. From 1960 through 1965, the United States intervened in Congo/Zaire. After Patrice Lumumba became Congo's first Prime Minister following independence gained from Belgium, he was assassinated in 1961 at the request of Dwight Eisenhower. During the same time in Brazil (1961-1964), President Joao Goulart was overthrown in a military coup which involved the United States. Again, the alleged reasoning for U.S. participation amounted to a fear of communism or, more importantly, anything that threatened this country's way of life. In the Dominican Republic (1963-1966), the United States sent in 23,000 troops to help stop a coup which aimed at restoring power to Juan Bosch, an individual the U.S. government feared had socialist leanings.

Of course, no one should forget about Cuba. When Fidel Castro came to power in 1959, the United States immediately sought to put another government in place, prompting some 40 years of terrorist attacks, bombings, a full-scale military invasion, sanctions, embargoes, isolations, and assassinations.

In Chile, the U.S. government sabotaged Salvador Allende's electoral campaign in 1964. In 1970, the U.S. government failed to do so and tried for years later to destabilize the Allende government particularly by building up military hostility. In September 1973, the U.S.-supported military overthrew the government, with Allende dying in the process. Some 3,000 people were executed and thousands more were tortured or disappeared. In Greece during the same period (1964-1974), the United States backed a military coup that led to martial law, censorship, arrests, beatings, torture, and killings. In the first month, more than 8,000 people died. All of this was executed with equipment supplied by the United States.

Back in Indonesia in 1965, fears of communism led the United States to back multiple coup attempts, which resulted in a horrendous massacre against communists. During this time the U.S. Embassy compiled lists of communist operatives-- as many as 5,000 names-- and turned them over to the Army. The Army would then hunt down and kill those on the list.

The U.S. government also has had its dirty hands connected to East Timor (1975 to present). In December 1975, Indonesia invaded East Timor using U.S. weapons. By 1989, Indonesia had slaughtered 200,000 people out of a population between 600,000 and 700,000. In Nicaragua (1978-1989), when the Sandinistas overthrew the Somoza dictatorship in 1978, the U.S. government immediately became involved. President Carter attempted diplomatic and economic forms of sabotage while President Reagan put the Contras to work. For eight years, backed by the United States, the Contras waged war on the people of Nicaragua.

Continuing on with Grenada (1979-1984), the United States intervened to stop a 1979 coup led by Maurice Bishop and his followers. The United States invaded Grenada in October 1983, killing 400 citizens of Grenada and 84 Cubans. Of course, the Libya example (1981-1989) must be mentioned. In the 1980s, the United States shot down two Libyan planes in what Libya regarded as its air space. The United States also dropped bombs on the country, killing more people, including Qaddafi's daughter. Yet that wasn't enough, as the U.S. government engaged in other attempts to eradicate Qaddafi. This included a fierce misinformation campaign, economic sanctions, and blaming Libya for being responsible for the Pan Am flight 103 bombing without any sound evidence.

The U.S. government, also in 1989, bombed Panama, leaving some 15,000 people homeless in Panama City. Thousands of people died and even more were wounded. Prior to the October 7, 2001 invasion of Afghanistan by the United States, the U.S. government had intervened there from 1979 to 1992.

During the late 1970s and most of the 1980s, the U.S. government spent billions of dollars waging a war on a progressive Afghani government, merely because that government was backed by the Soviet Union. More than one million people died, three million were disabled, and five million became refugees.

In El Salvador (1980-1992), the United States supported the government, which engaged in electoral fraud and the murder of hundreds of protesters and strikers. These dissidents, who had been trying to work within the system, took to using guns and declared a civil war in 1980. The U.S. government played an active role in trying to stop the uprising. When it was over in 1992, 75,000 civilians had been killed and the United States had spent six billion dollars.

In Haiti, from 1987 through 1994, the United States supported the Duvalier family dictatorship. During this time, the CIA worked intimately with death squads, torturers, and drug traffickers. Yugoslavia must also be mentioned, as no one should ever forget the United States' responsibility for bombing that country into annihilation.

In the early 1990s, the U.S. government continuously bombed Iraq for more than 40 days and nights. One hundred seventy-seven million pounds of bombs fell during this time on the people of Iraq. The remaining uranium deposits from weapons resulted in massive birth defects and incidences of cancer. Between 1990 and 1995, the United States was directly responsible for killing more than 500,000 Iraqi children under the age of five due to economic sanctions. Additionally, due to these sanctions, coupled with the continuous U.S. bombing that has occurred on Iraq since the Gulf War, more than 1.5 million innocent Iraqi people have been killed.

These few examples since 1950 of U.S.-sponsored and organized terrorism are horrendous, and unfortunately, these massive murderous tactics continue today. On October 7, 2001 the U.S. government began a full-scale military invasion of Afghanistan without even providing a shred of factual evidence linking Osama Bin Laden or Al Qaida to the attacks in this country on September 11.

To date, well over 4,000 innocent Afghani civilians have been killed by the U.S. government in this massive genocidal campaign. All along, U.S. government officials have claimed to possess concrete evidence proving the guilt of both Bin Laden and Al Qaida, but repeatedly said they cannot release this "proof" as doing so may endanger the lives of U.S. military personnel. This simply makes no sense, as there could not be any justifiable threat to U.S. personnel if they weren't already in inexcusable positions, violating the sovereignty of internationally-recognized nations.

The Taliban, which the United States helped put into power in 1994, has stated repeatedly to the U.S. government and the world that it would hand over Bin Laden to an international court if the United States provided proof of his guilt. The United States has refused and instead claimed the Taliban was not cooperating and was therefore harboring terrorists.

Can you imagine what would have happened if, prior to September 11,

2001, a structure in Kabul was bombed and the Taliban immediately suspected CIA director George Tenet as the prime suspect? Would the United States hand over Tenet to the Taliban if requested, if there was not substantial evidence provided of his guilt? Even if the Taliban supplied any shred of evidence, the United States still would refuse to hand over Tenet or any privileged citizen to an international court, because the United States does not abide by them or agree to them.

Regardless, the U.S. government believes that it has the right to provide no evidence of Bin Laden's or Al Qaida's guilt to the Taliban or the world before launching a massive genocidal campaign against Afghanistan civilians.

The true motives and the identities of those involved both in September 11, 2001 and October 7, 2001 are known only to a select few in power. However, evidence does exist in media sources as mainstream as the BBC (reported on September 18, 2001) that suggests the U.S. government was planning a military invasion of Afghanistan to oust the Taliban as early as March 2001. Furthermore, the intended deadline for the invasion was set for not later than October of the same year. The October 7, 2001, invasion by the United States into Afghanistan appears to have been right on schedule.

This war against terrorism, otherwise known as "Operation Enduring Freedom," is the latest example of U.S.-based terrorism and imperialism. It is clear that the events of September 11, 2001 were used as a chance for the U.S. government to invade Afghanistan, to attempt to increase U.S. regional and global power and to open up the much-sought-after oil reserves in the Middle East and Central Asia. The bonus, of course, was that this mission has given the United States the opportunity to target and attempt to annihilate any anti-U.S. sentiment within that region. As the war against terrorism expands, so does the possibility of more U.S. military bases and more security for the global economic powers.

If the U.S. government is truly concerned with eradicating terrorism in the world, then that effort must begin with abolishing U.S. imperialism. Members of this governing body, both in the House and Senate, as well as those who hold positions in the executive branch, constitute the largest group of terrorists and terrorist representatives currently threatening life on this planet. The only true service this horrific organization supplies is to the upper classes and corporate elite.

As an innocent child, I used to have faith in my government and pride in my country. Today I have no pride, no faith, only embarrassment, anger, and frustration. There are definite and substantiated reasons the U.S. government is not only disliked but hated by populations in many nations around the globe. The outrage and anger is justified due to the history of U.S. domestic and foreign policies.

Here in the United States, the growth of the empire, of capitalism, and of industry, has meant greater discrepancies between the wealthy and poor, a continued rise in the number of those considered to be a threat to the system, as well as irreversible harm done to the environment and life on the planet. Corporations in the United States literally get away with murder, facing little or no repercussions due to their legal structures.

The U.S. government, which sleeps in the same bed as U.S. corporations, serves to ensure that the "business as usual" policies of imperialism can continue with as little friction as possible. Anyone questioning the mere logic of this genocidal culture and governing policy is considered a dissident and, more often than not, shipped off to one of the fastest-growing industries of all, the prison industrial complex.

Internationally, U.S. policies have amounted to the same, often times worse, forms of violence. As I demonstrated herein with examples since 1950, the foreign policy track record has included genocide, assassinations, exploitation, military action, and destruction. Disguised as promoting or protecting freedom and democracy, U.S. foreign policies aim to directly control and conquer, while gaining power, finances, and resources.

U.S. imperialism is a disease, one that continues to grow and become more powerful and dangerous. It needs to be stopped. One of the chief weapons used by those protecting the imperialist policies of the United States is a slick, believable propaganda campaign designed to ensure that U.S. citizens do not question or threaten the "American way of life." Perhaps the strongest factor in this campaign is the phenomenon of capitalism. By creating a consumer demand for products, corporations-- greatly aided by the U.S. government-- can effectively influence people's dreams, desires, wants, and life plans. The very American Dream promoted throughout the world is that anyone can come to the United States, work hard, and become happy and financially secure.

Through the use of the propaganda campaign (designed, promoted, and transmitted by the U.S. ruling class), people are nearly coerced into adopting unhealthy desires for oftentimes unreachable, unneeded, and dangerous consumer goods. Through impressive societal mind control, the belief that obtaining consumer products will equal security and happiness has spread across the United States and much of the planet at this point, like some extreme plague. The fact that the policies of the United States murder people on a daily basis is unseen, forgotten, or ignored, as every effort is made by people to fit into the artificial model life manufactured by the ruling elite.

A universal effort needs to be made to understand the importance and execution of abolishing U.S. imperialism. This in no way refers to simply engaging in reformist efforts; rather, a complete societal and political revolution will need to occur before real justice and freedom become a reality. The answer does not lie in trying to fix one specific problem or work on one individual issue; but rather the entire pie needs to be targeted, every last piece looked upon as a mere representation of the whole.

If the people of the United States, whom the government is supposed to represent, are actually serious about creating a nation of peace, freedom and justice, then there must be a serious effort made, by any means necessary, to abolish imperialism and U.S. governmental terrorism. The daily murder and destruction caused by this political organization is very real, and so the campaign by the people to stop it must be equally as potent.

I have been told by many people in the United States to love America or leave it. I love this land and the truly compassionate people within it. I therefore feel I not only have a right, but also an obligation, to stay within this land and work for positive societal and political change for all.

I was asked originally if I would voluntarily testify before the House Subcommittee on Forests and Forest Health at a hearing focused on "ecoterrorism." I declined in a written statement. U.S. Marshals then subpoenaed me on October 31, 2001 to testify at this hearing on February 12, 2002, against my will.

Is this hearing a forum to discuss the threats facing the health of the natural environment, specifically the forests? No, clearly there is not even the remotest interest in this subject from the U.S. government or industry. The goal of this hearing is to discuss methodologies to improve the failed attempts law enforcement have made since the mid-1990s in catching and prosecuting individuals and organizations who take nonviolent, illegal direct action to stop the destruction of the natural environment. I have no interest in this cause or this hearing. In fact, I consider it a farce.

Since 1997, the U.S. government has issued me seven grand jury subpoenas, raided my home and work twice-- stealing hundreds of items of property-- and, on many occasions, sent federal agents to follow and question me. After this effort, which has lasted nearly five years, federal agents have yet to obtain any information from me to aid their investigations.

As I have never been charged with one crime related to these so-called ecoterrorist organizations or their activities, the constant harassment by the federal government constitutes a serious infringement on my Constitutional right to freedom of speech. This Congressional Subcommittee hearing appears to be no different, harassing and targeting me for simply voicing my ideological support for those involved in environmental protection.

I fully praise those individuals who take direct action, by any means necessary, to stop the destruction of the natural world and threats to all life. They are the heroes, risking their freedom and lives so that we as a species as well as all life forms can continue to exist on the planet. In a country so fixated on monetary wealth and power, these brave environmental advocates are engaging in some of the most selfless activities possible.

It is my sincere desire that organizations such as the Earth Liberation Front continue to grow and prosper in the United States. In fact, more organizations, using similar tactics and strategies, need to be established to directly focus on U.S. imperialism and the U.S. government itself. For as long as the quest for monetary gain continues to be the predominant value within U.S. society, human, animal, and environmental exploitation, destruction, and murder will continue to be a reality. This drive for profits at any cost needs to be fiercely targeted, and those responsible for the massive injustices punished. If there is any real concern for justice, freedom, and, at least, a resemblance of a true democracy, this revolutionary ideal must become a reality.

ALL POWER TO THE PEOPLE. LONG LIVE THE EARTH LIBERATION FRONT. LONG LIVE THE ANIMAL LIBERATION FRONT. LONG LIVE ALL THE SPARKS ATTEMPTING TO IGNITE THE REVOLUTION. SOONER OR LATER THE SPARKS WILL

TURN INTO A FLAME!

•

Darlene Hooley
5th Congressional District of Oregon
Testimony before the U.S. House Subcommittee on Forests and Forests
Health for the February 12, 2002, Hearing on "Ecoterrorism"

Thank you Mr. Chairman:

It is very appropriate that we are gathered here today on the birthday of Abraham Lincoln, one of our country's greatest leaders. His career -- and the turbulent times he brought the nation through -- exemplify the need to foreswear violence in the name of political causes and abide by the rule of law.

In the wake of an 1837 mob lynching of an anti-slavery newspaper editor, Lincoln urged his fellow Americans to "let reverence for the laws . . . become the political religion of the nation," to let legislatures and judges chosen by the people, rather than lynch-mobs motivated by passion and hatred, decide matters.

In the end, Lincoln's philosophy was vindicated. Our nation remains united, and we are committed to the rule of law.

But as is always the case, there is a minority of Americans who refuse to abide by this covenant.

They believe the rule of law does not apply to them, and in the forests and communities of Oregon and the Western United States, their actions are a rapidly growing problem.

Violence or intimidation directed against a Forest Service employee -- or arson in the name of protecting the environment -- are not lawful acts. They are crimes -- and their perpetrators should be apprehended and prosecuted to the fullest extent of the law.

Obviously, there are laws in place prohibiting assault or threatening harm against any individual, whether he or she is an environmental activist or

143

a Forest Service employee. It is inexcusable that a Park Service ranger would have to live in fear of having their home or office bombed, or that someone monitoring water quality on public land could be beaten and left for dead.

These are just some of the crimes on federal land which have occurred in the past few years.

As such, I strongly urge the members of the Committee to ensure that our local, state, and federal law enforcement officials are effectively upholding the law in this regard.

That said, eco-terrorism poses additional challenges for the law enforcement community.

It is a well-know fact that very few eco-terrorists, especially E-L-F representatives, have been caught. These groups have no formal organization, and act in small terrorist cells, which are autonomous from one another. Because these crimes are investigated with limited resources and manpower, local law enforcement officials have little success in successfully closing these cases.

Along with my colleague from Oregon, Congressman Greg Walden, I have sought to reverse the current situation by sponsoring H.R. 2583, the Environmental Terrorism Reduction Act. This bill would provide federal assistance where it is needed most, at the local level. H.R. 2583 would first require the Attorney General to establish a national clearinghouse for information on incidents of eco-terrorism, with the hope that investigators stay ahead of the curve in preventing additional acts of terror.

It should be noted the Bureau of Alcohol, Tobacco, and Firearms (ATF) already maintains a data-base of information on every explosive device found or triggered in the United States. As we consider moving this bill forward, it should be perfected to ensure the clearinghouse contain input from ATF so as not to reinvent the wheel.

In addition, H.R. 2583 would establish the Environmental Terrorism Reduction Program in the Department of Justice.

This program would authorize the Attorney General, upon consultation with the heads of Federal, State, and local law enforcement agencies and the Governor of each applicable State, to designate any area as a high intensity environmental terrorism area. After making such a designation local law enforcement agencies could access federal funding to assist them in solving and preventing these types of crimes in the future.

This program is similar to the Department of Justice's High Intensity Drug Trafficking Area program (HIDTA), which has been extraordinarily useful in Oregon and other states in helping make our communities better places to live.

Mr. Chairman and Mr. Ranking Member, thank you again for the opportunity to appear before the Committee. I would urge you and entire panel to co-sponsor H.R. 2583, and assist Congressman Walden and I in getting this legislation approved by the Judiciary Committee.

•

George R. Nethercutt, Jr.
5th Congressional district of Washington
Testimony before the U.S. House Subcommittee on Forests and Forests Health for the February 12, 2002, Hearing on "Ecoterrorism"

Mr. Chairman, I would like to thank you and the ranking member for taking the initiative to conduct this hearing today. Agroterrorism and the reprehensible actions of radical environmentalists have for too long been perceived as local concerns, concentrated in particular geographic regions. The sheer scope of this criminal activity escapes the focus it deserves, with arson, vandalism and intimidation often occurring in rural areas, with limited press coverage. We are left with anecdotal evidence and little sense of the vast criminal conspiracy that connects the members of organizations such as the Animal and Earth Liberation Fronts.

I would ask to include in the record three items, which I believe may be helpful to the Subcommittee in considering this issue. The first item is a letter to me from the National Center for Public Policy Research, along with copies of correspondence exchanged with national environmental groups about their positions on violent activism. Second, I am providing a Department of Agriculture report on the extent of animal and plant terrorism incidents at USDA funded facilities, with recommendations for improving security. This report responds to a requirement I sponsored in FY01, and represents only the very first tentative efforts by Federal agencies to grapple with this problem. Third, I am providing the 2001 Year-End Direct Action Report from the Animal Liberation Front.

I represent Washington state, which is blessed with rich natural resources and a vibrant biotechnology industry. Agriculture, forestry and science have been under assault by radicals for years in our state, and constituents have long expressed their concerns with criminal activity that threatens both their lives and their livelihood.

I met with one scientist who told me that she has been physically threatened by radicals and fears for her safety. "Yet, all I want to do is cure breast cancer," she says. Another scientist, from my district, fled with his family to Australia for a year after receiving death threats. These are people who want to make our lives better, cure diseases, make agriculture more sustainable and less ecologically damaging. But organizations like the Earth Liberation Front have put a bulls-eye on them.

In May of 2001, I finally had enough. At 3am on May 21, 2001, the University of Washington Center for Urban Horticulture was burned to the ground. In the twisted logic of the eco-terrorists, the Horticulture Center had done wrong by seeking to advance the protection and hardiness of urban forests and wetlands. The results of that crime are evident in this display. This facility suffered $5.3 million in physical damage -- some faculty members lost a lifetime of work that day, and that cost is inestimable. That same day, a poplar tree farm in Oregon was firebombed with almost identical incendiary devices. The interstate connections were made perfectly clear by that simultaneous action, and persuaded me that a strong federal response was required to contain this terrorism.

I will be eager to hear from Mr. Rosebraugh later this afternoon. Too many members of his organization lurk in the shadows, unwilling to engage in honest debate, but all to willing to resort to arson. I suspect that the purported intellectual underpinnings of this radicalism are insufficiently developed to weather the public condemnation that must accompany the associated violence. But before we go further, it may be helpful to have at least some sense of the ALF/ELF mind set.

In recent and telling magazine interview, Mr. Rosebraugh showed his sympathy with the victims of September 11, noting: "Anyone in their right mind would realize the United States had it coming." One of his ELF associates was more direct: "I cheered when the plan hit the Pentagon. Those people are in the business of killing people. It was like, Sorry, [expletive] happens." The connection with September 11 is not unwarranted, for like the murders in New York and Pennsylvania, members of these shadowy organizations have no respect for human life and will stop at nothing in pursuit of their dark vision of the future.

How best to deal with this home-grown brand of Al Qaeda? I propose that we use the model that has worked so well in Afghanistan. Improve our intelligence. Free the hands of law enforcement authorities. Isolate terrorists from allies and assistance. Cut off their funding. Give them no rest and no quarter.

National environmental groups need to know, you are either with us or against us. You need to choose which side you are on, and know we will be watching. Financing and harboring terrorists is no different from directly committing the acts. These dangerous and misguided zealots must be left without aid or comfort. This is the moral framework.

I have introduced legislation, H.R. 2795, the Agroterrorism Prevention Act, which would provide the necessary legal framework. I must here acknowledge the unflinching support of the lead cosponsors on this bill, Duke Cunningham and Saxby Chambliss. Our bill would broaden current definitions to protect all plant and animal research, enhance penalties for animal or plant enterprise terrorism, allow the FBI to investigate crimes under the Racketeer Influenced Corrupt Organizations Act, and establish an incident clearinghouse to strengthen local law enforcement efforts. The bill would also establish a research security program to extend technical assistance, threat and risk assessments to research universities.

Current law provides federal protection for some animal research, but H.R. 2795 would also include all plant research, including advanced genetic techniques, increasingly the targets of terror. We seek to broaden protection for facilities presently covered by the Animal Enterprise Terrorism Act, to include any commercial or academic enterprise that uses plants or animals. The ALF would now violate this section of federal law by bombing a livestock research lab, but not the Cattlemen's Association office down the street. We seek to end that inconsistency and would also expand the threshold for triggering violation of the act by recognizing ancillary economic damages.

Penalties for violations would be increased from one year to five years, and a new penalty is added for the use of explosives or arson, recognizing that firebombing is the preferred tactic of these groups. We expand restitution requirements and allow a possible death penalty sentence for violations resulting in a death. Firebombing is not a precise science, and I fear it is only a matter of time before a botanist is in the wrong place at the wrong time. This activity should be made a RICO predicate to give the FBI the tools it needs to unravel the web of criminal conspiracy. A information clearinghouse, administered by the FBI, would enhance Federal, state and local law enforcement efforts to draw connections from fragmentary evidence.

For too long, agroterrorism has been the stuff of anecdotes - short stories in the local paper, with no clear pattern or sense of the true scope of the activity. Yet, as this next chart makes clear, agroterrorism is a vast national problem. Each dot on this map represents one self-reported incident by the ALF/ELF during 2001.

Finally, H.R. 2795 would provide authorization for the National Science Foundation to provide competitively awarded grants to colleges and universities. We have a responsibility to protect our public investment in research, and this authorization would provide some initial "lessons learned" to educate the hardening of public research facilities.

Ultimately, the physical damage is secondary to the threat to innovation and scientific discovery. The academic disciplines that seek to improve human health, our food supply, and the environment are at greatest risk. Intimidation and violence have a predictable and unwelcome result, a chilling effect on scientific investigation and an impediment to discoveries that will improve our lives.

I would like to close with a few select words attributed to the ALF, following an attack on the property of a Michigan veterinarian working with fur farmers:

> We must all act our consciousness and inflict economic harm upon all of those who are responsible for the destruction of the earth and its inhabitants. We encourage others to find a local Earth raper and make them pay . . . The only language these people understand is money. We must inflict economic sabotage on all Earth rapers if we are ever

to stop the madness we live in. To do so is not a crime, it is a necessity.

Mr. Chairman, thank you again for holding this hearing and for supporting efforts to drain this fetid swamp of extremism.

●

Greg Walden
Second Congressional District of Oregon
Testimony before the U.S. House Subcommittee on Forests and Forests Health for the February 12, 2002, Hearing on "Ecoterrorism"

Thank you, Mr. Chairman, for your efforts to investigate the issues of eco-terrorism and lawlessness on our national forests. Let me say at the outset that regardless of which side of the political spectrum you reside on, breaking the law to further your views is wrong.

I represent the people in a district larger than any state east of the Mississippi, with more than half of the lands controlled by the government. Too often, the men and women in the federal service have been the targets of intimidation, ridicule and abuse by those who blame them for the federal policies they are paid to implement. They and their families deserve better than to live in fear because of the uniform they wear or the color of the truck they drive. We do not tolerate acts of violence against them. Just as we must speak out against acts of intimidation against Native Americans whose ancestral rights are in dispute.

But today I focus my attention on the eco-terrorism of two organizations which often jointly claim credit for acts of incredible destruction in my state. Let's call ELF and ALF what they truly are: TERRORIST ORGANIZATIONS. Their combatants wear no uniforms. They blend with the civilian population. They destroy private and government property. They teach others how to conduct dangerous and illegal acts. And they try to intimidate those who speak against them. Both Congresswoman Hooley and I are now featured on their affiliates' website.

I am sure some may question my inclusion of the Animal Liberation Front (ALF) in my testimony. However, several terrorist acts nationwide and within my district have been jointly claimed by both groups' spokespersons.

When Mr. Rosebraugh stepped down as the ELF spokesperson, David Barbarsh, the spokesperson for ALF, filled the void from his location in Vancouver, British Columbia. Two of the three specific acts I will be referring to today were jointly claimed by ELF/ALF. Mr. Chairman, my district has seen three acts of terrorism committed by ELF or ELF/ALF in recent years. Numerous other acts of violence and destruction of private property remain unclaimed but appear in the recent ALF 2001 Year-End Direct Action Report.

On July 21, 1997 an arson fire at Cavel West meatpacking plant in Redmond, Oregon resulted in $1.4-million in damage, a jointly-claimed act. According to Captain Wayne Shortreed of the Redmond Police Department, at one point the blaze was so hot that it threatened a propane storage facility approximately 100 yards away in a densely populated area.

Four months later, this firebombing was followed by a November 29, 1997 jointly-claimed attack on several BLM horse corrals in Burns, Oregon, also in my district. This direct action resulted in over $450,000 in damage and the release of 539 horses and burros; it also resulted in the scuttling of a planned adoption of 100 wild horses and 40 burros that had been scheduled to take place on December 6-7, 1997.

And on December 27, 1998 ELF firebombed the U.S. Forest Industries headquarters in Medford, Oregon, causing more than $900,000 in damage. It is this last attack on U.S. Forest Industries, claimed only by ELF, that I'd like to focus on in my testimony.

On the morning of December 28, 1998, the employees of U.S. Forest Industries arrived at work to find their offices smoldering. The scene is reminiscent of what we saw of the damaged part of the Pentagon after September 11th. It didn't take a jetliner to destroy this office; an ELF firebomb did the job. And while fortunately there was no loss of life, the destruction was just as severe.

As pictures speak louder than words, I thought it might be helpful to see the damage inflicted on U.S. Forest Industries. This first picture you see shows the aftermath of the firebomb on the exterior of the building with the yellow, crime-scene tape. In this second picture you see the interior devastation from the attack, though it's hard to see because the intensity of the fire has blackened the walls. Company files, office equipment, all

150

destroyed to further someone's political agenda.

Amazingly, Mr. Chairman, and by sheer force of will, U.S. Forest Industries operations were shut down for only four hours on Monday, December 28, because the company was able to relocate its 15 employees to its mill operations plant in White City, Oregon.

In the words of U.S. Forest Industries President, Jerry Bramwell, "We didn't want to give ELF the satisfaction of putting us out of business."

It didn't take long for ELF to claim responsibility for this attack as this January 16, 1999 ALF press release illustrates. We had to delete the expletives used in the ALF press release, as such language is not appropriate for this hearing. I would like to read some excerpts from this release.

In the second paragraph the press release states, "To celebrate the holidays we decided on a bonfire. Unfortunately for US Forest Industries it was at their corporate office headquarters in Medford, Oregon."

The press release then states in the fourth paragraph: "This was done in retribution for all the wild forests and animals lost to feed the wallets of greedy (expletive deleted) f-ks, like Jerry Bramwell, U.S.F.I President."

The attack was not because USFI was harvesting timber from public lands. No, they were harvesting timber off of private lands in Colorado.

The so-called communiqué continued, and I quote, "This action is payback and it is a warning to all others responsible, we do not sleep and we won't quit" (end quote).

Clearly, Mr. Chairman, the threat remains.

Mr. Chairman, if there are still some out there who feel that these acts by ELF/ALF should not be classified as terrorist acts, perhaps this next poster will sway their opinion.

This is an enlargement of a page taken straight from ELF's website (www .earthliberationfront.com). As you can see, the title of the page is "Setting Fires with Electrical Timers: An Earth Liberation Front Guide." I think the intent of the guide is dramatically and blatantly clear. They're actively enlisting and training others to carry out additional attacks in our country.

Now, ELF and ALFs claim that no human or non-human animal will be hurt by their attacks. But this assertion is incredulous in light of the severity and violent nature of many attacks perpetrated over the last four years.

I think an editorial in the January 24, 1999, edition of the *Oregonian* said it best when it stated, "ELF's followers think they have the power to plan their violence so that no ['human or non-human animal'] will ever be hurt. What are they going to say if man, woman or child just happens to be in the wrong place when ELF makes its next statement by fire? There is no sense in what ELF offers to the world and no honor."

Mr. Chairman, I couldn't agree more with the words expressed in this editorial. It is only a matter of time before an innocent life is lost in a future ELF/ALF attack. That is why it is imperative to treat all acts of terrorism equally. The terrorists behind the attacks of September 11, 2001, and December 27, 1998, both used terror and destruction to further their cause.

Terrorism is terrorism whether it is international, domestic, economic, religious, social or environmental. I call on our Justice Department to redouble its efforts to track down, apprehend and convict those responsible for these acts. It's time to break up this terrorist network, too.

Mr. Chairman, I commend you once again for holding this hearing and I yield back the balance of my time.

•

Questions asked to Craig Rosebraugh at the U.S. House Subcommittee on Forests and Forests Health for the February 12, 2002, Hearing on "Ecoterrorism"

Chairman Scott McInnis:

-Are you currently affiliated with the ELF?

-Did you play any role in the making of the ELF "training film?"

152

-Is that your voice on the film?

-Who paid your attorney fees?

-Are your attorney fees being paid for by the ELF?

-(Referring to the danger of fires spreading to unintended targets) Did you say "they are always dangerous"?

-Do the ELF and ELF Press Office have tax status?

-Are they non-profits?

-Did the ELF Press Office receive outside donations for costs, legal expenses, etc.?

-What are sources of money?

-Has the North American ELF Press Office ever received financial support from animal rights groups?

-Do you know Michael Conn?

-Have you ever been arrested for trespassing at the Oregon Regional Primate Research Center?

-Why was there a card with Michael Conn's address in your house?

-Was the ELF/ALF planning an act against Conn?

-Are the ELF planning future acts?

-Do you know Leslie James Pickering?

-Is Leslie James Pickering the new spokesperson for the ELF?

-Do you know if he has ever taken part in an ELF/ALF action?

Mr. Inslee:

Noted that witness had filed written testimony and asked if he had thus waved his Fifth Amendment rights.

Mr. McInnis:

Stated that council is not allowed to testify, can only advise client.

-On September 7, 2001, the *Associated Press* quoted you in reference to this committee, "These people are trying to stop the work of the ELF." Do you have information that can lead to the capture of the ELF?

-Are you aware that your answer could lead to the incarceration of the ELF?

-Quoted contempt code then asked, "Do you still wish to take the Fifth Amendment?"

Mr. Inslee:

Asked again for the Fifth Amendment issue to be addressed. Then reads Martin Luther King quote, "Riots cannot win and their participants know that."

-Do you agree with that statement?

-Are you familiar with a group...? (Talked about a group that could have chosen to blow something up or to do things another way and ended up passing an anti-trapping initiative in Oregon.)

-Are you going to take the Fifth Amendment on everything?

Mr. Holt:

"It would not be productive to ask questions at this time"

Ms.?:

-Did you submit this document? (Holds up testimony; Craig answers that he submitted testimony but does not know if that is it). Read quote from p. 5 of testimony, second to last paragraph, "by any means necessary" and last paragraph, "It's my sincere desire..."

Mr. Soler:

Statement about right and wrong way to do things, legal/illegal and stated that environmental extremists have hurt working people.

Suggested we move on to "legitimate witnesses" who have the "guts and courage not to hide behind the Fifth Amendment."

Mr. Inslee:

Statement about this type of action damaging to those of us working on environmental law, damages caused by forcing them to focus on these acts instead of focusing on legislation.

Mr. Simpson:

"Nice to have a witness so proud of the work he does he's afraid to talk about it."

Mr. Tancredo:

-Would you take this opportunity to ask these groups to stop what they are doing?

Mr.?:

-Read from testimony: "All power to the people..." Is this a call to revolutionary action?

-Do you believe arson and violence are reasonable acts in a free society?

Quoted Mark Sands who was convicted of eco-arson, "...no environmental or religious excuse for terrorism of any kind."

Comment about the irony of taking the Fifth Amendment, "if one has the courage of one's convictions, shouldn't they have the courage to risk conviction?"

Mr. McInnis:

Commented referring to Fifth Amendment issue, "We do intend to take full course on this matter."

Mr. Walden

Commented that taking the Fifth seems uncommitted to the cause, "...run and hide behind the laws of the Constitution...there is no commitment there".

-Are you related to Ken Lay?

-You say protections for the environment are not provided by the government; what protections are needed?

-Is there something in that answer that could incriminate you?

-What evidence do you have that the national forests are decimated?

-Do you think science provides any thing positive to society?

-Are you familiar with the communiqué about the St. Paul arson?

-Are you familiar with the communiqués bearing your name?

-Have you ever given an interview regarding the ELF?

Read last sentence of testimony again. Is that your testimony?

-You indicated that you submitted the testimony and now you won't answer?

Stated, "I see no further point in proceeding with this witness at this time"

Mr. Nethercutt:

-Mr. Rosebraugh, are you a citizen of the United States of America?

Mr. McInnis:

Requests that Stuart Sugarman (Rosebraugh's legal counsel) instruct his

156

client about his behavior and that "we will pursue this."

Commented that this is the kind of forum to express your opinions, hoped we could have a civil debate.

Mr. Nethercutt:

-Are you a citizen of the United States of America?

-Is the U.S. Constitution the law of the land?

Mr. McInnis:

"Obviously the witness has no intention of cooperating. There will be consequences."

Stated that they will submit written questions, if he refuses we will resubmit; then if he refuses we will proceed with contempt of Congress. Commented that there are a few people that "you probably know" who were just sentenced; reads quotes expressing regrets and adds, "One of yours has now come across" and expresses hope that Craig will 'come across': "I look forward to the day that you 'cross that line' and become constructive and contribute to the environmental cause."

Stated that within next 5 days they will submit questions to sort out which fall out of Fifth Amendment privilege, then he will ask for a vote of contempt of Congress.

●

James F. Jarboe
Domestic Terrorism Section Chief,
Counter-terrorism Division
Federal Bureau of Investigation
Testimony before the U.S. House Subcommittee on Forests and Forests
Health for the February 12, 2002, Hearing on "Ecoterrorism"

Good morning Chairman Mcinnis, Vice-Chairman Peterson, Congressman Inslee and members of the subcommittee. I am pleased to have the opportunity to appear before you and discuss the threat posed by ecoterrorism, as well as the measures being taken by the FBI and our law enforcement partners to address this threat.

The FBI divides the terrorist threat facing the United States into two broad categories: international and domestic. International terrorism involves violent acts or acts dangerous to human life that are a violation of the criminal laws of the United States or any state, or that would be a criminal violation if committed within the jurisdiction of the United States or any state. Acts of international terrorism are intended to intimidate or coerce a civilian population, influence the policy of a government, or affect the conduct of a government. These acts transcend national boundaries in terms of the means by which they are accomplished, the persons they appear intended to intimidate, or the locale in which perpetrators operate.

Domestic terrorism is the unlawful use, or threatened use, of violence by a group or individual based and operating entirely within the United States (or its territories) without foreign direction, committed against persons or property to intimidate or coerce a government, the civilian population, or any segment thereof, in furtherance of political or social objectives.

During the past decade we have witnessed dramatic changes in the nature of the terrorist threat. In the 1990s, right-wing extremism overtook left-wing terrorism as the most dangerous domestic terrorist threat to the country. During the past several years, special interest extremism, as characterized by the Animal Liberation Front (ALF) and the Earth Liberation Front (ELF), has emerged as a serious terrorist threat.

Generally, extremist groups engage in much activity that is protected by Constitutional guarantees of free speech and assembly. Law enforcement becomes involved when the volatile talk of these groups transgresses into unlawful action. The FBI estimates that the ALF/ELF have committed more than 600 criminal acts in the United States since 1996, resulting in damages in excess of 43 million dollars.

Special interest terrorism differs from traditional right-wing and left-wing terrorism in that extremist special interest groups seek to resolve specific issues, rather than effect widespread political change. Special interest extremists continue to conduct acts of politically-motivated violence to force segments of society, including the general public, to change attitudes about issues considered important to their causes. These groups occupy the extreme fringes of animal rights, pro-life, environmental, anti-nuclear,

158

and other movements. Some special interest extremists—most notably within the animal rights and environmental movements—have turned increasingly toward vandalism and terrorist activity in attempts to further their causes.

Since 1977, when disaffected members of the ecological preservation group Greenpeace formed the Sea Shepherd Conservation Society and attacked commercial fishing operations by cutting drift nets, acts of "eco-terrorism" have occurred around the globe. The FBI defines eco-terrorism as "the use or threatened use of violence of a criminal nature against innocent victims or property by an environmentally-oriented, subnational group for environmental-political reasons, or aimed at an audience beyond the target, often of a symbolic nature."

In recent years, the Animal Liberation Front (ALF) has become one of the most active extremist elements in the United States. Despite the destructive aspects of ALF's operations, its operational philosophy discourages acts that harm "any animal, human and nonhuman." Animal rights groups in the United States, including the ALF, have generally adhered to this mandate.

The ALF, established in Great Britain in the mid-1970s, is a loosely-organized movement committed to ending the abuse and exploitation of animals. The American branch of the ALF began its operations in the late 1970s. Individuals become members of the ALF not by filing paperwork or paying dues, but simply by engaging in "direct action" against companies or individuals who utilize animals for research or economic gain. "Direct action" generally occurs in the form of criminal activity to cause economic loss or to destroy the victims' company operations. The ALF activists have engaged in a steadily growing campaign of illegal activity against fur companies, mink farms, restaurants, and animal research laboratories.

Estimates of damage and destruction in the United States claimed by the ALF during the past ten years, as compiled by national organizations such as the Fur Commission and the National Association for Biomedical Research (NABR), put the fur industry and medical research losses at more than 45 million dollars. The ALF is considered a terrorist group, whose purpose is to bring about social and political change through the use of force and violence.

Disaffected environmentalists, in 1980, formed a radical group called

"Earth First!" and engaged in a series of protests and civil disobedience events. In 1984, however, members introduced "tree spiking" (insertion of metal or ceramic spikes in trees in an effort to damage saws) as a tactic to thwart logging. In 1992, the ELF was founded in Brighton, England by Earth First! members who refused to abandon criminal acts as a tactic when others wished to mainstream Earth First!.

In 1993, the ELF was listed for the first time along with the ALF in a communiqué declaring solidarity in actions between the two groups. This unity continues today with a crossover of leadership and membership. It is not uncommon for the ALF and the ELF to post joint declarations of responsibility for criminal actions on their web-sites. In 1994, founders of the San Francisco branch of Earth First! published in the *Earth First! Journal* a recommendation that Earth First! mainstream itself in the United States, leaving criminal acts other than unlawful protests to the ELF.

The ELF advocates "monkeywrenching," a euphemism for acts of sabotage and property destruction against industries and other entities perceived to be damaging to the natural environment. Monkeywrenching includes tree spiking, arson, sabotage of logging or construction equipment, and other types of property destruction.

Speeches given by Jonathan Paul and Craig Rosebraugh at the 1998 national animal rights conference held at the University of Oregon promoted the unity of both the ELF and the ALF movements. The ELF posted information on the ALF website until it began its own website in January 2001, and it is listed in the same underground activist publications as the ALF.

The most destructive practice of the ALF/ELF is arson. The ALF/ELF members consistently use improvised incendiary devices equipped with crude but effective timing mechanisms. These incendiary devices are often constructed based upon instructions found on the ALF/ELF websites. The ALF/ELF criminal incidents often involve pre-activity surveillance and well-planned operations. Members are believed to engage in significant intelligence gathering against potential targets, including the review of industry/trade publications, photographic/video surveillance of potential targets, and posting details about potential targets on the internet.

The ALF and the ELF have Jointly claimed credit for several raids, including a November1997 attack of the Bureau of Land Management wild horse corrals near Burns, Oregon where arson destroyed the entire complex, resulting in damages in excess of four hundred and fifty thousand dollars and the June 1998 arson attack of a U.S. Department of Agriculture Animal Damage Control building near Olympia, Washington, in which damages exceeded two million dollars.

The ELF claimed sole credit for the October 1998, arson of a Vail, Colorado ski facility in which four ski lifts, a restaurant, a picnic facility and a utility building were destroyed. Damage exceeded twelve million dollars.

On 12/27/1998, the ELF claimed responsibility for the arson at the U.S. Forest Industries office in Medford, Oregon, where damages exceeded five hundred thousand dollars. Other arsons in Oregon, New York, Washington, Michigan and Indiana have been claimed by the ELF. Recently, the ELF has also claimed attacks on genetically-engineered crops and trees. The ELF claims these attacks have totaled close to $40 million in damages.

The name of a group called the Coalition to Save the Preserves (CSP), surfaced in relation to a series of arsons that occurred in the Phoenix, Arizona area. These arsons targeted several new homes under construction near the North Phoenix Mountain Preserves. No direct connection was established between the CSP and ALF/ELF. However, the stated goal of CSP—to stop development of previously-undeveloped lands-- is similar to that of the ELF. The property damage associated with the arsons has been estimated to be in excess of $5 million.

The FBI has developed a strong response to the threats posed by domestic and international terrorism. Between fiscal years 1993 and 2003, the number of special agents dedicated to the FBI's counterterrorism programs grew by approximately 224% (to 1,669—nearly 16 percent of all FBI special agents). In recent years, the FBI has strengthened its counterterrorism program to enhance its abilities to carry out these objectives.

Cooperation among law enforcement agencies at all levels represents an important component of a comprehensive response to terrorism. This cooperation assumes its most tangible operational form in the Joint Terrorism Task Forces (JTTFs) that are established in 44 cities across the nation. These task forces are particularly well-suited to responding to terrorism because they combine the national and international investigative resources of the FBI with the street-level expertise of local law enforcement agencies.

Given the success of the Joint Terrorism Task Force (JTTF) concept, the FBI has established 15 new JTTFs since the end of 1999. By the end of 2003 the FBI plans to have established JTTFs in each of its 56 field offices. By integrating the investigative abilities of the FBI and local law enforcement agencies, these task forces represent an effective response to the threats posed to U.S. communities by domestic and international terrorists.

The FBI and our law enforcement partners have made a number of arrests of individuals alleged to have perpetrated acts of eco-terrorism. Several of these individuals have been successfully prosecuted. Following the investigation of the Phoenix, Arizona arsons noted earlier, Mark Warren Sands was indicted and arrested on 6/14/2001. On 11/07/2001, Sands pleaded guilty to ten counts of extortion and using fire in the commission of a federal felony.

In February 2001, teenagers Jared McIntyre, Matthew Rammelkamp, and George Mashkow all pleaded guilty, as adults, to title 18 U.S.C. 844(i), arson, and 844(n), arson conspiracy. These charges pertain to a series of arsons and attempted arsons of new home construction sites in Long Island, NY. An adult, Connor Cash, was also arrested on February 15, 2001 and charged under the same federal statutes. Jared McIntrye stated that these acts were committed in sympathy of the ELF movement. The New York Joint Terrorism Task Force played a significant role in the arrest and prosecution of these individuals.

On 1/23/2001, Frank Ambrose was arrested by officers of the Department of Natural Resources with assistance from the Indianapolis JTTF, on a local warrant out of Monroe County Circuit Court, Bloomington, Indiana, charging Ambrose with timber spiking. Ambrose is suspected of involvement in the spiking of approximately 150 trees in Indiana state forests. The ELF claimed responsibility for these incidents.

On September 16, 1998, a federal grand jury in the western district of Wisconsin indicted Peter Young and Justin Samuel for Hobbs Act violations as well as for Animal Enterprise Terrorism. Samuel was apprehended in Belgium and was subsequently extradited to the United States. On August 30, 2000, Samuel pleaded guilty to two counts of Animal Enterprise Terrorism and was sentenced on November 3, 2000, to two years in prison, two years probation, and ordered to pay $364,106 in restitution. Samuel's prosecution arose out of his involvement in mink releases in Wisconsin in 1997. This incident was claimed by the ALF. The investigation and arrest of Justin Samuel were the result of a joint effort by federal, state and local agencies.

On April 20, 1997, Douglas Joshua Ellerman turned himself in and admitted on videotape to purchasing, constructing, and transporting five pipe bombs to the scene of the March 11, 1997 arson at the Fur Breeders Agricultural Co-op in Sandy, Utah. Ellerman also admitted setting fire to the facility. Ellerman was indicted on June 19, 1997 on 16 counts and eventually pleaded guilty to three. He was sentenced to seven years in prison and restitution of approximately $750,000. Though this incident was not officially claimed by ALF, Ellerman indicated during an interview subsequent to his arrest that he was a member of ALF. This incident was investigated jointly by the FBI and the Bureau of Alcohol, Tobacco and Firearms (BATF).

Rodney Adam Coronado was convicted for his role in the February 2, 1992 arson at an animal research laboratory on the campus of Michigan State University. Damage estimates, according to public sources, approached $200,000 and included the destruction of research records. On July 3, 1995, Coronado pleaded guilty for his role in the arson and was sentenced to 57 months in federal prison, three years probation, and restitution of more than $2 million. This incident was claimed by ALF. The FBI, BATF and the Michigan State University Police played a significant role in the investigation, arrest, and prosecution.

Marc Leslie Davis, Margaret Katherine Millet, MarcAndre Baker, and Use Washington Asplund were all members of the self-proclaimed "Evan Mecham Eco-Terrorist International Conspiracy" (EMETIC). EMETIC was formed to engage in eco-terrorism against nuclear power plants and ski resorts in the southwestern United States. In November 1987, the group claimed responsibility for damage to a chairlift at the Fairfield Snow Bowl ski resort near Flagstaff, Arizona. Davis, Millet, and Baker were arrested in May 1989 on charges relating to the Fairfield Snow Bowl incident and planned incidents at the Central Arizona Project and Palo Verde nuclear generating stations in Arizona, the Diablo Canyon nuclear facility in California, and the Rocky Flats nuclear facility in Colorado. All pleaded guilty and were sentenced in September 1991.

Davis was sentenced to six years in federal prison, and restitution to the Fairfield Snow Bowl ski resort in the amount of $19,821. Millet was sentenced to three years in federal prison, and restitution to Fairfield in the amount of $19,821. Baker was sentenced to one year in federal prison, five months probation, a $5,000 fine, and 100 hours of community service. Asplund was also charged and was sentenced to one year in federal prison, five years probation, a $2,000 fine, and 100 hours of community service.

Currently, more than 26 FBI field offices have pending investigations associated with ALF/ELF activities. Despite all of our efforts (increased resources allocated, JTTFs, successful arrests and prosecutions), law enforcement has a long way to go to adequately address the problem of eco-terrorism. Groups such as the ALF and the ELF present unique challenges. There is little if any hierarchal structure to such entities. Eco-terrorists are unlike traditional criminal enterprises, which are often structured and organized.

The difficulty investigating such groups is demonstrated by the fact that law enforcement has thus far been unable to affect the arrests of anyone for some recent criminal activity directed at federal land managers or their offices. However, there are several ongoing investigations regarding such acts. Current investigations include the 10/14/2001 arson at the Bureau of Land Management wild horse and burro corral in Litchfield, California, the 7/20/2000 destruction of trees and damage to vehicles at the U.S. Forestry science laboratory in Rhinelander, Wisconsin, and the 11/29/1997 arson at the Bureau of Land Management corral in Bums, Oregon.

Before closing, I would like to acknowledge the cooperation and assistance rendered by the U.S. Forest Service in investigating incidents of eco-terrorism. Specifically, I would like to recognize the assistance that the Forest Service is providing with regard to the ongoing investigation of the 7/20/2000 incident of vandalism and destruction that occurred at the U.S. Forestry Science Laboratory in Rhinelander, Wisconsin.

The FBI and all of our federal, state and local law enforcement partners will continue to strive to address the difficult and unique challenges posed by eco-terrorists. Despite the recent focus on international terrorism, we remain fully cognizant of the full range of threats that confront the United States.

Chairman McInnis and members of the subcommittee, this concludes my prepared remarks. I would like to express appreciation for your concentration on the issue of eco-terrorism and I look forward to responding to any questions.

•

Porter Wharton, III
Sr. Vice President of Public Affairs
Vail Resorts, Inc.
Testimony before the U.S. House Subcommittee on Forests and Forests Health for the February 12, 2002, Hearing on "Ecoterrorism"

On the morning of October 19, 1998, at approximately 3:30 a.m., the first of eight fires were set. At 4:00 a.m., the first alarms came into Vail dispatch and by 4:20 a.m., the first firefighters were on their way up the dirt road to the 11,200-foot ridgeline where the fires raged at two locations a mile and a half apart.

By 4:40 a.m., the first firefighters were on the scene. What they were confronted with was five buildings and three ski lifts engulfed in flames. Hampered by a lack of water on the ridgeline, six inches of fresh snow and fires that by that time had almost an hour's head start, their task was virtually impossible.

Eventually 195 firefighters from 11 fire departments and our company were engaged throughout the night and into the day. They came from six counties and stayed for over eight hours engaged in the battle.

When the morning sun rose over the Gore Range, it illuminated a shocking amount of damage. Foremost was the complete loss of the resort's flagship on-mountain restaurant, Two Elk. A 24,000 square foot, majestic log structure, with seating for 550.

Four additional buildings housing dining and ski patrol functions were also totally consumed. Three chairlifts were damaged. The total value of lost assets was over $12 million, making this the most costly act of eco-terrorism in this country's history.

Most fortunately, only one of the almost 200 firefighters involved was injured. And a hunter who had left his friends at their nearby campsite to sleep in a small restroom building for warmth awoke to find himself in the only structure not engulfed in flames.

As one witness to the carnage said later, "The only thing we can be thankful for is that we aren't having services."

Former Colorado Governor Romer was the first to call the fires an act of terrorism. Then, on Wednesday October 21st, two days after the fires, an e-mail was received by Colorado Public Radio

The e-mail, purportedly sent by ELF, the Earth Liberation Front, an eco-terrorist group responsible for tens of millions of dollars of destruction across Europe and the United States, claimed responsibility for the fires.

Why had Vail drawn the attention of ELF? Three days before the fires, a federal court had given final approval for the construction of the Category III expansion of the ski area. The expansion had been controversial, with some environmentalists opposing it for reasons including possible impacts to Canadian Lynx habitat - even though no lynx had been seen in the area since 1973.

The expansion had been contemplated since the resort's founding in 1962. It was desired by our guests and supported by an overwhelming majority of our community. The approval process took over seven years and five million dollars in expenditures by our company. It was the most scrutinized ski area expansion in history with over 65 studies conducted on soil, air, wildlife and water issues. Two administrative reviews and three court challenges all supported the expansion. It was approved by four federal agencies, one state agency and two local governments.

But ELF did not accept the results of this exhaustive process.

The ELF communiqué stated the fires had been set, "... on behalf of the lynx. Putting profits ahead of Colorado's wildlife will not be tolerated. This action is just a warning." And then our guests were warned, "For your safety and convenience, we strongly advise skiers to choose other destinations."

The property damage has now been repaired. But the scars on our community and our company remain. A former Vail mayor said at the time, "This was not only an attack against Vail Resorts; this was an attack against the people who live and work in Eagle County." It is the wealthy visitors to Vail that are a part of its image, but when the guests are gone, there are 30,000 hard-working very normal people that remain in the valley they call home. Those are the people ELF terrorized. The sense of violation and the feelings of outrage remain.

The investigation is still open. No arrests have been made. ELF boasts it is above the laws of this country and claimed they were, "… effecting social change" and that, "… decreasing profits by destroying property has been very effective."

But let's call it what it really is. No matter what the supposed justification, this was terrorism. This is a fringe group saying in essence that they are more important than the laws that are the foundation of this society and this country. Any effort on the part of this administration and this Congress to assure homeland security must include a response to domestic environmental terrorism. These faceless, cowardly criminals must be stopped.

If they are not, more property will be destroyed. More threats of extortion and worse will be issued. More law-abiding citizens will live in fear. And eventually, inevitably there will be a loss of life. It's a miracle it hasn't happened already.

●

Richard B. Berman
Executive Director
Center for Consumer Freedom
Testimony before the U.S. House Subcommittee on Forests and Forests Health for the February 12, 2002, Hearing on "Ecoterrorism"

ECOTERRORISM, ITS CONNECTIONS TO ANIMAL-RIGHTS TERRORISM, AND THEIR COMMON ABOVE-GROUND SUPPORT SYSTEM

Mr. Chairman, Members of the Subcommittee, my name is Richard Berman. I am the Executive Director of the Center for Consumer Freedom, a nonprofit organization based in Washington, DC. The Center does not accept and has never received government funds.

On behalf of American restaurant operators and food producers, I would like to thank you for holding this hearing today. Eco-terrorism is indeed alive and well in the United States of America, and it shares a common heritage with violent animal-rights extremism. These radical movements have been responsible for well over 1,000 documented criminal acts in the U.S., most of which would be prosecuted as felonies if the perpetrators could be brought to justice.

I am not talking about peaceful protest, pickets, sign waving, slogan chanting, or forms of civil disobedience that are protected by the First Amendment. Rather, America's present environmental and animal-rights terrorists have committed arsons, assaults, vandalism on a massive scale, and a host of other property crimes that cripple food producers and resource providers, and occasionally lay waste to entire restaurants.

On September 11th of last year, on the very day America mourned the loss of thousands of lives to foreign terrorists, our own homegrown version (the Earth Liberation Front and the Animal Liberation Front, known as "ELF" and "ALF") took joint credit for firebombing a McDonald's restaurant in Tucson, Arizona.

There is no doubt now, and the FBI concurs, that the Earth Liberation Front is associated with the Animal Liberation Front. Special Agent David Szady (now the U.S. counterintelligence executive) has told CNN that "by any sense or any definition, this is a true domestic terrorism group that uses criminal activity to further their political agenda."

During the past three years alone, ELF and ALF have claimed responsibility for smashing bank windows, torching a chicken feed truck, burning a horse corral at a Bureau of Land Management facility, firebombing dealer lots full of sport utility vehicles, destroying valuable scientific laboratory equipment and many years worth of irreplaceable research documents, "spiking" trees in the Pacific Northwest, and even setting bombs under meat delivery trucks. There should be no sympathy for intentionally-committed felonies of this magnitude. Eco-terror and animal-rights crimes have become everyday events in America, yet they are among our most under-reported and least-punished offenses.

Members of the Subcommittee, on rare occasions the criminals responsible for these violent and unlawful acts are captured. Just two weeks ago a pair of animal-rights terrorists were sentenced to prison terms for attempting to blow up a dairy truck near San Jose, California. They were caught red-handed, with homemade bombs just as deadly as those being exploded by other terrorists in the Middle East. But the vast majority of crimes like these go unpunished. The underground ELF and ALF even have the gall to brag publicly about their felonies. ALF actually released a report in January, claiming responsibility for 137 crimes in 2001, and causing an estimated $17.3 million in damages.

ALF and ELF won't stop with damage to people and businesses with whom they disagree. Rather, they are aggressively recruiting new criminals to their vicious gang. Incredibly, the group's leaders have begun to distribute "how-to" manuals on the Internet, describing how to build bombs and incendiary devices, how to destroy fields of genetically-engineered food crops, and how to commit "arson," "thievery," and other felonies without leaving clues at the crime scene. There is even a volume on the easiest way to sink a ship.

Any 10-year-old with a computer can download much of this reading material. For a few dollars and the cost of postage, ALF "spokesperson" David Barbarash will mail the rest of the materials to anyone who asks. Mr. Chairman, I have submitted a copy of Mr. Barbarash's disturbing catalog for the record.

Equally troubling is the extent to which some eco-terrorists and animal-rights criminals have managed to garner support, both philosophical and financial, from above-ground activist organizations, including those that enjoy the same tax benefits as our nation's churches and universities.

Between 1994 and 1995, for instance, People for the Ethical Treatment of Animals gave over $70,000 to an Animal Liberation Front criminal named Rodney Coronado, who was convicted of arson, a felony, in connection with the $1.7 million firebombing of a Michigan State University research facility. This amount, by the way, is more than ten times the total that the same organization (PETA) devoted to animal shelters during those two years. In addition, both PETA and its president, Ingrid Newkirk, are acknowledged financial supporters of an organization called No Compromise, which operates on behalf of, and for the "underground" supporters of the Animal Liberation Front.

PETA raised over $15 million last year from the general public, all of it tax-exempt. When will PETA be held accountable?

Another eco-criminal, Dave Foreman, pleaded guilty in 1991 to felony conspiracy in a plot to blow up the power lines of three nuclear power generating stations. Mr. Foreman was a co-founder of the radical "Earth First!" organization, the group from which the Earth Liberation Front split during a 1992 meeting in the United Kingdom. Among its other claims to fame, Earth First! actually published the newsletter articles (in the *Earth First! Journal*) from which "Unabomber" Ted Kaczinsky chose his last two victims.

An organization called the Ruckus Society was started by another Earth First! co-founder named Mike Roselle. This group was largely responsible for the 1999 anti-WTO protests in Seattle, which ended in mass rioting and the destruction of Starbucks and McDonald's restaurants. The Ruckus Society trains young activists in the techniques of "monkeywrenching," which, when applied, result in property crimes of enormous financial cost.

The Ruckus Society and the Rainforest Action Network (another outfit founded by Mr. Roselle) are tax-exempt organizations that have enjoyed contributions from such mainstream sources as Ted Turner and Ben & Jerry's. When will this breeding ground for environmental criminals be held accountable?

Ruckus, by the way, also gets funding from a San Francisco outfit called the Tides Foundation, which distributes other foundations' money while shielding the identity of the actual donors. Our tax law permits this sort of money-laundering. If the public is prevented from learning where a tax-exempt organization like the Ruckus Society gets their money, then the legal loopholes that permit foundations like Tides to operate as it does should be closed.

Mr. Chairman, these are all serious charges that I am making, and I urge this Committee to fully investigate the damage that ALF, ELF, and other like-minded terrorist groups have caused to American businesses, American livelihoods, and the American psyche. I would also urge the appropriate Congressional committee to explore the tax-exempt status of groups that have helped to fund - directly or indirectly - these domestic terrorists.

Thank you, Mr. Chairman, for holding this hearing.

•

William F. Wasley
Director of Law Enforcement and Investigations (LEI)
Forest Service United States Department of Agriculture
Testimony before the U.S. House Subcommittee on Forests and Forests
Health for the February 12, 2002, Hearing on "Ecoterrorism"

MR. Chairman and members of the Subcommittee:

My name is Bill Wasley, and I am the Director of the Forest Service Law Enforcement and Investigations (LEI) program. Thank you for the opportunity to appear before you today to discuss eco-terrorism acts on Forest Service facilities and how the Agency is addressing employee safety.

The Forest Service manages approximately 192 million acres of land in the United States. Protecting people and natural resources is part of our mission. This mission has become more difficult over the years as crimes occurring on national forests and to federal property have increased, especially criminal acts against research projects and government facilities. LEI is responsible for protecting and serving the public and agency employees; protecting natural resources and other property under the jurisdiction of the Forest Service; and cooperating with other law enforcement agencies.

Escalation of Incidents

Over the past 10 years, destructive civil disobedience and destructive criminal acts have increased, damaging resources and placing people in harm's way. Destructive criminal acts have primarily been related to protests against commercial logging activity on National Forest System (NFS) lands. These acts have included the illegal occupation of NFS lands and roads that place protestors at great risk; spiking trees designated for cutting; damaging or destroying natural resources, public roads, and facilities; damaging private property; and threatening and interfering with timber sale purchasers and timber operators. Since 1998, the Earth Liberation Front (ELF) has claimed responsibility for at least five such acts to Forest Service resources, facilities, or vehicles.

Forest Service research programs have also been the targets of recent criminal acts. The Agency has an extensive research and development program that conducts basic and applied research on an array of subjects that complement the diverse mission of the Agency, including research on biological pathogens or forest genetics.

In FY 2000, two acts of vandalism resulted in damages to the Forest Service Research facilities in Minnesota and Wisconsin, estimated at over $1.3 million. Over 850 pine and broadleaf trees, and saplings from "superior" tree stock and cross-pollination research were cut down, ring-barked and trampled. ELF claimed responsibility for this act.

In November of 2001, two explosive arson devices were planted near university and Forest Service research buildings at Michigan Technical University, but fortunately were located by security personnel prior to detonation. No one has yet been charged with this crime.

Prevention is critical to the Agency's action plan against destructive criminal acts. Currently, the Forest Service is conducting facility security assessments to identify those facilities that are vulnerable. These assessments will address employee, facility, asset, transportation, special use permitting, and resource protection concerns.

Safety in the Workplace

Since the mid 1990s, the number of threats and attacks on Forest Service employees have increased. Examples of these attacks include the bombing of an employee's residence and the complete destruction by arson of two Forest Service offices. These attacks have raised fears and concern among Agency employees for their personal safety. The Agency is addressing these concerns by securing government facilities; producing and distributing safety pamphlets, brochures, and videos; holding safety meetings; providing information to employees on steps that are being implemented to improve employee security; and providing violence awareness training. The Forest Service has an agreement with the Office of Inspector General (OIG) regarding investigations dealing with employee safety. The safety of Agency employees and the public on Forest Service lands is the top priority for the Forest Service.

Efforts to Ensure Coordinated Security

In cases of domestic terrorism the FBI has primary jurisdiction. LEI assists the FBI by serving on the joint task force investigating domestic terrorism acts.

Agency law enforcement officers and criminal investigators coordinate closely with line and staff officers to provide and implement security procedures for Forest Service facilities, resources, employees, and the public. Security measures undertaken by LEI include: conducting threat assessments; providing personnel and facility security details during protests or high risk events; providing first responders to incidents; responding to protest and civil disobedience activities; investigating criminal acts; conducting search and rescues; responding to shooting incidents and drug and alcohol possession and use problems; and responding and investigating all reported instances of intimidation, threat, or assault against agency employees.

In investigating criminal acts, LEI has developed many cooperative agreements with other Federal, State, and local agencies for performance of routine law enforcement patrols, drug enforcement, timber theft investigations, and coordination of other enforcement activities. LEI participate in many task forces, particularly the FBI's counterterrorism taskforce mentioned above and the Office of National Drug Control Policy's (ONDCP) High Intensity Drug Trafficking Area (HIDTA) program.

Conclusion

The Forest Service is committed to work with the FBI to combat acts of domestic terrorism. We also are committed to ensuring safety and security of the public and our employees. The job is immense, but we will continue to work at providing these services and expend resources consistent with this priority.

This concludes my statement. I would be happy to answer any questions you or Members of the Subcommittee might have.

●

Michael S. Hicks
Northwest Oregon Area Logging Manager
Boise Cascade Corporation
Testimony before the U.S. House Subcommittee on Forests and Forests Health for the February 12, 2002, Hearing on "Ecoterrorism"

Mr. Chairman and committee members:

I am Michael S. Hicks, Northwest Oregon Area Logging Manager for Boise Cascade Corporation. Boise Cascade owns or controls over 2.3 million acres of forest land using science based, state-of-the-art forestry practices. In addition to being a major distributor of office products and building products, Boise Cascade also manufactures building products and paper products to meet the demands of the American public. Over 19,000 people work for Boise Cascade in the United States.

My area in Monmouth, Oregon is part of the Western Oregon Region with the regional office located in Medford Oregon. In my position as Logging Manager, I am responsible for obtaining a reliable source of log supply for our three Northwest Oregon veneer mills. The logs are obtained from our own lands, from contracts sold by a number of government and private sellers, and from open market log deliveries. My responsibilities also include the management of 160,000 acres of timberland and management of a staff of 25 to 30 professional foresters and biologists. Our office is a field office, primarily housing field foresters, engineers, field biologists, and administrative support staff.

Thank you for allowing me to provide my testimony on domestic terrorism. The title of this hearing is "Ecoterrorism and Lawlessness on National Forests." However, from my perspective, we are dealing with just plain TERRORISM AND LAWLESSNESS. It really does not matter what the cause is, or how one's actions are justified. There is no prefix anyone can put before the word terrorism that justifies a cause. We are a nation of laws and due process. Terrorism is terrorism, plain and simple. I am here today to relate my experience with domestic terrorism, as I call the activities that were carried out against our company. It was Christmas morning, 1999 and this was to be the first time my wife and I would enjoy the chance to sleep in on Christmas morning since the 1970's. However, the phone rang at about 5:15 a.m. It was our local Boise Cascade Employee Relations Manager telling me our office was on fire.

174

Needless to say, my string of early awakenings on Christmas morning remained intact. This time, however, it wasn't because of kids or grandkids running around to see what Santa and his elves had brought. As we found out a few days later, it was elves of a different stripe. The evil and cowardly elves of the Earth Liberation Front (ELF) had brought their gift of terror to our lives. ELF, through their spokesperson at the time, Craig Rosebraugh, claimed responsibility for the fire. Their claim was verified by ATF and FBI investigators.

That Christmas morning was cold and dry, made even colder by a stiff wind from the north. ELF could not have had better conditions to start a fire. When I arrived about 25 minutes after receiving the call, the fire had been burning for over an hour. The roof had caved in and the firefighters were busy trying to put out several hot spots. Incendiary devices placed on opposite sides of the building by the arsonists, presumably for maximum effect, had ignited the arson fire. Our office was primarily wood construction with many interior walls lined with cedar. The office was built in 1978 and the construction was meant to display the wood products industry. The alcoves in the front and rear provided corners for maximum ignition heat and the vents above the ignition point allowed the fumes and flames to carry throughout the dry, wood framed attic. It was clear that ELF had sized up our facility and had known their standard fire setting practices would cause the office to burn easily, once ignited.

There were at least three alarms called during the fire, with many firefighters working several sides of the 7,500-square-foot structure. After a quick look, I called my boss to give him an update and then started to call all my staff. One by one, the staff—and in many cases their families—came in during the morning, interrupting their holiday festivities. We all stared in disbelief and wandered around as close as the firefighters dared to let us. The fire departments were concerned about our safety as we instinctively moved closer and closer, driven by the need to save what we could. Throughout the early morning we comforted each other and tried to comprehend what was happening. At the time, we did not know it was an arson fire. As we gazed at the smoldering rubble, we all wondered what we could have done to prevent it.

The fire department kept us from entering the perimeter, but I was able to engage a fireman on the periphery about how things were going and when they thought it would be contained and finally extinguished. As I was discussing the situation with the firefighter, I noticed one area containing all our easements, lease documents, real estate papers, rights-of-way files and other important files. It was not heavily damaged by the fire, but was getting a lot of water going in and around it. I asked the fireman if there was any way we could get a tarp over the file cabinets to protect them from water damage. We broke out the remaining glass of the window and crawled in to the office and draped a tarp over the cabinet. We were very fortunate that the fire originated well away from this area. With the exception of a little water in the file cabinets, these files were saved from fire or water damage. I wish we could have done the same for many others.

Several hot spots were particularly difficult to extinguish. The firefighters, many of them volunteers, had to separate the outside wall from the building to extinguish the fire. It was difficult and dangerous work. They were trying to pull the wall down while preventing the firemen from getting trapped by the falling wall. They pulled an exterior wall down in at least two locations. After seeing all the dangers up close, I remember thinking that morning about all the hazards the firemen endured. We gained a renewed appreciation for the dedication and bravery of our firefighters on that chilly Christmas morning.

By late morning the fire was declared out. The fire marshal indicated he wanted us to stay away from an area he thought might have been the source of the fire, the copy machine room. With the caution to stay clear of this area, we were allowed to enter and retrieve what we could salvage. Because safety is one of our company's core values, we held a safety meeting before we embarked on the salvage project. One of the first things I brought out was a display case with a folded American flag from the office of Sergeant Major Rudy Frazzini, one of our foresters, who is also a Gulf War veteran and active in the Marine Reserves. This was the flag that had draped his father's coffin, and I knew how important this was to Rudy and the rest of us. I made sure it was safe in the seat of my pickup.

Many of the staff had to postpone their Christmas activities to spend the day salvaging all the items they could. It was especially tough on four of my grandchildren because we were due to open presents with them at 10:00 a.m. in the morning and they had to wait until I arrived that evening. The fire was on a Saturday and we were expecting rain by the following Monday. We knew we had to get everything under cover by then. We worked all day Saturday and came back on Sunday to move as much as we could to our mill site. Our goal was to salvage the files and what we could for our temporary quarters. I recall pulling out file drawers that were still smoldering and attempting to extinguish the embers so that we could salvage the files. We filled a large room (approximately 2,000 square feet) in the nearby veneer mill with file drawers, computers in varying degrees of meltdown, and other office equipment that we thought we could salvage.

There were many hazards associated with salvaging all the usable remains of a fire. We had to contend with broken glass, floors that gave way and overhead ceilings that had caved in and were resting on file cabinets. We contended with the ever-present tangle of wires, debris and remnants of the ceiling and roof trusses. The conditions were difficult for salvaging, but we worked cautiously and had a good share of the salvageable material removed by Sunday evening.

On Monday our access to the office and its contents was cut off completely by investigators from the FBI and ATF, as well as the Oregon State Police. Not only could we not get close to the rubble, we could not even talk to any of the investigators. The Federal folks were quite focused and extremely professional in their investigation. The evidence gathered and the fine work by the Federal agencies eventually led to confirmation that ELF did, in fact, start the fire. As noted earlier, ELF, through their spokesman, Craig Rosebraugh, claimed responsibility for the fire, and their claim was independently confirmed by Federal investigators.

When you think about losing your home to fire, what is the first thing you wish you could save, assuming all the family members and pets are out? In my house, my first concern would be the irreplaceable art work, family heirlooms, and of course, all the photos and slides of family and friends. Our offices are very much like our homes. Many of us spend as much time in our office as we do our home. We have collectibles, art and other individual items that reflect ourselves. The very personal nature of our offices being destroyed by a cowardly arson attack has as much of an emotional impact as losing one's home. That may sound too strong, but the point is we all lost personal items that were important to our professional lives that make us balanced and productive contributors to our society.

In my case, I lost a whole file drawer of photographs and slides taken over a 25-year career. These pictures were a great treasure to me and I was able to salvage little of that precious drawer. I clearly remember welling up with tears, looking at the fused mass of pictures and shriveled slides, thinking that this history of my work life, much like a daily journal, is gone. I had intended to use these pictures to write my professional history when I retired. I just do not think about it any more because I get depressed. In addition, I was very proud of my contributions to various boards and organizations. The certificates recognizing those contributions were hanging on my wall, as I am sure they do in many of your offices. They were all incinerated into a pile of ash and rubble. I did manage to salvage one thing I treasured and brought it with me today to the hearing on Ecoterrorism and Lawlessness in National Forests. I hold a copy of the proceedings on hearings of the sale of timber from Federal lands held in the spring of 1979. I was able to testify at a similar Congressional hearing and was given a copy of those proceedings. It is a little worse for wear, but that was one little treasure I did get to keep.

Other colleagues have similar stories, such as one who lost the only photo he has of his two very pregnant daughters posing tummy to tummy. Another person lost a one-of-a-kind map of the original railroad route that accessed the heart of our forest lands during the times when the only access was by railroad. One person lost the picture of his father dressed in his army uniform, and a diploma with the summa cum laude banner was damaged. Numerous family pictures and small mementos were lost. This was not just an attack on a corporate entity; it was an attack on all the individuals who called our office home for 40 to 60 hours a week. Our personal possessions were destroyed. Our lives were severely disrupted.

As far as the corporation was concerned, the attack did not alter our business strategy. We were up and running within a week, on the first operating day in January, with all new copies of contracts, an office, phones, and all the office equipment necessary to keep us in business. It did, however, change how we view security. We take our security much more seriously than we did before December 25, 1999. Our new office contains state-of-the-art security measures inside and out. We all have a heightened sense of awareness. We lost our sense of security and became more keenly aware of the risks we have on our lands, at our mills, and around our equipment. The timber industry is a proud and industrious segment of society. Even though the industry has been battered on many fronts, it is still relatively strong and viable with an incredible will to survive. A few terrorists will not stop our efforts to be good stewards of the land, or stop us from providing quality products the public demands. The domestic terrorists have only strengthened our resolve to remain a strong, viable part of the U.S. economy.

To replace the office, we went through months of analysis, negotiations, and internal discussions before we settled on a structure that was very much the same floor layout as before, but very different in building design. Since ELF attacked our facility, security has become a huge factor in how we site, secure and manage our facilities. Existing streets, access, cooperation of local government, and current zoning of adjacent properties all played into our decision to relocate in the same spot as before. In the end, we were not going to allow terrorists to dictate where we conduct business. The company spent approximately $1.5 million dollars replacing the office and contents. A significant portion of that cost was expended on internal and external security. Boise Cascade has been a target once; we felt we could once again be in someone's cross hairs. As a result of the arson fire, the company chose to build using more materials such as concrete, steel, and aluminum, which are non-flammable and non-renewable energy consuming. Ironically, when the effects of the air pollution from the fire are added to the use of energy consuming non-renewable building products, the effects on the ecosystem are doubled. ELF impacted our lives, as well as our office building, and now we are more cautious. Life goes on and we are continuing to harvest, plant and nurture our forests for future generations. Our mills continue to make and distribute high quality forest products that we all use. After such an event, we look at life differently, but we must continue managing our forestlands. After all, they are not going anywhere.

We also manage our timber sales differently, as this 1999 arson was not our company's first experience with lawless behavior by radical activists. For example, our company has experienced these negative effects on our operation in southern Oregon in the early 1990s with the Sugarloaf timber sale on the Siskiyou National Forest. During logging operations we hired extra security and our operations were delayed. We even had protesters force one of our contractor's log trucks to come to a halt so an accomplice could lock himself underneath the truck. Trees were spiked with metal spikes. We have seen the results of lawless activities in the National Forests firsthand. From our perspective, purchasing timber from the National Forests has increased Boise Cascade's risk of being targeted by organizations like ELF.

In summary, ELF burned our office building. It was reported on December 31, 1999 by the *Oregonian* newspaper that Craig Rosebraugh received the ELF communiqué and that "he was pleased with the arson." ELF is a

179

terrorist organization willing to break laws that we all live and work by. Boise Cascade lost little time getting back to the business of growing, harvesting, planting, and nurturing the forests in our charge. It did not change the company's desire to meet our customer's wood, paper and office products needs in the market place.

The terrorists did have an impact on how we view the world from a security perspective. And it also cost the company $1.5 million. The primary impact of burning our office was on the personal lives of our staff. However, it also placed my staff, the firefighters, and me in harm's way, and it is only a matter of time before someone is seriously injured or killed. We have biologists who frequented that office at all hours of the night, coming or going on their rounds to survey for Spotted Owls and Marbled Murrelets. Any one of those workers could have been present, and injured or killed by ELF's terrorist activities.

Our personal and professional losses cannot be measured, so we are moving on. We only hope the cowards are caught and held accountable for the terror and destruction they have caused. Congress and others should recognize that these groups are terrorists and these groups should be sought out and prosecuted to the full extent of the law.

Thank you for the opportunity to comment on such an important and timely topic.

•

Gloria Flora
Public Employees for Environmental Responsibility
Testimony before the U.S. House Subcommittee on Forests and Forests Health for the February 12, 2002, Hearing on "Ecoterrorism"

On behalf of Public Employees for Environmental Responsibility Before the House Resources Subcommittee on Forests and Forest Health Hearing on "Eco-Terrorism and Lawlessness on National Forests" February 12, 2002

To spread their message and inflate their importance, "eco-terrorism" groups must command a prominent public stage. Unfortunately, this subcommittee hearing is aiding these so-called eco-terrorists by giving them the United States Congress as a forum.

This craving for attention is illustrated in a recent self-promoting report on the exploits of eco-terrorists that seeks to magnify the number and impact of their activities. This hearing serves the media agenda of these groups by assigning a greater importance to their role and by attempting to falsely suggest that they are a major force on the vast public lands within the National Forest System.

If you ask Forest Service employees to rank the problems they must confront daily, "eco-terrorism" would not even make the chart. I know because for over 22 years, I was a Forest Service employee and have worked in national forests throughout the West.

My name is Gloria Flora and, in my career in public service, I have occupied many positions including Forest Supervisor on the Lewis and Clark National Forest in north-central Montana and on the Humboldt-Toiyabe National Forest in Nevada and eastern California. I resigned from the Forest Service in 2000 specifically to call attention to the far greater threat of harassment, intimidation and lawlessness that haunts Forest Service employees. I have started a non-profit organization, Sustainable Obtainable Solutions, dedicated to ensuring sustainability of public lands and the communities that depend on them.

I am here today testifying on behalf of Public Employees for Environmental Responsibility or PEER. PEER is a national service organization for the scientists, land managers and law enforcement officers working on our state and federal public lands. Speaking on behalf of the organization, PEER condemns terrorism in any form as do I.

There is a problem of lawlessness facing Forest Service employees and the citizens who visit, work within or live near national forests -- but it has little to do with eco-terrorism. This afternoon I would like to discuss the nature and extent of these challenges, outline the causative factors and conclude with steps we all need to take together toward solutions.

Conflicts over public land management continue to escalate and challenge even the most innovative land stewards and community members. When values collide, the first casualty is the ability to communicate our views with civility and respect. Sometimes, and with a seemingly growing frequency, violence, or threats thereof results. Federal agents across the

West deal with hostile, even dangerous working conditions fanned by the flames of anti-government sentiment.

Each winter, California's Imperial Valley swarms with off road vehicle riders on long holiday weekends. As Bureau of Land Management agents struggle to mitigate the environmental damage caused by thousands of vehicles, more and more, they are forced to protect themselves from the ever-increasing incidents of violence against their ranks. In recent years, rangers have been attacked by mobs, run down by vehicles and assaulted with weapons by off-roaders yelling anti-government epithets.

This past Thanksgiving a record crowd of 200,000 off-roaders descended on the desert wilderness. By the end of the weekend, BLM agents had dealt with two deaths, 220 medical emergencies, 50 arrests, nearly one thousand citations, several shootings, and one ranger run over by an angry 3-wheeler.

As reported in the *New York Times* on January 2nd, Forest Service managers voiced doubts about the safety of sending their own law enforcement personnel into certain areas of these public lands because the danger is too extreme. Internal agency memos describe the situation as near-riot conditions.

Federal agents are often targets because it is their job to enforce environmental policies. In the California desert, some off-roaders resent federal decisions to close portions of the desert to vehicle use to allow the land to recover and protect the habitat of the threatened desert tortoise. As I have witnessed in other parts of the country, some people extend their anger about federal policy into violence against federal employees.

While this annual chaos in the California desert is a dramatic example, it is certainly not an isolated case. According to agency records collected and tabulated by PEER, beatings, shootings, threats and other incidents of violence against federal resource managers, primarily in the West, rose sharply in 2000, and have risen in all but one year since the Oklahoma City bombing in 1995.

Overall, attacks aimed at U.S. Forest Service employees and facilities rose by more than 20% in 2000, the latest year for which we have statistics. Incidents at Fish & Wildlife Service rose by half, while incidents at the Bureau of Land Management (BLM) rose by a third. For all three agencies combined, serious incidents rose by nearly a third in 2000.

PEER assembles these numbers because the U.S. Department of Justice has yet to implement statutory requirements that it compile and report on attacks against government workers. PEER has established its own database on violence against federal resource agency employees using the Freedom of Information Act to collect incident reports.

These numbers, however, do not begin to tell the story. Employees have reported to PEER many incidents not reflected in the official counts. The agencies have no incentive to aggressively monitor employees' working conditions. To some large extent, agencies often reflect a "no news is good news" attitude with regard to these incidents. As a result, PEER believes that the official numbers significantly understate the true number of events.

Moreover, the bare numbers do not convey the impact even one incident can have on affected employees, agency operations and public perceptions. Take one case: Guy Pence who, until his transfer, was district ranger of the Carson District on the Toiyabe National Forest (before it was combined with the Humboldt National Forest), which includes Nye County, Nevada, the heart of the anti-environmental "wise use" movement.

A Forest Service employee since he graduated college more than 25 years ago, Pence started working on the Toiyabe in 1984, and he developed a reputation as a no-nonsense manager. He suspended or canceled the permits of grazers, loggers and miners who violated permit conditions and environmental laws. One of the users Pence cited for violation was Dick Carver, a Nye County commissioner, private rancher and an outspoken "wise use" leader. Carver gained national attention (including the cover photo of *Time* magazine) in the mid-90s when he drove a bulldozer towards Forest Service rangers in an attempt to open a road that had been closed by the agency. This act added to an already alarming level of tension surrounding public land management issues in Nevada.

A few weeks before the tragedy in Oklahoma City, a bomb exploded at the Carson City ranger station. Fortunately, no one was in the office at the time. The bomb was set outside Guy Pence's office sending a clear signal as to who was the target. No suspects were ever arrested, and no group claimed responsibility.

In August 1995 a bomb exploded under Pence's personal vehicle, which was parked in his driveway. Miraculously, no one was hurt. The blast destroyed the family van and blew out the front windows of the Pence home. Luckily, Pence's wife and daughters had just left the living room. Again, no arrests were ever made and the case remains unsolved.

The Forest Service transferred Guy Pence to its Boise office where his new duties include aviation, fire, and law enforcement. The Forest Service says Pence's transfer was not a demotion, and it maintains that it did not move Pence out of fear. Most people, however, can read between the lines.

Since Pence's transfer, the Boise office has been evacuated several times due to bomb threats. And the employees on the Carson District still fear another attack. They implemented security measures that are now commonplace for protection from terrorist attack.

No matter where they are or how far they go, neither Pence, nor his family, will ever be able to forget what happened in Nevada. While Pence admits that the safety issue looms large, he is much more concerned about his family's safety than his own. He is worried more about the effect the move to Idaho has had on his wife and three daughters. His wife had to give up her teaching job, and his daughters, who grew up in Carson City, have lost life-long friendships.

Pence said, "The bombings really made us take stock of our life. Things that seemed routine or normal now seem so fragile and more precious than ever. Actions are so interconnected and their impact can ripple out to affect everyone involved."

The legacy of the Guy Pence was still very much alive when I became the Supervisor of the now-combined Humboldt-Toiyabe National Forest in 1998. By the end of 1999, I resigned my position as Forest Supervisor in protest of the pervasive and escalating intimidation and harassment of Forest Service employees. Let me be clear that I did not allege that there were prosecutable threats of direct violence that were being ignored. In the previous 18 months, there were none of which I was aware. Rather it was the insidious and increasing acts of hostilities, fueled by media sensationalism, private vendettas and political posturing which made life extremely difficult for many Forest Service employees and their families… 24 hours a day, 7 days a week.

Instead, the legacy of the previous incidents contributed to something almost more insidious: a syndrome I came to call "Fed-bashing." Fed-bashing is a tough phrase. I define it as destructive actions or words meant to hurt and belittle federal employees, personally and/or collectively. It is not much different than racism. You pick a class of people, you decide they are the source of your problems and you proceed to systematically make them unwelcome in your community. I do not begrudge anyone for being upset with certain federal laws or policies but how we handle that dislike is measure of our own personal integrity and ultimately, the yardstick of a community. Because I resent a tax, I do not have the right to personally vilify the tax collector or members of his family.

Some say that I over-reacted. In an atmosphere of hostility, how do you decide when your employees are truly at risk? How do you calculate how many insults, personal attacks in the media, refusal of service in public establishments, are "acceptable" and how many equal a precursor to violence? When actively hostile citizens threaten to break the law using "Remember Waco" as a rallying cry and the local sheriff, the FBI and the Justice Department warn you and your employees to stay 100 miles away instead of doing your job... is that the warning salvo that violence is just around the corner? The last time someone "remembered Waco" in a very visible manner, over 180 people lost their lives in Oklahoma City. None of them reported a "prosecutable threat" prior to losing their lives.

My point is simple. More than overt acts of violence should be of concern. When frustrations grow and dialogue becomes uncivil, nasty and personally demeaning toward individuals of a certain group of people, an unsavory element is attracted to the fray, like sharks to the smell of blood. There are far too many boastful threats about armed insurrection and civil uprising in the rural West to be sanguine about this situation.

Perhaps my biggest frustration was the behavior of many public officials at all levels who either turn their backs or openly condone such behavior. In response to my expressed concerns about the treatment of my employees and their families in Nevada, a member of Congress, casually quipped, "You're federal employees: What do you expect?"

This phenomenon of elected officials egging on the tensions is certainly not confined to Nevada. Recently, an elected official in Montana likened a Forest Service manager to a Nazi for not openly opposing the roadless initiative.

To evoke the image of fascism and compare it to contemporary public land management in America is at best delusional and, at worst, a disgrace to the memories of those who suffered unimaginable terror at the hands of the Nazi regime. Try to convince the relatives of millions of people who lost their lives that the situations that we face in the rural West are comparable.

To my knowledge, all elected officials, as well as Forest Service employees, sign an oath of office to uphold the Constitution and the laws of the United States. That oath should not be taken lightly. Those who wish to selectively support the laws, that is, only the ones that please them personally, should recognize that they are violating their oath of office and are doing a disservice to the public.

No matter how disturbing, these events are only the symptoms of deeper causes. Federal resource employees are targeted because of conflicts surrounding those resources. While the acreage within the National Forest System is vast, the natural resources contained within it are finite.

In many places, public lands are degraded: non-functioning, denuded riparian areas, dropping water tables, degraded water quality, sediment in streams, excessive fuel build-up, loss of biodiversity, and species heading towards extinction confront us. There are still hundreds of abandoned mines leaking acidic water with a pH of 2 and poisoning ground water, despite billions of dollars spent on clean up.

Look at the cattle industry on public land, for example. Public land grazing is a struggling industry that produces less than 4% of the nation's beef supply. In many areas, the public range can no longer sustain traditional levels of grazing. Plant species are lost, riparian areas shrink. When the lands suffer from overgrazing, people get alarmed and demand that basic stewardship be enforced. The Forest Service re-evaluates the allotment management plan and reduces allowable numbers in some places. The result is that the range con and district ranger are cast as villains attacking custom and culture. Wrong. What is the real story?

The real story is economic and social. The market for beef does not keep pace with inflation, production costs rise and middlemen profit while price on-the-hoof plummets. Trade policies loosen. Cheap, subsidized beef from other countries flood the borders. People have grown concerned about their health; they no longer trust chemicals, they want less fat in their diet. Although they buy significantly less red meat, they are willing to pay more for chemical free, low-fat beef. In reality, these changes in public taste, market forces and international trade agreements affect ranchers' livelihood far more than the laws of Congress or Forest Service policies.

Some ranchers understand that the Forest Service is not the enemy. Rather than attacking the Forest Service, ranchers figure out how they can use the research capabilities of the government and universities to help determine better techniques to graze cattle, improving weight gain while maintaining habitat diversity. They switch to lower fat breeds, and stop using chemicals. They find a niche market for the product in demand, sell directly to the retailer and get twice the price. These folks work with the agencies and organizations to develop a certification program for beef raised in environmentally sustainable methods, creating a cache for concerned consumers and higher demand. They sell a conservation easement on the ranch and keep it in the family. They thrive, the community thrives and so do their cattle and the wildlife.

By contrast, some of their neighbors try a different approach. These ranchers make sure everyone in the community knows what "those Forest Service bastards" have done to them. They violate the commitments they signed off on in their grazing permit, overgraze the land and their cattle do not thrive. They mortgage the ranch to sue the Forest Service based on what they believe is a Constitutional right to run as many cattle as they want, wherever they want on public land, because their grandfather did. They refuse to change. They lose the suit and the ranch is subdivided. They suffer and the community suffers. Whose fault is it?

When seeking the roots of complex natural resource problems, I find it worthwhile to step back and look at the larger context. This often helps us to understand why we are where we find ourselves. We must look at local and regional history, social trends, and environmental changes, while examining the national and global trends that affect us.

Looking at the social situation in the rural west, the operative word here is change. Life as we know it has changed dramatically and the pace continues to accelerate with every new technological development. Even during the recent period of broad national economic prosperity, there are plenty of pockets within the rural west with lots of folks still struggling to get by. The "haves" are getting richer while the "have nots" see their buying power and political influence waning.

A shift in demographics is also evident; geography for many is no longer essential to job. Many people can work anywhere, and you know exactly the places they want to live-- where the air is cleaner, and the mountains tower majestically over their new home in the last, best place. Indeed local culture is changing: name a town that does not have at least one place to buy espresso.

The population is shifting and growing. This requires a greater degree of tolerance and sharing; a greater degree of tempering individual demands for the sake of community. This means getting along with others by working out equitable solutions for sharing public resources.

History is replete with examples of civilizations having to share or lose their "traditional" uses. It has only been a little more than 100 years since this society appropriated all resources from the First Americans. Now, a century later, we are again thrusting massive change upon the western landscape, its people and what our culture considers "traditional use" communities. There is much to value in these hard-working decent communities and much we can do to ensure these communities continue to be viable.

Any conservation plan or policy for public lands that does not consider the economic health of both the rural communities of the intermountain west and struggling tribal nations is woefully inadequate. It is not too much to ask for the world's wealthiest nation to have a sound economic transition strategy when we change the way we value and manage the resources on public land. We cannot throw people out of work with just a shrug and a brief apology. However neither can citizens expect that their chosen way of life is an inherent right that all others must protect regardless of the consequences?

Life has never been easy for those who choose to make their living off the land. Prior to the Industrial Revolution, the vast majority of the population depended directly on natural resources for their livelihood. Since the Industrial Revolution, labor related to natural resources has been steadily declining. Now, basic extractive industries account for less than 5% of our gross national product.

This shift means that life keeps getting tougher for those who want to

188

continue to make their living off the land while contesting the changes that society mandates. This shift is just as inevitable as the massive societal transformation of the industrial revolution, the invention of the computer and introduction of mass communication. We have accelerated the rate of change--change that is inevitable.

It is not my intention to be harsh or cavalier. I have worked in small communities for over twenty years; I know how badly these dislocations can hurt. It is how we manage that change is critical for both the rural communities in the West and the surrounding landscapes. We, as a nation, cannot consume and waste, populate and communicate at this rate and expect that the rural west will be just like it was when we were growing up. There is no going back.

So, what are the solutions? Civil discourse is step one. There is no bogeyman out there. We are all in this together, like it or not. Respectful civil dialogue is an essential tool in establishing and reaching long-term goals for the preservation of our nation's natural treasures. In my opinion, this approach is essential in convincing the American public that an investment in the health of their children's inheritance is wise -- a sound fiscal strategy. Such an investment in restoration and natural wealth accumulation will also bring a sustainable prosperity to the communities previously dependent solely on extraction.

The time is right for the nation and especially the Intermountain West to adopt a new strategy in the management of public lands through civil discourse because the alternative is a widening chasm between the majority of Americans and a shrinking but steadily more extreme collection of groups fighting to maintain a fading status quo of resource extraction at the expense of clean water, productive soil and vibrant wildlife.

I recently read that a Montanan proclaimed that "we, the people, will decide" what uses will be permitted in a heated protest against the roadless initiative. He promised armed conflict and bloodshed if uses were restricted. He is right on the first item, the people will decide. And most of you know that "We, the People..." are the first words in the Constitution. It applies to all Americans. All the Americans who have been paying for the care and maintenance of the national forests, and subsidizing every use for more than 100 years will decide what we leave for the future.

We are facing predicaments that can only be resolved by civil discourse.

Through a series of events, natural and social, we are trying to make the land do more than it is capable of in terms of supporting us for the next hundred years.

Clearly one of the least effective ways of seeking resolution is to vilify the federal employees who are stewards of this land we all share. What sense does it make to shoot the messengers?

The second essential step is to end the Fed-bashing. Public officials at all levels need to provide moral and political support for the district ranger, field biologist, range conservationists and other professional struggling to faithfully execute the law and serve the public in trying circumstances.

Politicians must resist the natural urge to "pile on" when the mob demands "heads should roll." We need more rare acts of courage when public officials are willing to stake their own careers on telling people what is right when it is not popular. We need more leaders willing to stand shoulder to shoulder with embattled public servants, to let them know they are not alone and that someone in the public they serve appreciates the struggle.

In my Forest Service career I met too few real leaders. In Nevada, when my staff really needed support from higher-ups in state and federal government, there was precious little. I resigned to draw attention to that lack of support, and in that I succeeded.

What concerns me is what happens the next time? Will lessons have been learned? Are my successors in the Forest Service doomed to walk the same path, share the same frustrations and meet the same fate? I see signs and fervently hope that collaborative solutions are emerging not just on the Humboldt-Toiyabe but on the other challenging resource faults lines in national forests throughout the West.

The final step is to look to the future. We cannot lose sight of our responsibility to leave a quality environment for the future. The superfund sites and abandoned mines that we spend billions on to stabilize and prevent further damage are perfect examples of waiting until the damage is done to face the issue -- and then shifting the higher cost to the taxpayer and the legacy of pollution to our children.

I do not mean to over-simplify, there are fundamental problems that even the hardest-working folks cannot easily overcome. One is the lack of market incentives to help transition to sustainable methods in industries. Shifting from dependence on non-renewable energy sources is one area that shows promise: fuel cell technology and solar advancements are emerging methods of providing energy, while reducing demand for a non-renewable resources, reducing air pollution and ultimately global warming, as well as providing jobs that can be located in rural areas. Organic agricultural products reduce ground and water pollution, bring higher prices and can be an economical small business in rural areas. There are many deteriorated landscapes and areas of poor forest health. Restoration using the equipment and skills of forest workers is a very viable idea that needs an influx of money and a change of perspective.

A paradigm shift is required in the political leadership of the rural West. In making decisions, local leaders need to take natural capital, i.e., the real dollar value or replacement value for the goods and services that we get from the land, into account. The cost of restoring degraded landscapes frequently far exceeds the value of what has been extracted. But, a plan for managing public land as a long-term trust, ensuring we are living off the interest and not depleting the capital, is possible only with the willing, civil participation of all interested parties.

We need to be willing to collaborate on solutions rather than wanting to overpower and win. Freedom to share and hear all viewpoints was clearly seen by the crafters of the Constitution as an imperative. We need to accept the fact that we do not know everything. There is a golden opportunity to learn from our neighbors and for us to share with them our experience and knowledge. The bottom line is showing respect and civility towards others despite what you think about their opinion or in how they express their relationship with their landscape.

I suggest that our personal relationship with the land is an excellent barometer of how we relate to other people. I believe there are different levels of maturity in land relationships. A child-like attitude may lead one to take the land and its resources for granted, as if it will always be there and it will meet all of your needs. A mature attitude recognizes that you are much more transient than the land. With maturity comes the understanding that you must give and sacrifice for the sake of the relationship. What you take must be returned and never take more than you absolutely need for the sake of those who come after you. Solutions are tough. We need to recognize that no one is going to win it all. But I remind you, this is not about winning, it is about finding balance through sustainable practices.

We are in this for the long-run.

Demeaning each other will not bring about solutions, nor will it suggest to the rest of the nation that we in the West are thoughtful, reflective, inclusive individuals; people who can be trusted to make good choices and therefore deserve greater local control. If we can demonstrate to the rest of the nation that we collectively are far-sighted, cooperative stewards, we will gain the support of the rest of the nation in our efforts to reach sustainable solutions to our considerable natural resource challenges...civilly.

•

Michael Roy Pendleton, Ph.D.
Government Accountability Project
Testimony before the U.S. House Subcommittee on Forests and Forests Health for the February 12, 2002, Hearing on "Ecoterrorism"

Representing My Role As A Social Scientist and The Research I conducted While A Professor At The University Of Washington,

Thank you Mr. Chairman and committee members for inviting me here today. My name is Michael Pendleton and I am representing my work as a social scientist while at the University of Washington, and specifically my published research on forest based crime, enforcement, lawlessness and timber theft. I would like to add, however, that my testimony also reflects my experience as the grandson of a legendary North West Logger, whose small logging business was bankrupted by strategic vandalism of his equipment, and my service as a working police officer in the State of Oregon where the importance of real enforcement were made apparent. This is my testimony.

The hundreds of hours that I have spent in patrol trucks with land management enforcement officers strongly indicates that public policy on these matters would be greatly enhanced were we to broaden our understanding of crime and terrorism in our national forests. It isn't that your concern with "eco-terrorism" is wrong. Rather, it is incomplete. What I know and every "on the ground" forest officer will tell you is that the vast majority of property crime and violent acts are committed not by "eco-terrorist", but by a relatively small but known group of local residents that subscribe to a twisted view of wisdom and use. The drive-by shooting of a ranger station where the offenders emptied their automatic weapons only to stop and reload for a second pass was explained by the offenders, upon arrest, as their answer to federal management of forest and parklands. In effect those inside the ranger station nearly gave their lives for performing their jobs. The drive-by shooting is but one among many examples of blown gates, car bombings and arsons where land management employees and federal property are the clear targets of violence. The examples I cite are not, however, the work of eco-terrorists but crimes committed to service a radical right philosophy that clearly advances the "take over" of national lands from federal management and the American people. I would submit that such a view is at least as worthy of a public policy response as the one advanced by eco-terrorists.

In spite of these well known, and documented cases of domestic terrorism, little has been done to address these concerns. In fact, in the wake of the Oklahoma bombings, federal legislators actually advanced legislation to disarm land management officers to include Forest Service Law Enforcement Officers. In my article concerning crime, criminals and guns in these settings, I point out the nonsensical nature of this proposed policy. Documented crime in these settings has been escalating since 1990. During my research, 255 known offenders were identified of which 85% lived in close proximity to the National Forest under study. Forest Law Enforcement Officers, on average, contacted at least one individual during their daily patrol that was visibly armed. Of all the people encountered during this research by Forest Law Enforcement Officers, 37% were visibly armed. Criminal history research on weapons offenders encountered in natural settings reveal an astonishing profile where, on average, these offenders have 7.8 prior offenses of which half were felonies. One individual in this research accounted for 48 prior offenses. To actually suggest disarming Law Enforcement Officers in the face of this reality sent a strong message to those charged with land management.

Other, very strong signals have been sent to Forest Service Law Enforcement Officers to suggest that addressing forest crime in a meaningful way will not be rewarded. While the $40 million dollars of damage attributed to eco-terrorist groups such as the Earth Liberation Front is clearly unacceptable and should be addressed, it pales in comparison to the $100 million dollar annual loss attributed to timber theft from National Forests. Yet in spite of this chronic and well documented property crime, efforts to address this loss by Forest Service Enforcement Officers have been overtly stopped. The disbandment of the Forest Service

Timber Theft Investigations Branch in 1995, and the retaliation against its whistle blowers, was perhaps the most visible effort to stifle meaningful enforcement. But others exist as well such as the systematic dismissal of large timber theft cases, and the recent presidential pardon of a convicted timber theft offender.

Even more profound efforts to limit a law enforcement response to timber theft occur as part of a complicated system of internal Forest Service practices based on the view that timber theft is nothing but a folk crime committed by basically good people. Such a view empowers organizational practices that encourage officers to "look the other way" or face real organizational pressures to conform or get out. Law enforcement officers consistently pointed to such practices as a 10% over-cut provision in timber sale contracts, known monetary thresholds of $50 thousand dollars below which there would be no follow-up investigation by central office investigators, and fatal flaws in the handling of cases submitted to law enforcement officers thus preventing prosecution. When combined with poorly equipped and funded enforcement programs these operational practices effectively discouraged meaningful pursuit of timber thieves.

The effect of systematically ignoring timber theft has been to create an uneven playing field in the timber industry for those that choose to play within the rules. More importantly to systematically ignore the theft of trees worth millions of dollars each year is as blatantly wrong and immoral as looking the other way while a corporation fix's the price of electricity as it is also stealing its employee's retirement. In both cases greed promises to bankrupt the future lives of those to follow. If there is doubt about this, all one has to do is compare the impact of unsustained forests on a displaced logger, with the views of a 59 1/2 year old Enron employee.

Based upon my research and experience it seems clear to me that meaningful policy to address the full range of crime, terrorism and lawlessness is long overdue in America's forests. The first step is to empower and fully fund meaningful law enforcement in the National Forests. The core of this effort should be built around the policy of "blind justice". This policy would simply require the full and effective enforcement of the law against ALL who choose to offend regardless of where on the political spectrum one might shop for their justification. Specifically, terrorists who offend in the name of the environmental protection or terrorist who offend in the name of the wise use movement should be found and prosecuted to the fullest. Criminals who steal trees should be treated in the same way as those criminals who destroy property. They are both crimes and those who do those things are criminals.

Anything short of the policy of blind justice will reveal a policy that is at a minimum based upon a distorted view of crime and lawlessness in our nations forests. It follows that these distortions will promote irrelevant means to manage the full array of crime that exists, often vilifying some to the exclusion of others. At its worst, anything short of a policy of blind justice will lay transparent the bias's it serves and further undermine Americans respect and confidence in the rule of law and the commitment to doing the right thing. I urge you to adopt and fully fund a policy of "blind justice" in our nations forests.

In support of my testimony I have requested that three of my articles be placed in the record. These articles are entitled: 1) "Crime, Criminals and Guns in Natural Settings: Exploring the Basis for Disarming Federal Rangers", American Journal of Police, Vol. XV, No. 4, 1996. 2) "Looking the Other Way: The Institutional Accommodation of Tree Theft", Qualitative Sociology, Vol. 20, No. 3, 1997. 3) "Taking the Forest: The Shared Meaning of Tree Theft", Society and Natural Resources, Vol. 11, 1998.

Thank you for your attention to this most important issue.

●

The following statement and responses were sent to Congress on March 15, 2002, by Craig Rosebraugh, answering the follow-up questions demanded by Scott McInnis after the Subcommittee on Ecoterrorism.

These are Craig Rosebraugh's responses to questions posed on 3/1/2 by a person or persons unknown. In the event any response is deemed non-responsive, Mr. Rosebraugh asserts the following objections, rights, and privileges in declining to answer all questions posed at the 12 February 2002 Subcommittee on Forests and Forest Health hearing and to all questions posed by a person or persons unknown by mail and facsimile on 1 March 2002:

- Mr. Rosebraugh asserts his right to have the subcommittee's clearcut ruling on all objections interposed.

- Congress shall make no law respecting an establishment of religion, or prohibiting the free exercise thereof; or abridging the freedom of speech, or of the press; or the right of the people peaceably to assemble, and to petition the Government for a redress of grievances. First Amendment to U.S. Constitution.

- No person shall be held to answer for a capital, or otherwise infamous crime, unless on a presentment or indictment of a Grand Jury, except in cases arising in the land or naval forces, or in the Militia, when in actual service in time of War or public danger; nor shall any person be subject for the same offense to be twice put in jeopardy of life or limb; nor shall be compelled in any criminal case to be a witness against himself, nor be deprived of life, liberty, or property, without due process of law; nor shall private property be taken for public use, without just compensation. Fifth Amendment to U.S. Constitution.

- The enumeration in the Constitution, of certain rights, shall not be construed to deny or disparage others retained by the people. Ninth Amendment to U.S. Constitution.

- The powers not delegated to the United States by the Constitution, nor prohibited by it to the States, are reserved to the States respectively, or the people. Tenth Amendment to the U.S. Constitution.

- A committee of Congress can have no general powers to probe the affairs of the citizen.

-The penumbral constitutional right to privacy.

-The question is double and/or complex, please rephrase it.

-The question is asked for an improper purpose, and/or is prejudicial and/or is designed to make witness commit perjury, contempt, or state untruths.

- Mr. Rosebraugh is entitled to a transcript of the 12 February 2002 hearing, and to any other statements made on the record under oath by Mr. Rosebraugh to avoid inconsistent testimony under oath.

- The question is not pertinent or relevant to an authorized subject matter of the hearing.

- The bounds of the power of the committee have been exceeded. The subcommittee, committee, or the House of Representatives are not authorized to conduct this hearing or conduct this investigation.

- House rules and committee rules do not authorize these questions.

- The subcommittee has failed to properly apply the House Rule Xl(k)(5) to the effect that it shall investigate the witness in executive session if a public hearing might unjustly injure the reputation of a witness.

- No probable cause existed for the issuance of the subpoena.

- The question is unnecessary for the investigation.

1) Do you view violence against individuals, organizations and other enterprises that work and play on the national forests as a legitimate means of seeking public policy change, specifically with respect to management of the nation's forests?
    Yes.

2) Do you believe that destroying Forest Service property is a legitimate means of pursuing public policy change?
    Yes.

3) You claim to have never had any role in an ELF related attack, and yet you loudly proclaim the virtues of "direct action" against government and industry. If you believe so deeply in ELF's cause, so much that you encourage and recruit others to partake in that cause, why aren't you willing to engage in the acts of environmentally motivated aggression yourself?
    I do not adopt any factual assumptions made in the preamble to your question. I would not be effective as a spokesperson if I were so involved.

4) There is a widely held belief that, if ELF's attacks continue to increase in frequency and magnitude as they have in recent years on the national forests and other places, it is very likely only a matter of time before human life is lost. The FBI has said this, as have many others. Do you

share in the view that it's just a matter of time before someone is badly hurt or killed by the ELF?

I do not adopt any factual assumptions made in the preamble to your question. I do not know.

5) Do you still agree with this statement attributed to you in The Bear Deluxe Magazine? "If you are talking about fires, and the use of incendiary devices, there is the danger of people being near or inside that building, or the fire could spread to another building. There are always dangers."

I do not adopt any factual assumptions made in your question. Yes.

6) In late October 1996, a Forest Service truck was firebombed, and an incendiary device that failed to detonate was found planted atop the roof of the Willamette National Forest Building. Fortunately, the device was located and removed and no one was injured. Are you familiar with this attack on the Willamette National Forest? You claim that ELF seeks to protect all life on earth, yet if this device had detonated, it is possible - indeed probable - that someone could have been seriously injured or killed. How can ELF reasonably claim to defend all life, and yet so routinely and recklessly endanger it?

I do not adopt any factual assumptions made in the preamble to your question. See all objections, rights, and privileges asserted above.

7) Do you find it disconcerting that, when ELF firebombed forestry research labs at the Universities of Washington and Minnesota in 2001 and 2002 respectively, the fire quickly spread to other areas on both campuses, potentially endangering lives in buildings not targeted by ELF? In the case of the University of Washington, the fire spread to an adjacent library. And in the case of the University of Minnesota, the man-made fire spread to a soils testing center in the near vicinity.

I do not find it disconcerting that ELF firebombed, without physically harming anyone, research into genetic modification of our natural world for profit. Genetic engineering is a threat to life on this planet. As to the other factual allegations, I do not know whether or not they are true, so I do not feel comfortable commenting on them.

8) Are you personally concerned that one day an ELF or ALF perpetrated attack will wind up killing or wounding someone?

No, I am more concerned with massive numbers of people dying at the hands of greedy capitalists if such actions are not taken.

9) Do the Earth Liberation Front and the Earth Liberation Front's North American Press Office have a tax status? Are they non-profits?

    a) I do not know. Can't you ask the IRS?

    b) I do not know. Can't you ask the Oregon Secretary of State?

10) Do the Earth Liberation Front and the Earth Liberation Front North American Press Office receive outside donations that fund operations, income for ELF press office employs, travel expenses, legal expenses or other incidental costs? IF so, what are the sources of these donations?

    I do not know.

11) Has the North American Earth Liberation Front ever received direct financial support from any animal rights or environmental groups to support program activities?

    I do not know.

12) Has the Earth Liberation Front Press Office ever received contributions from the People for the Ethical Treatment of Animals? Did you ever sign, endorse, cash or deposit a check from PETA on behalf of the Earth Liberation Front Press Office?

    I do not recall.

13) To the best of your knowledge, has the Earth Liberation Front or the Earth Liberation Front North American Press Office ever filed income tax returns with the IRS?

    I do not know.

14) Did you have any prior knowledge whatsoever that the Earth Liberation Front intended to destroy the Vail lodge with fire?

    See all objections, rights, and privileges asserted above.

15) Subsequent to the attacks, have you had any conversations, received any written or electronic communications, or acquired any first or second hand information through any means identifying the perpetrators of the Vail arson?

    See all objections, rights, and privileges asserted above.

16) Hypothetically, if you would have had prior knowledge or after the fact knowledge about the Vail arson, or any other ELF attack, would you report it to the authorities?

See all objections, rights, and privileges asserted above.

17) Do you know who Michael Conn is?

Michael Conn is a researcher at the Oregon Regional Primate Research Center in Beaverton, Oregon. Conn wastes hundreds of thousands of federal tax-dollars torturing and killing monkeys, a practice that has in no way benefited human health.

18) Were you ever arrested for trespassing on the Oregon Regional Primate Center where Mr. Conn works?

See all objections, rights, and privileges asserted above.

19) Why was there an index card with Mr. Conn's name and home address in your residence? Was either ELF or ALF planning to take "direct action" against Mr. Conn or his property? If not, why was Mr. Conn's name and address in your possession?

See all objections, rights, and privileges asserted above.

20) Leslie James Pickering is the new spokesperson for the Earth Liberation Front. To the best of your knowledge, has Mr. Pickering ever been involved in, had prior knowledge about, aided, abetted or in any way assisted in the commission of an ELF or ALF attack?

See all objections, rights, and privileges asserted above.

21) David Barbarash is the spokesperson for ELF's sister organization, the Animal Liberation Front. To the best of your knowledge, has Mr. Barbarash ever been involved in, had prior knowledge about, aided, abetted or in any way assisted in the commission of an ELF or ALF attack?

See all objections, rights, and privileges asserted above.

22) Rodney Adam Coronado was convicted for his role in a 1992 arson at Michigan State University. To the best of your knowledge, has Mr. Coronado been involved in, had prior knowledge about, aided, abetted or in any way assisted in the commission of an ELF or ALF attack since 1992?

See all objections, rights, and privileges asserted above.

23) In a September 7, 2001 AP story you said of the February 12 hearing: "These people are trying to stop the work of the Earth Liberation Front. I'm not going to participate in any effort that is going to incarcerate any of the people involved in the ELF or stop their work." Do you have specific

information that might lead to the incarceration of members of the Earth Liberation Front? If not, why are you afraid of saying something that might lead to the incarceration of ELF members? Is this the reason you chose to repeatedly plead the 5th Amendment in response to questions offered by Members of Congress during the February 12th hearing?

a) No

b) I do not accept your factual assumption in this question. It is clear you want to incarcerate ELF members. I was stating that I was uninterested in helping you.

c) I do not recall.

24) As you know, several members of this Committee wrote a number of national environmental groups, urging them to publicly condemn eco-terrorism, ELF, and, by extension, you. As you also know, all of the organizations did. Does this lack of support among national environmental groups frustrate you? What would you say in response to their condemnations of ELF and ALF?

Are you asking what I know or telling me? Did you really ask them to condemn me or did your letter not even mention me? Are you sure all of the organizations did, or are you exaggerating? Did you select only groups that must rely on the good graces of Congress for "success?"

a) No

b) Throughout the history of social movements globally, struggles have relied upon a variety of tactics, both legal and illegal in nature. I would hope that if those groups are actually concerned with stopping the destruction of the natural environment, they would understand and support this diversity.

25) In your press statement about the Vail lodge firebombing, you said that the area slated for ski area expansion was some of the last, best lynx habitat in North America. Do you know how long it has been since anyone - environmentalists, biologists, wildlife enthusiasts - has seen a lynx in the area that you called some of the last, best habitat for the lynx in North America?

No I do not, but that is irrelevant to the fact that the area is some of the last, best Lynx habitat in North America.

26) What role if any did you play in creating, writing and speaking in the Earth Liberation Front training video "Igniting the Revolution?" Who paid the production costs? What was the underlying purpose of this video?

a) I spoke in it.

b) I do not recall.

c) Educating the public

27) In that video, and in a number of interviews and other written accounts, you talk about how ELF prefers arson to all other forms of "direct action" because it inflicts maximum economic and symbolic damage on the target. Please elaborate on this.

I think this is accurate. I have no further elaboration to offer.

28) In the ELF's recruitment video and in other public documents, you also talk about the need to attack symbols of corporate capitalism that promote the spread of what you call "the destructive American Dream." Is this correct?

Yes.

29) When you were still serving as the Earth Liberation Front's Spokesperson, a Q & A page appeared on ELF's website called "Frequently Asked Questions About the ELF." Is this document familiar to you? Did you write this? If not, do you know who did?

I do not recall.

30) In the "Frequently Asked Questions" piece the authors listed Mt. Rushmore, the Statue of Liberty and Wall Street on a short list of "forms and symbols of capitalism [that] can be targeted successfully to greatly influence the impact the capitalist state has on life." Remember, in your video and in other places you have frequently said that firebombing is the best tactic to use in a direct action. Taken together, aren't you encouraging ELF's cronies to go out and firebomb the Statue of Liberty? Since ELF has shown no signs of slowing down since 9-11, do you still think that, on an abstract level, it would be a good or desirable thing for the ELF to attack other symbols of capitalism in New York City, like Wall Street offices?

a) I don't know.

b) Yes.

31) Ted Kazcinski, the Unabomber, admitted in Court that he located his last two murder victims on published Earth First! hit lists. Kazcinski is now listed on an Earth Liberation Front related Website (www.spiritoffree dom.org.uk/elf.htm) as a "Prisoner of War." Do you consider Kazcinski a "Prisoner of War" and a comrade-in-arms in the struggle against corporate capitalism?

See all objections, rights, and privileges asserted above.

32) In your opinion, is Kazcinski a member of the Earth Liberation Front?

    See all objections, rights, and privileges asserted above.

33) How do you explain this quote taken directly from an ELF-related website (www.spiritoffreedom.org.uk/elf.htm)? "Donations of support (for Kazcinski) are needed and sincerely appreciated. If you'd like to send support funds, please write Dr. Kazcinski (if you'd like to include a few blank sheets of lines writing paper, NO stamps, it would help him avoid other bureaucratic hassles as well). Thereafter please send donations as a postal money order, blank cheque, etc. (including his name and ID number), DIRECTLY to the address listed below."

    My explanation is that there is an attempt to raise donations for Dr. Kazcinski.

34) How long has ELF asked its membership to write and make donations to Kazcinski? How does this support for the Unabomber square with ELF's purported adherence to non-violence toward humans?

    a) I am not aware of the ELF asking its membership to make donations to Dr. Kazcinski.

    b) I don't know.

35) The Oregonian reported recently that you are attending school at Goddard College and that your master's thesis is "Rethinking Nonviolence: Arguing for the Legitimacy of Armed Struggle." With regard to your thesis, what do you mean by "armed struggle?" "Armed" in what way? In your thesis, will you argue that the time has come for armed resistance against the U.S. government?

    a) a movement involving political violence.

    b) I am not arguing for one specific sort of political violence.

    c) I don't know, it's still a work in progress.

36) Jeffrey Luers was sentenced last year to 23 years in prison on ecoterrorism-related charges. Have you ever met or had any direct or indirect contact with Mr. Luers? What advice would you give this young man as he wastes away in prison for the next 2-plus decades? Are you at all concerned that your fate may be the same as Mr. Luers?

    a) See all objections, rights, and privileges asserted above.

    b) I don't know.

    c) No.

37) When Luers was asked how he first became involved in eco-terrorism in a recent interview conducted by EarthFirst! Journal, he responded: "I was radicalized by anti-authoritarian, anarchist beliefs as well as animal rights. I got involved first in 1997 working for CalPIRG and canvassing for the Sierra Club... Power cedes nothing without demand. The only way to bring about change is to fight for it... Using fire does two things. It destroys 'the targets,' which not only stops the destructive practice they are engaged in, but also causes severe economic damage to those responsible. It also receives media attention. Nothing is more effective at drawing attention to an issue than violence... The mainstream media has been all over it, and sympathetic. I've been given a forum to radicalize other people." Do you share these sentiments?

See all objections, rights, and privileges asserted above.

38) On January 29, 2002, ELF took credit for firebombing the University of Minnesota's Microbial and Plant Genomics Research Center, which at the time was under construction. According to the Dean of the University's College of Biological Sciences, the building was being built to house genomics research focused on "finding ways to reduce use of pesticides and fertilizers in agriculture, find renewable alternatives to fossil fuels, identify new strategies for cleaning the environment, and preserve ecosystems." In what way is reducing reliance on pesticides and looking for clean energy alternatives bad for the environment?

I don't know how those objectives would be bad, but I don't take the dean's words as gospel.

39) What gives the ELF the right to impose its incredibly narrow view of environmentalism on researchers at the University of Minnesota who have literally spent their lives searching for ways to keep our environment safe, clean and healthy? What's more, what gives ELF's henchman the right to firebomb another person's property based on differences of opinion about what constitutes "true environmentalism?"

a) I do not agree with your factual assumptions and biased opinions. I am not convinced that researchers at the U of Minnesota have literally spent their lives searching for ways to keep our environment safe, clean, and healthy. I believe the ELF has the right to uphold natural law, protecting those substances that allow all of us to survive on the planet - clean air, clean water, and clean, healthy soil.

b) See answer to 39a.

40) The Southern Poverty Law Center, a renowned organization dedicated to the preservation and enhancement of civil rights, had this to say about the Earth Liberation Front in its Summer 2001 Intelligence Report: "...ELF's use of underground violence strongly resembles ex-Klansman Louis Beam's concept of 'leaderless resistance.' The ELF is composed of autonomous and secretive 'cells' that initiate terrorist acts independently, and do not communicate with or even know one another... like most groups on the radical right today, the ELF sees global capitalism as the enemy... There is an obvious ideological gulf separating the radical right, with its racist and fascist appeals, from the left-wing, environmentalist Earth Liberation Front, which advocates 'equality, social justice and... compassion for all life.' But when it comes to the current economic and political system, the two groups increasingly find themselves on the same side." How do you feel about ELF being compared to the Klu Klux Klan? IS this an accurate comparison? Do you feel a kinship of cause with "racists and fascists," as the Southern Poverty Law Center contends?

    A) That is ridiculous and insulting. I would expect the Southern Poverty Law Center to have more intelligence than that.

    B) No.

    C) No.

41) Please define "direct action."

    An action that is direct. Something done or accomplished without intermediary agents or conditions.

42) Do acts of eco-terrorism typically follow after a call for "direct action?"

    I don't know.

43) When the ELF called for "direct action" to protest this hearing, and included the photos, names, and addresses of Members of Congress on the same website (www.protectcivilliberties.com), what was its purpose? Were they seeking to intimidate the Members of this Subcommittee and the witnesses?

    A) I was not aware that the ELF "called for 'direct action' to protest this hearing.

    B) I do not know.

44) Did you play any role in the construction of the aforementioned website calling for "direct action' in conjunction with this hearing? Did you ever have a conversation with anyone regarding the construction, of

www.protectcivilliberties.com?
>A) Yes.
>B) I don't recall.

45) You claim that our environment has gotten progressively dirtier over the years. But the facts don't support that. The facts tell us that air quality has improved by 64% from 1970-2000, toxins released have declined by 45% between 1988 and 1998, and erosion was reduced 32% between 1982 and 1997. Presently, few trees are harvested off the National Forests than has been the case in a very, very long time. Isn't it true that ELF's rationale for firebombing homes and schools and government buildings is grounded in lies and self-serving propaganda rather than in facts?

>No. I question the truth of the above stated "facts."

46) In an ABC News interview last year, you said that "every single social movement that has actually gained success has used a variety of tactics." In your mind, then, is ELF's relationship with mainstream environmental groups akin to a one-two punch? If so, what is your response to the countless environmental organizations who condemned ELF, and by extension you, prior to the February 12 hearing? Do you feel any disdain for mainstream environmentalists based on their unwillingness to take direct action to protect, the environment?

>A) No.

>B) I am not aware of countless environmental organizations condemning me and ELF prior to the February 12 hearing. I prefer to respond to groups after I know what they have said. Can you please send me each organization's response?

>C) No.

47) An Indiana based Internet news-service (Nuvo.net) ran a story on ELF following an April 30, 1999 ELF attack on construction and logging equipment associated with a highway expansion project near Bloomington, Indiana. The story featured the comments of an individual associated with an environmental group called Valley Watch. With regard to ELF's attack on the construction site, he said" "As a non-violent environmental activist, I can tell you that's not my style. But we're all upping our pressure these days, and I can certainly understand the frustration that leads someone to take these kinds of actions... I'm not going to condone ELF, but I'm not going to condemn them either. After all, violence against property is not violence against people." Publicly, the vast majority of mainstream environmental groups have condemned ELF, and you personally for that

matter. Do you think a lot of mainstream above ground environmental groups share the sentiments of this individual from Valley Watch, public condemnations notwithstanding?

I have no idea.

48) On April 30, 2000 ELF, through you Mr. Rosebraugh, took credit for sabotaging construction and logging equipment used for a highway expansion project 45 miles from Indianapolis, Indiana. Do you remember issuing a statement of credit for ELF in conjunction with the Indiana attack?

I don't recall.

49) In an interview with an Indiana Internet news provider (www.nuvo.net) following the aforementioned attack, you went beyond merely admitting that ELF was responsible for the April 30 siege. You told the news outlet this: "I wouldn't be surprised to see more ELF direct action in the future over there." Those comments are interesting because exactly two months later, on June 30, ELF took part in a large-scale tree spiking in the same great State of Indiana, just as you had forecasted. Your prediction of additional attacks on April 30 was one of three things: (1) an incredibly good guess; (2) a prescient moment on your part; or (3) the product of direct knowledge that ELF would attack again in the area. Which one was it: a good guess, a prescient moment or direct knowledge?

No. I question the truth of the above stated "facts."

46) In an ABC News interview last year, you said that "every single social movement that has actually gained success has used a variety of tactics." In your mind, then, is ELF's relationship with mainstream environmental groups akin to a one-two punch? If so, what is your response to the countless environmental organizations who condemned ELF, and by extension you, prior to the February 12 hearing? Do you feel any disdain for mainstream environmentalists based on their unwillingness to take direct action to protect, the environment?

A) No.

B) I am not aware of countless environmental organizations condemning me and ELF prior to the February 12 hearing. I prefer to respond to groups after I know what they have said. Can you please send me each organization's response?

C) No.

47) An Indiana based Internet news-service (Nuvo.net) ran a story on

ELF following an April 30, 1999 ELF attack on construction and logging equipment associated with a highway expansion project near Bloomington, Indiana. The story featured the comments of an individual associated with an environmental group called Valley Watch. With regard to ELF's attack on the construction site, he said" "As a non-violent environmental activist, I can tell you that's not my style. But we're all upping our pressure these days, and I can certainly understand the frustration that leads someone to take these kinds of actions... I'm not going to condone ELF, but I'm not going to condemn them either. After all, violence against property is not violence against people." Publicly, the vast majority of mainstream environmental groups have condemned ELF, and you personally for that matter. Do you think a lot of mainstream above ground environmental groups share the sentiments of this individual from Valley Watch, public condemnations notwithstanding?

    I have no idea.

48) On April 30, 2000 ELF, through you Mr. Rosebraugh, took credit for sabotaging construction and logging equipment used for a highway expansion project 45 miles from Indianapolis, Indiana. Do you remember issuing a statement of credit for ELF in conjunction with the Indiana attack?

    I don't recall.

49) In an interview with an Indiana Internet news provider (www.nuvo.net) following the aforementioned attack, you went beyond merely admitting that ELF was responsible for the April 30 siege. You told the news outlet this: "I wouldn't be surprised to see more ELF direct action in the future over there." Those comments are interesting because exactly two months later, on June 30, ELF took part in a large-scale tree spiking in the same great State of Indiana, just as you had forecasted. Your prediction of additional attacks on April 30 was one of three things: (1) an incredibly good guess; (2) a prescient moment on your part; or (3) the product of direct knowledge that ELF would attack again in the area. Which one was it: a good guess, a prescient moment or direct knowledge?

    A good guess.

50) Who first contacted you about serving as the spokesperson for the Earth Liberation Front? How did he/she contact you?

    a) Jesus Christ
    b) It was a spiritual sort of thing.

51) During the time you served as spokesperson for the Earth Liberation Front, how did you support yourself?

      muffins.

52) During your time with the Earth Liberation Front Press Office, how large was the staff? If there were other staff, were they volunteers or working on a paid basis?

      See all objections, rights, and privileges asserted above.

53) Why did you resign as a spokesperson for the Earth Liberation Front?

      To step back from the spotlight and allow others to come forward and demonstrate their ideological and philosophical support of the ELF.

54) Do you still communicate with the Earth Liberation Front and Animal Liberation Front Press Offices? If so, how often?

      See all objections, rights, and privileges asserted above.

7.

GUERRILLA NEWS NETWORK INTERVIEW • SPRING 2002

EARTH LIBERATION FRONT 1997-2002

Burn, Baby, Burn
The ELF: Terrorists or Defenders of the Planet?
Guerrilla News Network
Spring 2002

Quick-- name the FBI's number-one domestic terrorist organization.

If you said a cabal of radical Muslims or a posse of white supremacists, you'd be the weakest link. The U.S. government's most-wanted, homegrown terrorist group is the Earth Liberation Front (ELF).

First formed in England from an Earth First! splinter group in the mid-90s, the highly-secretive, non-hierarchical organization has been responsible for a well-orchestrated campaign of arson attacks against businesses and organizations that they claim are destroying the planet.

Basing much of its structure and ethics on those of the Animal Liberation Front (ALF), the ELF's first official attack in the U.S. was in 1997. Since then, it has caused tens of millions of dollars in damage, notably including the burning of a ski resort in Vail, Colorado ($28 million); various genetic engineering labs and a Republican Party office in Indiana. Its web site takes credit for more than three dozen acts and even includes a handy primer on "setting fires with electrical timers."

Because of its autonomous cell structure, the ELF has so far been extremely successful in eluding law enforcement. But last summer, Jeff "Free" Luers, a 22-year-old ELF operative (*editorial note; inaccurate*), was convicted of setting fire to a Chevrolet dealership in Eugene, Oregon and attempting to ignite a gasoline tanker nearby. The fire torched three pickup trucks, while the tanker failed to ignite. No one was hurt. Luers was sentenced to 22 years & 8 months. Three days before he was sentenced, as he sat in jail, another ELF cell hit the same dealership, causing ten times the damage - burning 36 SUVs.

To its growing roster of powerful critics, the ELF is a group of terrorists who, like Al Qaeda, pose a threat to America's very "way of life." The loaded rhetoric has only increased since 9/11. Armed with increased powers from the USA/PATRIOT Act and other more recent easings of restrictions on government snooping, law enforcement appears willing to do whatever it takes to take the group down. During a Feb. 12

212

Congressional hearing, Rep. George Nethercutt (R-WA) stated, "The best way to deal with eco-terrorists is to use the same tactics we're using in our current war on terrorism."

The criticism is not just from inside the Beltway; some moderate Greens call the ELF reckless, immature and ultimately harmful to an environmental movement trying to gain mainstream support.

But the ELF doesn't seem to care what either thinks. Members see themselves as eco-warriors perpetrating "health ops" - the vanguard of a radical fringe willing to put their freedom on the line to save an increasingly threatened environment. Their attacks are meant to send a message, and they hit polluters, clear-cutters, and others they see as enemies of the planet where it hurts the most: in the wallet. They claim to take all necessary precautions to avoid any human or animal casualties. So far none of their arson attacks have hurt anyone.

With all the heat, you might think tracking down the ELF's new spokesperson, Leslie James Pickering, would be difficult. In fact, the group welcomes getting the word out. So recently, GNN's info-guerrillas in the misty Northwest, Charles Maol and Roland Glasgow, met up with the bespectacled Pickering at a Portland café and listened as he outlined the group's ideology of economic sabotage, their blistering critique of moderates, the government's seeming inability to infiltrate them and the long road ahead.

This month, the UN issued a disturbing new report in which it stated that if current development continues unabated, in the next 30 years the Earth could be littered with a wasteland of urban slums, see the extinction of a quarter of its mammal species and have significant populations dying of thirst and water-borne disease.

Is the ELF our last, best hope for avoiding this horrifying vision? Or is the group just a bunch of aggro-treehuggers armed with outdated ideas and a dangerous propensity to burn things?

You decide . . .

Charles: *What's your reaction to the FBI and Congress listing the Earth Liberation Front and Animal Liberation Front as the primary domestic terrorist organizations in the United States?*

LJP: The first thing that comes to my mind is the FBI and the system in general are taking the ELF and ALF very seriously because they perceive them as a threat, and in a way that's just what the ALF and ELF want.

I mean, they're attempting to change the system. They're trying to say that we have a completely different value system. We value clean air and clean water, clean soil and the environment more than property and profits and therefore we're the antithesis of the system. For them to say we are a threat is reassuring of our effectiveness as an organization.

At the same time they are basically just targeting industries and corporations in particular. They're not necessarily aimed at the overthrow of the United States government. It's a way for the system to blow the whole thing out of proportion so they can get more funding, more resources, and effectively criminalize the group in the eye of the public... The FBI wants more money to combat this. They want more resources. They want to put anyone who might be an anarchist or a revolutionary or an activist in jail or behind bars or whatever. So it's a big issue.

I personally wish that the ELF/ALF weren't the biggest domestic terrorist threat in the United States. I wish there were an organization that really was targeting the system at large and was being really active in the overthrow of the system because it seems as though we really need to stop and re-evaluate what we're doing and start taking actions that are going to start bringing revolutionary change.

Roland: *How much is public opinion important to the ELF and ALF?*

LJP: I don't know if public opinion is as necessary as getting real and honest and factual information to the public. It's not necessary that the public love the ELF and have ELF t-shirts. It's more important that people understand the motivation and desperation and the tactics that the ELF are engaging in and say, "Well, whether or not I would personally engage in that type of activity, the system is on a suicidal path and we need to do something to stop it immediately and therefore I can at least relate to the ELF on a level."

Roland: *What's the defense to attacks by more mainstream groups who argue the ELF's tactics are creating a backlash to the movement and actually worsens the cause even more?*

LJP: That's another big question. It's based on what I consider is the false assumption that the mainstream movement is actually succeeding on the path that it's engaging in.

We've seen throughout history several examples of successful social justice movements, and every one I've been able to study had an element of radical direct action, economic sabotage and property destruction to it. It can be anything from the Boston Tea Party to stuff that the Black Panthers were doing, and for these mainstream groups to completely come out and condemn the ELF personally shows that they're not part of any revolutionary movement whatsoever. They're happy with their petty crumbs that they're licking off the floor from lobbying and doing national day for animal rights or whatever. They're happy with their minor successes and they are just going to keep going bringing in their non-profit dollars until they retire.

I don't really care what the Sierra Club says. They're monopolizing ideology as to how to effect change and that is essentially why movements aren't successful.

Charles: *Let's talk about tactics for bit. What kinds of tactics are typical in the ELF? What kinds of tactics have been most successful and what tactics have failed miserably?*

LJP: The ALF, throughout the 80s and 90s and up until today, it seemed like they focused on the actual liberation of animals, the freeing of animals which usually consisted of burglary, you know, breaking and entering, freeing animals and finding new homes for them. They also did other kinds of sabotage which didn't entail freeing animals or might have been coupled with the freeing of animals. They destroyed meat trucks for example, or after they freed animals from the vivisection labs they would burn that lab down.

But the ELF is a different story. While it's structured like the ALF and has lots of similarities to the ALF, it's coming from a different background. It comes from-- dare I say-- the Earth First! Background, where there was an element of economic sabotage going on already that was very different. It was sort of unclaimed, quiet, sneak in there in the middle of the night and sabotage a bulldozer, cut down a billboard or spray paint something on a billboard and never take responsibility for it and never try to connect it to

215

the movement. It seems as though that was going on in the 80s and people involved in that thought, "Well, this is a good idea but we're not taking it far enough."

It's said that in 1992 a group broke off of Earth First! in Europe and started the first Earth Liberation Front chapter. Since then, ELF has come to the United States.

The first claimed action was in 1997, and they've mainly engaged in arson because it has a major effect in a few ways: It causes massive economic damage to its targets. On average, I think it's a million dollars per action that the ELF has caused. It's also very good at getting attention. Now, whether that attention is positive or negative is another issue, but it does draw attention to things like genetic engineering, which basically goes on behind closed doors. The third and most powerful aspect to it is that it is actually, really beginning to be a threat. The system views it as a movement that is very radical in their tactics and is potentially escalating them even further and therefore pays attention to them.

People hear about arson, not just going in with spray paint or freeing some chickens; it's something that's very serious and takes a lot of dedication and sincerity to risk your own personal freedom for that kind of thing. And it affects the public consciousness and the political climate in a way that really makes people stop and think, "Wait a minute. Maybe the United States isn't perfect. There's a group out there that's completely the opposite of what they're trying to perpetrate—the ideas they're trying to perpetrate in people's minds—and they're taking militant direct action against them and they've not stopped."

It's been going on for over four years now, and that has an effect on the population, not just the liberal activist population but also the mainstream population and the right wing or whatever you want to call the industry-minded, capitalist people. It's a threat. It's a sense that maybe I can't just build this massive genetic engineering compound without getting it torched. So I think it's effective on a lot of different levels.

Charles: *How does the structure of the ELF/ALF, the anonymity of its members, protect the cells carrying these actions out?*

LJP: First and foremost, the structure of the autonomous, loose-knit, non-hierarchical Earth Liberation Front/ Animal Liberation Front protects them from capture. There is no leader. There's nobody they can pin down. They have no idea if the person or people that are responsible for Vail are also responsible for Boise Cascade. They have no idea whatsoever. Nobody does, and that's the beauty of it.

But at the same time it goes beyond that, because what they're displaying is a non-hierarchical structure, which is essentially a model of a solution to the sort of oppressive aspects of hierarchy which we are living under in this society. For organizations like the Sierra Club or whoever to just mimic the system's structure while trying to change the system is almost a joke. You know, you have to reevaluate where the problems are coming from in the first place and the ELF has done that. They've created a structure that's completely different. It's the antithesis of the system.

Charles: *Could you speak about the security culture of groups like the ELF?*

LJP: Security culture is a vague term. It can mean anything from knowing what to do if an agent knocks at your door, knowing how to talk or not talk to police officers. In what kind of situation is it okay to engage in certain types of activities and what kind of situation isn't that okay.

The ELF, more specifically, their model of security is that there is no hierarchy. It's basically an ideology. You know if you believe in the values and ideas that are vaguely expressed by the ELF then you can follow their guidelines—their three guidelines. You can follow those guidelines, form your own cell and begin taking action in the name of the Earth Liberation Front.

Therefore, in the case I already used, the people who are responsible for Vail might not know-- and most likely have no idea-- who was responsible for Boise Cascade. And that makes it so the people who get busted for Vail are unable, even if they wanted to, which I'm sure they don't, they are unable to lead the authorities to the people who are responsible for Boise Cascade.

That's a model that I think evolved out of the failures of a lot of groups in the 60s and 70s: The groups that were militant in their tactics but were still based on a hierarchical system which is able to be taken out, the same way government is able to be taken out, the same way corporations are going to be taken out.

217

This is a group where even if all the ELF cells were taken out tomorrow, next week someone could come across the ELF guidelines, form their own cell and start taking action. Or ten years from now, someone could come across it and start taking action. Or twenty years from now, someone could start a group based on the same thing and could be very powerful the way the ELF is very powerful.

Charles: *What are the ELF guidelines?*

LJP: They're essentially to engage in economic sabotage against corporations and government agencies profiting from the destruction of the environment. The second one is to take any necessary precautions to prevent injury to humans or animals. Like, if there was a fish tank in the building or a dog or something like that, they would eliminate the threat of harm to that animal, let alone a security guard or someone sleeping in the building or whatever.

And the third is to express to the public through the media or through whatever source they feel necessary their intent and their reasoning and their logic behind whatever they are doing, to expose the oppression they are fighting against.

As a spokesperson, when a communiqué comes in to the press office I have to evaluate it and make sure I consider it to be an official ELF communiqué—It has to fall into those three guidelines. If there is no communiqué to the action and there is something like ELF spay painted on the scene, it might have been an excellent action, it might have been the best thing that could have been done for that action, but I'm not going to come out and say it was an official ELF action because it didn't follow that last guideline.

Sometimes there might be a good reason to not claim responsibility for something and I think that is necessary in some situations, but as a spokesperson I can't say that is ELF just because there is spray paint.

Roland: *The ELF has been labeled "eco-terrorists" by the media. Does the ELF have a preferred term and what do you think of that label?*

LJP: That label is something I don't even imagine we can ever shed at this point without a complete revolution. The media has grabbed onto that and they are not letting go until they get taken down. And they do that, again, because they perceive the ELF as a threat and they want to label them and create as negative a stigma around them as they possibly can. I don't believe the ELF is a terrorist organization simply because they don't engage in terror. They engage in economic sabotage.

Those corporations, those government entities, those individuals who are destroying the Earth and oppressing people are doing so because they are making a lot of money at it. That's their motivation. Corporations are in existence specifically to make money. So what the ELF does to counteract that is engage in economic sabotage. They want to eliminate the profit motive.

They have never intended to harm anyone and that's why they never have harmed anyone. If they wanted to conduct a terrorist act they would, because basically they are facing the same charges as a terrorist is if they ever get caught. They are already getting life in prison. If Rep. Nethercutt has anything to do about it, they will be getting the death penalty. If they actually believed that type of activity would be the most effective to engage in, they would be engaging in it. So clearly to me they are a sabotage organization.

They are arsonists. They are vandals. They are criminals. I don't have any qualms about that. I don't want to make them look any less radical then they are, because frankly, the radical aspect of it is what gets them attention and makes them effective. But they aren't terrorists; they just aren't. And if you think about what you are saying when you are calling them eco-terrorists or just terrorists in general, you realize that they are not engaging in terrorism.

Charles: *Who are eco-terrorists?*

LJP: Eco-terrorists are people who are terrorizing the environment, which is basically everyone in the government right now. Basically, everyone in any of the pollution industries. Any capitalist out there right now. Eco-terrorists are the people getting burned by the ELF.

Charles: *Do you think the ELF and ALF can be stopped?*

LJP: No. I think there might be the occasional ELF/ALF cell that slips up, and we have seen a couple examples of that. Specifically with the

ALF, there was a group in Salt Lake City that was composed of a bunch of individuals who had personal issues, and that effected the organization. I don't know what specifically happened, but they were involved in subcultures and some other things that were very sort of rumor oriented, and too many people knew about what was going on and people ended up getting busted.

The situation in New York with a series of development homes and there were a bunch of luxury condominiums being developed on like wetlands in Long Island and there were three juveniles prosecuted and convicted for some of those actions and a forth individual who wasn't a juvenile, was an adult, and is fighting it, claims he didn't have anything to do with it. Essentially one of those individuals was bragging about it-- I think to their friends-- and that is what led to it.

I think that most of the people involved in these activities aren't of that nature. That's just an assumption on my part. I don't think that most people involved in the Earth Liberation Front or Animal Liberation Front are going around bragging about it and that's why they aren't getting caught. I just don't think that the really effective, really serious people involved in the ELF are going to get caught. And that is because the system is created to deal with common criminals, people who are reactionary - someone who gets drunk and goes out and smashes up his girlfriend's car.

In the ELF, action is completely premeditated; not just that, but it's assumed to be rehearsed. They figure out everything they can to avoid security alarms. They figure out everything they can do to avoid leaving fingerprints or traces of hair or footprints at the scene.

There have been over four years of actions here in the United States, over three dozen of them claimed by the ELF, over 40 million dollars in damage and they virtually have no suspects and have captured or prosecuted virtually nobody.

Roland: *Could you speak to the discrepancies in sentencing between common criminals and ecologically-minded economic saboteurs?*

LJP: Say somebody gets drunk or whatever or gets depressed and just randomly burns down a building. That person is facing arson charges and maybe a couple years in jail at the most, depending on how much criminal history they have, or how much damage they caused, or how malicious the court thinks they are or what have you.

Well, say that a different person does a very similar action of the same economic damage, the same potential risk to individuals or whatever and does that with a political motivation because that corporation is polluting their drinking water for example. That person's facing much more time now because of the legislation that has passed. It's basically discrimination.

If you burn down a building and cause a million dollars worth of damage, a person believing in this democracy would think that you would get the same charge as anyone else who burns down a building and causes a million dollars worth of damage.

Charles: *We talked about the activities of law enforcement being ineffective for the most part; so if what they are doing isn't accomplishing their stated objective, what have their actions accomplished?*

LJP: What they have been doing is basically harassing Craig Rosebraugh and myself and anybody else who might be in public support of the ideology of the group. They have also been profiling anybody who might look like a radical environmentalist, or anybody who might look like an anarchist. On the *60 Minutes* piece that they did on the ELF that Craig Rosebraugh participated in, a representative for the FBI came on and he was saying that their main hope was to infiltrate the group. If they have their heads screwed on straight, they really don't expect to infiltrate an ELF cell, because there is virtually no likelihood of that ever happening.

What they do expect to do is infiltrate the larger anarchist environmental movement. They want to have people in there with dreadlocks and Carhartt pants, and they want to have them go to all of the conferences and try to figure out who is really doing things. The ELF doesn't talk about it, and they are probably not even involved for the most part in the mainstream environmental movement because that would eventually lead to their capture. I think they are people who have nothing to do with the environmental movement and that's because they disagree with it. They don't think it's effective.

As far as my own personal experiences go, they have raided the ELF press office twice since I have been involved with it. They have raided my car. They have taken thousands of dollars of my property that will never be returned. They've taken three or four of my computer systems in particular, and lots of personal items, photographs, what have you. I have had these "chance meetings" with federal agents at the local health food store.

They say, "Oh, how's your health doing," and mention a specific health problem I might have had years ago and just letting me know that they know about that.

It's a sort of psychological harassment. It's like, "Were on to you." They try to make me nervous—try to get me to crack.

The first raid happened when Craig and I left an organization here in town (Portland, OR) that he in particular founded with some other people and I joined shortly afterwards. We left that group and started the press office up and moved our stuff out of that organization and had it in his house in his basement.

His house was raided. The press office was in hiatus between one spot and another and they knew that was a weak point so they raided his house. He was able to give me a call before they kicked the door in, and I came over immediately and before I was able to come into the house, an agent—who had a brain hemorrhage and who is no longer an active agent any more—came storming out at me, and he said "Hey Leslie. How's your leg doing? How's your heart doing?"

Basically letting me know he knew all this stuff, and he wouldn't let me get close to the house. He was one who was really active in the personal harassment side that was going on for a while, and like I said, he isn't with the FBI anymore so that has backed down a bit.

There is another agent specifically from the ATF who for a long time was really up in our face when we started passing on communiqués.

He came up to our house and he was saying, "You guys are walking a fine line. You're on thin ice."

He was trying to make us scared to pass on these communiqués—trying to get us nervous. When we first started getting communiqués we were all living in a house in Portland and it seemed like for a couple months there was a car outside constantly, and it was very nerve racking psychologically.

But it's not something that's going to deter me or Craig. If anything, it's going to make people fight harder. When you're really being oppressed and it's as blatant as possible, it's really going to make you fight back as hard as you possibly can and that is exactly what happens. There were times we would get really frustrated and Craig and I came out of the house and went up to the car and started yelling, "Get the fuck out of here!" and sometimes they'd leave and sometimes they didn't.

There's two kinds of surveillance and two kinds of harassment. There are the obvious - what you're meant to see and feel the psychological trauma from. And then there is the kind you're intended not to see and not to know about. The type they are heavily engaged in right now is the other kind of surveillance, the second kind, the kind you are not supposed to see or understand or know how it's going. Because they have tried the first kind for years and it hasn't deterred us or deterred the movement in general. So I think they are really heavily engaged in secret surveillance—the tapping of phones--not just ours, but everybody's. Having agent provocateurs or infiltrators at meetings or such types of things.

Charles: *Since 9-11 they have focused more attention on anything they can possibly label terrorism. Have you noticed a marked difference in your life, in your vocation operating the press office?*

LJP: It's definitely different, and as soon as I saw those planes crash into those buildings I knew it was going to be different. And this ties into the other question I answered. When they start coming down on people, it's only going to radicalize people. When they come down on the ELF, calling them terrorists, what that might spawn is-- and I'm not saying this as a personal threat-- but what that might spawn is a more radical, more militant organization. When the oppressor rises so do the forces of the people—the forces of liberation.

While it might have been okay to destroy property but not okay to harm individuals in one person's mind, if you beat that person down a little bit more they might change their mind. I think that's what it's going to do to people with this type of legislation, with this type of talk they have on TV all the time, with all these flags they're convincing people to put in the back of their car windows.

Myself, I feel like there's way more pressure. There was already a high risk involved in this position but it seems like it just got a whole lot higher overnight. That doesn't mean it's not worth fighting for, or not worth doing anymore. But it does mean that eventually this position that I'm in, this liberty I have to speak my mind, might be completely eliminated. There might not be, here in the USA with our freedom of speech and our freedom of the press, there might not be that kind of freedom anymore. There already isn't. I'm already facing all kinds of labeling, potential threats and potential imprisonment in this position.

I can foresee the day really soon where anybody that is in this position that I am in would be imprisoned immediately for a "terrorist thought crime" or whatever they want to call it. Specifically, the Feb 12th Congressional hearing was the first of its kind. It's something that they never went to the extent of before—conducting a Congressional hearing specifically on eco-terrorism where they subpoenaed anybody.

Roland: *Can you describe how the mainstream media has filtered the message of the ELF/ALF? And what's been your dealing with the press?*

LJP: I think that there is the rebel appeal going on. They want to make us look like villains or rebels. There has always been an appeal in American society to the rebel, James Dean or whatever. People just like somebody who's fighting back or standing up—the underdog. And we were just milking that as much as we could because that's all they're going to give us.

They're not going to put us on *CNN* or *60 Minutes* and say, "Feel free to speak your mind. What's wrong with the environmental situation right now?"

And they're not going to give us twenty minutes of free space. What they do is give us ten seconds of free space after saying "You're a violent eco-terrorist. Defend yourself."

I could go on forever about the mainstream media. It's extremely frustrating.

Charles: *Have there been any occasions that went off and something came back to the press office that it was clear that there was an objective but the action went SNAFU?*

224

LJP: Offhand, there was at least one communiqué sent where there was an incendiary device that didn't ignite. They claimed credit anyway because they knew it would still get attention. And that was for a Nike distribution center or something, and they had incendiaries on the roof, I believe, and the weather prevented them from igniting.

They sent out a communiqué anyway that said that, "Until Nike stops their sweatshop practices, etc., we're not going to stop fighting against you."

That's the extent of it though. They haven't ever caused as much as a scratch to anyone, so that type of mistake hasn't happened and I don't think it will happen, and I'm worried about it if it does personally, like I said. If the ELF did ever harm anyone all kinds of people would jump on their case.

They would say, "That's the worst thing that could have happened," "It wasn't justified."

During the Vietnam War there was an army-funded Mathematics Research Center in Madison Wisconsin that was bombed by an underground group. They used a massive bomb, almost as big as the Oklahoma City bomb, and one person was accidentally killed from that action. It was a student that had nothing to do with the Mathematics Research Center. But what they were doing was essentially mathematical equations that were going to result in the death of thousands of people in Vietnam. And the repercussions of that bombing were that many in the anti-war, anti-imperialist movement were saying that it was the worst thing that could have happened and that it wasn't justified.

Well, yes that is terrible. I think it's terrible when someone dies. I hate when people are oppressed. That's why I am here doing what I am doing. But what they're fighting against is a system that kills people daily and the intention was not to hurt anybody and that was an accident in that particular case. The intention was to liberate people and it's a completely different picture.

You don't see masses of people in the environmental movement condemning the entire system every time someone dies of cancer, but the system and industry caused that and they are completely responsible for it. You don't see people flipping out every time someone in Afghanistan dies, but they should. It's a flip-flop of values and a flip-flop of what is really significant.

That person who died in that particular Madison bombing, like I said, that's extremely sad and extremely unfortunate, and the people who were responsible for that expressed grievances about it and have been dealing with it for the rest of their lives. The whole movement has suffered because of that. But how many people died in Vietnam? How many kids got sent to Vietnam to fight an unjust war that got slaughtered for nothing?

And I've been speaking on a personal level, and that's not going to gain widespread public support. I wouldn't say that to *CNN* because people would not even let themselves think on that level and try to understand what I am saying. But you have to evaluate the reality of the situation and the levels of oppression that are going on. Because the level of oppression that the system is perpetrating on the people is so massive that anything the Earth Liberation Front could ever do to anybody wouldn't even compare. And the motivations of the system are capitalistic. They're imperialistic.

The motivations of the ELF are liberty, freedom, and justice, and health and fresh air and all the rest. It sickens me to think that an anti-imperialist movement or an environmental movement that is just really coming into its own could get completely stomped out because of one mistake or one thing that wasn't perfect. Revolutions are not perfect. When you are fighting for what you need to survive you are going to make some mistakes along the way. You might hurt somebody. You might burn down some buildings along the way. That's just the way it is because what you have to do to liberate yourself from the oppression that you are under is so intense.

You know when you look to nature you know there's all kinds of violence at a sustainable level. Species eat other species they feed off other life forms and violence exists in nature and that's just the way it is. We can't imagine that there's anything outside of that. That's ridiculous. That's completely anthropocentric. It's based all on the belief that humans are somehow better than everything else in nature and somehow apart from nature and that, I think, is the foundation of oppression in my opinion. It's the foundation of this system. That's what caused Westernized society to rise out of the rest of the human culture. I just think it's ridiculous.

Charles: *What do your folks think of the ELF?*

226

LJP: (laughs). I love that question.

Charles: *You get it a lot?*

LJP: Yeah, especially by reporters who are older and view me as young, you know, (imitating an uptight voice) "What do your parents think about this?"

Craig (Rosebraugh) did a piece on 20/20 and they called him a juvenile delinquent; "What do your parents think of this?" (laughs). They were just really mean to him…

I am a product of American society. I grew up rebelling against my parents because they were the most obvious oppressive force in my life and I ran away from home when I was 17 to join an environmental movement. I thought I was never going to talk to my parents again. I dropped out of school and all the rest. Well, since then I've realized a lot of things and I've rebuilt relationships with my family and it's difficult because your family, just like rest of the people you deal with in this society, are greatly affected by American propaganda, by the American dream. They're brainwashed by the system and to get through to them is sometimes the hardest thing you can really do, but you can't have a revolution without engaging in personal sacrifices and trying to cause a lot of personal changes.

You can't be a true revolutionary if you're not challenging yourself and really doing what's hardest to do and oftentimes, the hardest things to fix are your personal relationships. You know my parents are scared that I might end up in jail. They don't want to see me in jail, but they have gotten to the point where I really believe they are, how do say, proud of me in a way—proud that I'm standing up for what I believe and that despite the negative stigmatism or bad reputation that I might get and the risks I'm taking in doing this, I'm still fighting for what I believe and speaking the truth and not taking into account the sort of fear factor.

Roland: I imagine that those who share your ideology and those who engage in ELF actions must feel rather isolated. Could you speak to that?

LJP: Yeah, it is really difficult. It's not something that just anybody can up and do. Let me give you a little history. There's a group that Craig and I were involved in Portland. It was a social justice group that attempted to

227

expose that all the various social issues like feminism, animal rights and environmentalism are all coming from the same root cause—the system's oppression-- and that was the intention of the organization. But one of things we did was speak out in support of the Animal Liberation Front, which was active at the time. We'd explain to people that we thought they were no different from the Boston Tea Party— that what they were doing was just and should be commended and after doing that a while I think we got a bit of a reputation.

You try to just go to a regular protest and it's like, "Oh, there's so and so. Don't go near them because they're being heavily surveyed. Don't associate with them. That person is so high on their horse and that they think they're so great and what they have to say is so important," because if somebody sees you on *CNN* they're going to think, "Oh that person thinks they're better than me."

Sometimes that's the reaction to me being seen on mainstream media. Yeah, it's completely isolating and I really wish that there was a stronger revolutionary community that would really give myself and Craig and anybody and everybody more support. And wouldn't be so duped into the sort of jealousy or whatever, because really this, what I do, is extremely stressful, extremely unexciting. After the third or fourth time you've had big cameras in your face and you've met people you saw on TV, all of the sudden you're not looking forward to that next interview, especially when they're calling you a terrorist over and over. I mean, it's not glamorous. These extreme personal sacrifices you take because you really believe in what you're doing, and I really believe in what I'm doing, and that's why I take those sacrifices.

8.

RESIGNATION STATEMENT

Final Statement of Leslie James Pickering as Spokesperson for the North American Earth Liberation Front Press Office
Earth First! Journal
June/July 2002

More than any other event in my life, the actions of the Earth Liberation Front (ELF) have been the most eye-opening, inspirational and empowering. The actions of the ELF have restored a hope in me that had otherwise been beaten into submission by the oppressive cycle of daily life within contemporary American civilization.

When I was a teenager in suburban New York state, I, like many of my peers, would do almost anything thinkable to break the mundane reality of my existence. One of the activities that drew my attention was attending loud, angry, independent music events. These events appealed to me because they were welcoming atmospheres for me and my peers to vent our legitimate frustrations with the social and political situations we had been born into and forced to swallow. At one of the first of these shows I attended, I was handed some literature about an organization called the Animal Liberation Front (ALF).

At first, I didn't think much of it—a souvenir to bring home—and I stuffed it in my backpack. It wasn't until I had the time to look it over that I realized the implications these stapled photocopies would have on my life. It turned out that the ALF was an underground organization that struggled for the freedom of animals by "liberating" them from factory farms, vivisection labs and other abusive institutions. The ALF was a group of fugitives who broke the law to fight for freedom, much like many of our cultural heroes: George Washington, Thomas Jefferson, the Boston Tea Partiers, Robin Hood, etc. I was fascinated.

At this point, I naturally had an appreciation for nature, but I was not especially what one would call an "animal lover," nor have I ever been. I had never considered being a vegetarian and had no awareness of any popular movement for animal rights. The tactics of the ALF simply made sense to me on an honest and fundamental level, based on my natural instincts for self defense and the little that I had learned about revolutionary/social movements from school and conversations. My fascination with this sensational organization soon led me to learn of the popular movements for the freedom of animals and environmentalism and later to study any and all revolutionary/social movements that I could

230

scrounge up information on.

In 1997, the ELF began taking "direct actions" similar to the actions of the ALF. From the onset, the direct actions of the ELF were causing millions in damages to corporations and government agencies that were profiting from destroying the Earth. The actions and existence of the ELF created an enormous wave of attention across the U.S., as authorities fruitlessly scrambled for evidence, often barely beginning one investigation before the ELF would strike again.

I have been privileged to be in the position of spokesperson for the North American Earth Liberation Front Press Office (NAELFPO) since the spring of 2000. The press office has been referred to by the media as a "clearinghouse" for the anonymous communiqués of the ELF. For me personally, it has been an opportunity to publicly speak my belief in direct action and to help the movement gain the public's attention and support.

I support the actions of the ELF and the ALF wholeheartedly. I unwaveringly support revolutionary action to bring about the liberation of the Earth and its animal nations, including the liberation of the human race. I feel that illegal actions, like those of the ELF and ALF, are 100 percent necessary for liberation, and I hope to see the continuation and the rapid escalation of their activities until the Earth and all of us who live here are free of institutionalized oppression.

That being said, shortly after co-founding the NAELFPO, I vowed to speak the truth about the ELF. I have since done the best job I could with limited resources and opportunities to fulfill this promise, and I will continue to do so. However, I have come to realize that being in the position of spokesperson for the organization has presented me with difficulties in speaking this truth.

There is an existing diversity of opinions among those who support the activity of the ELF on the manner in which the underground organization should be represented. I am only able to honestly represent the movement in the light in which it appears to me, which is not necessarily the same light in which all others who support the ELF view it.

As I see it, the ELF is a loose network of clandestine guerrilla groups that are a part of a larger movement struggling for global revolutionary change. The tactics that they engage in, which many consider nonviolent sabotage, are a direct result of their analysis of the oppression they struggle against and the level of activity they perceive to be effective within the particular context of their actions.

I see and personally hope that there is no proof that the movement in general should view the tactics of the ELF as the end-all of action for liberation. I see absolutely no logic in a judgment that struggle perceived as nonviolent is the only legitimate kind to be waged. In addition, I have no problem admitting that I personally do not consider the actions of the ELF and ALF as nonviolent, as any dictionary will clearly spell out.

Again, this does not mean that I do not wholeheartedly support all of these actions, only that I do not consider them nonviolent and do not believe nonviolence is the only legitimate means by which to struggle for liberation.

Any dictionary will tell you that violence is, more or less, any act that aggressively harms or threatens harm to anyone or anything. Therefore, if actions were truly nonviolent, they would fail to even threaten harm to anything, which I certainly do not consider to be the case with the ELF. The entire intention of the ELF is to bring about liberation through engaging in effective acts of sabotage against oppressive institutions. To not even threaten harm to these institutions would therefore be failure.

But regardless of what the dictionary says, I believe that attaching the nonviolence label to these actions is based on a misguided understanding of public opinion and fear of a liberal backlash that comes anyway. I also believe the blind endorsement of this label is counterrevolutionary. Any notion that alleged nonviolence is the only way by which to achieve liberation is ill-informed and condemning of the many other effective tactics that have, can and must be put into practice in successful revolutionary movements.

Throughout history, liberation has been achieved through a healthy balance of a variety of tactics, many which have been considered nonviolent and many which have been considered violent. Even the most popular examples of nonviolent resistance were far from existing in a vacuum. During the same periods that Gandhi and Martin Luther King, Jr. were waging their nonviolent struggles, numerous other organizations were struggling for the same liberation through what were considered violent means—undeniably having a massive effect on the progression

232

of the overall movements. In fact, I've yet to find a historical example of a successful revolutionary movement that consisted strictly of nonviolent activity, and I do not believe that one is possible in our contemporary setting.

Recently, I appeared on a short television spot regarding the February 12 hearing held by the Congressional Subcommittee on Forests and Forest Health. Also on this clip appeared an unnamed representative of an unnamed organization allegedly from the mainstream environmental movement.

Among other less interesting things, he said, "Violence, when used in this country, is simply wrong."

I have found that a lot of the ideological basis for nonviolence in the U.S. is fundamentally nationalist.

Why is it that when it comes to clearly violent struggle outside the borders of the U.S.-- such as that waged by the Zapatistas in Chiapas, Mexico-- the majority of liberals are quick to lend their ideological support, while those same liberals adamantly condemn the actions of the ELF and ALF here within the borders of such a powerful and oppressive government? I believe this is because they have been brainwashed by the system into buying the line that within U.S. borders, somehow revolutionary change can magically be achieved through reformist activity. I think we need to wake up and realize that the U.S. is a global power, force-feeding its suicidal capitalist American Dream down the throats of everyone on the face of the planet. Revolutionary change has never been achieved through reformist activity and is certainly not going to be handed to us on a silver platter by the U.S. government.

I have also found that almost all of the popular cheerleaders of nonviolence are/were strongly religious people who endorsed the tactic because of their religious beliefs, not necessarily because of its effectiveness in bringing about revolutionary change. Recognizing the connection of nonviolence to religion was important to me, because it helped me realize the larger intentions of the philosophy.

The belief that one species, the human race, can somehow live an entirely nonviolent existence on this planet-- when it is perfectly clear that no species throughout all of nature is capable of this-- is blatantly anthropocentric. The belief that humans are separate and somehow exempt from the laws of nature is a major cause of the disastrous imbalance that our species now suffers from.

Often it seems that blind adherence to nonviolence philosophy is based on a reactionary denial of the level of resistance that it'll take to bring about revolutionary change. When many begin to comprehend the level of oppression we face today, nonviolence philosophy gains appeal as a very comfortable Heaven/fairyland where liberation can be achieved strictly through personal changes. I consider this state of denial a kind of psychological illness common among liberal North Americans. I strongly feel that anyone hypnotizing the people with the nonviolence-as-gospel dog-and-pony show is a criminal, disarming us in a time when we desperately need to defend ourselves.

This denial of what really needs to happen to liberate the Earth and ourselves from the deadly path that the system is leading us all down is a major factor in our inability to achieve that liberation. The outright condemnation of violent revolutionary action in America needs to come to an end before a true revolution can effectively take place. The system knows this, and its pigs are working harder than ever to brainwash the public by calling the ELF "terrorists" and the Pentagon a "force for freedom."

More than anything, I simply recognize the right and, at times, the necessity and duty of all people to defend ourselves when taking a beating, to fight for our very lives. This right is not only extended to those being crushed by the hands of this beast, but also to those of us being digested in its belly.

In addition to the nonviolence issue, I do not believe that the actions of the ELF are strictly environmental in their scope. It has probably already become clear that I recognize the actions of the ELF as acts of revolution, not reform. I have attempted to express this in every piece of literature, interview, public presentation and conversation that has occurred as a result of my participation in the NAELFPO—and increasingly so in recent months.

I cannot perceive the Earth without conjuring up images of all life taking root within this atmosphere. The liberation of the Earth equals the liberation of every one of us. And as I see it, the liberation of the Earth and the liberation of all species of the Earth is the goal of the ELF.

234

RESIGNATION STATEMENT

I do not see the organization as simply an environmental group satisfied with the economic damages it inflicts and attention it draws from each of its individual actions. I do not see the ELF as only caring about the oppression caused by Vail Resorts, Inc. and Boise Cascade. These are just platforms for a much larger message to get out on a global scale, and that message is, "We're not taking anymore."

I see the objectives of any revolutionary movement for liberation being to off the oppressor, to smash the system of oppression and to create a free and just society in its place. I see no exception to this in the case of the ELF, and I certainly do not hope that I am wrong.

Currently, the FBI considers the ELF and the ALF the "number one priority" among domestic terrorist threats. This is nothing new; the same thing has been said about revolutionary organizations in the past that the system perceived as a threat. This is, however, a noteworthy point in the struggle for liberation: It is recognition from the oppressor. The system does perceive this movement as a threat and is using an increasing amount of its resources to stomp it out. This is a point at which the struggle needs to evolve in order to survive, so as not to suffer the same fate as revolutionary struggles of previous generations.

This system has clearly proven itself to value its "progress" above and beyond anyone and anything. It represents a pursuit of profits and property at the expense of the people, the natural elements of the Earth that sustain our lives and of the planet as a whole. This "American Dream" is a death wish, and we cannot allow it to nail our coffins shut.

The struggle must constantly assess and reassess the oppressor and the oppressor's perception of the struggle. New tactical directions must evolve with these assessments. I, for one, have begun to question the power and use of any official press office for an autonomous organization or movement. If the purpose of a press office is to draw much-needed attention to a movement, then is there a point at which that press office is no longer needed or practical? Where is the point at which, within the context of an existing movement, the direct actions of the movement are able to speak for themselves?

I recognize that all forms of institutional oppression flow from the same source, the institution, the system that dictates nearly every facet of our lives under its twisted objectives. Therefore, I am not an environmentalist;

I am not an activist; I'm not a reformist or any form of liberal. I am a revolutionary. I advocate the return of all power to the hands of the people by any means necessary on a global scale. I see anything short of this as failure and as disastrous. And I'm not about to deny this reality because of any existing atmosphere of opinion within the popular liberal environmental movement. To deny this reality is to limit the ability of this movement to evolve into one that truly has the capacity to achieve the objective of liberation.

Arguing for a nonviolent, single-issue revolution has placed us in a position of hypocrisy and has allowed us to be backed into corners with our arguments. I believe that the movement hasn't gained the public support that it needs to be successful because the intelligent public can see these glaring holes in our arguments. I have found that public opinion is not as the media represents it, and it is far from what liberals perceive it to be.

I recognize that the only way to build a successful revolutionary movement is to present a sound and powerful argument, backed up by effective action. I believe that once this movement is presented to the oppressed peoples of the Earth, public support will be powerfully behind it.

Nonviolence, economic sabotage and armed propaganda are tactics, not strategies, not gospel and certainly not the only effective actions to be taken as part of a successful revolutionary movement. Like the tools of a toolbox, each has a specific use and specific results. Depending on the job you have, you choose a tool (or a set of tools) from your toolbox. You don't choose only the tools that fit most comfortably in your hand or that are the prettiest; you choose the ones that'll get the job done. Sometimes these tools do fit comfortably in your hands, but most of the time they give you blisters. No matter what, though, at the end of the day, the objective is always to have the job completed. It's idiotic to shun the sledgehammer when you're working to knock down a wall,

Our arguments and actions need to be sound, thorough and brutally honest. We need to awaken from our coma and struggle for a realistic, not utopian, solution. No matter how uncomfortable this may seem to many of us, it's nothing compared to what will happen if we don't and what is happening already.

Long live the Earth Liberation Front! Long Live the Animal Liberation

RESIGNATION STATEMENT

Front! Down with this insane system that plagues the Earth and its peoples! Revolution is liberation!

With this statement I officially resign from my role with the NAELFPO, but I am by no means silencing myself. I intend to continue with increasing effort to struggle for revolutionary change without being bound to any dogmatic atmospheres of opinions. I encourage and welcome communication of any kind and can be reached at leslie@arissa.org.

Leslie James Pickering quit high school at seventeen to struggle against "this system that stops at nothing to profit from the destruction of everything." After five years of continuous civil disobedience and protest, he grew frustrated with the lack of results in his activity and helped to found the North American Earth Liberation Front Press Office (NAELFPO) in early 2000.

He served as press officer with the NAELFPO until his final resignation in summer of 2002. During this period, the NAELFPO sustained two raids by the Federal Bureau of Investigations (FBI) and the Bureau of Alcohol Tobacco and Firearms (ATF), responded to half a dozen grand jury subpoenas; conducted pubic presentations; produced booklets, newspapers, magazines, and a video on the ELF and handled the release of dozens of ELF communiqués.

Through the NAELFPO, Pickering was the editor of *Resistance, the Journal of the North American Earth Liberation Front Press Office*, as well as many other independently-produced materials regarding the Earth Liberation Front. Pickering served twice as ELF Spokesperson, handling countless local, national, international, corporate and independent media inquires, which resulted in coverage in the *New York Times*, the *Washington Times*, The *Los Angeles Times*, *USA Today*, *Christian Science Monitor*, *Rolling Stone* magazine and many more.

He has also appeared in televised interviews with the ABC, NBC, CNN, FOX, CBC and BBC networks, as well as National Geographic TV and many others. He has given lectures at various conferences and at Lewis & Clark College, Saint Michael's University, Rochester Institute of Technology, Bard College, Yale University, New York University and many other institutions of learning.

In 2003, Pickering resigned from the NAELFPO, issuing a lengthy statement renouncing nonviolence philosophy and single issue-politics, but he continues to support the ELF as a component of a revolutionary movement. He is now involved in an emerging revolutionary effort known as Arissa.

IF NOT YOU... WHO?

IF NOT NOW... WHEN?

ALSO AVAILABLE FROM ARISSA MEDIA GROUP

SOCIAL CRISIS AND SOCIAL DEMORALIZATION
The Dynamics of Status in American Race Relations
Ronald Kuykendall

This insightful book provides an alternative perspective on American race relations - that race relations are status relations creating a series of behavioral consequences. Kuykendall argues that the racial problem is a political class conflict and must be resolved through revolutionary political class struggle.

THE LOGIC OF POLITICAL VIOLENCE
Lessons in Reform and Revolution
Craig Rosebraugh

An in-depth study of political violence and nonviolence used historically in justice struggles; includes a critical examination of the limitations of single-issue reformist pursuits in the United States.

THE LOGIC OF POLITICAL VIOLENCE
Craig Rosebraugh Live at Laughing Horse Books
Spoken Word CD

This lecture examines the historic roles that political violence and nonviolence have played in social and political movements in the United States and internationally. A 65-minute spoken word cd recorded live at Laughing Horse Books in Portland, Oregon on Janurary 10, 2003.

TO ORDER GO TO:
www.arissamediagroup.com